Bruce Chatwin

Twayne's English Authors Series

Kinley Roby, Editor

Northeastern University

TEAS 542

BRUCE CHATWIN
Courtesy of Jerry Bauer

Bruce Chatwin

Patrick Meanor

State University of New York–Oneonta

Twayne Publishers
An Imprint of Simon & Schuster Macmillan
New York

Prentice Hall International
London • Mexico City • New Delhi • Singapore • Sydney • Toronto

Twayne's English Authors Series No. 542

Bruce Chatwin
Patrick Meanor

Twayne Publishers
An Imprint of Simon & Schuster Macmillan
1633 Broadway
New York, NY 10019

Library of Congress Cataloging-in-Publication Data

Meanor, Patrick.
  Bruce Chatwin / Patrick Meanor
    p. cm. — (Twayne's English authors series ; 542)
  Includes bibliographical references (p.   ) and index.
  ISBN 0-8057-4568-8 (hardcover : alk. paper)
  1. Chatwin, Bruce, 1940–1989—Criticism and interpretation.
  2. Travelers' writings, English—History and criticism.
  3. Travelers in literature.   4. Travel in literature.   I. Title.
  II. Series.
  PR6053.H395Z76   1997
  823'.914—dc21   97-10211
                                                 CIP

10 9 8 7 6 5 4 3 2 1

Printed in the United States of America

In honor of

*Alexander Toradze, one of the world's great pianists,
teachers, and friends—who always comes through,*

*and in loving memory of best friend, mentor, and lifesaver
Dr. Edward H. Kelly (1930–1987)*

*and dearest possible friend
Jack Bissell (1962–1995)*

Contents

Preface

Bruce Chatwin has been widely recognized as one of England's most brilliant travel writers, novelists, essayists, and journalists. He undoubtedly revived the art of travel writing in the late twentieth century by producing books every bit as compelling and stylishly rendered as the best of Graham Greene's and D. H. Lawrence's travel books. In many ways, he regenerated and augmented Lawrence's persistent concern over the devastating effects of Western cultural imperialism on native cultures, such as the Australian aboriginals and the Araucanian and Tehuelche Indians in southern Chile and Patagonia.

But it is in Chatwin's sense of moral outrage—though always muted and kept distinctly objective—that he demonstrates his unapologetic romantic sensibility and philosophical belief in the innate goodness of human nature. There is little question that Western civilization and its legacy of mechanization and ownership have done enormous damage to the natives of both Australia and South America and also to the delicate ecological balance among the human, animal, and botanical life forms that cohabit in vital symbiotic relationships.

In Chatwin's consistent attempts to locate the genesis of these problems, he found it necessary to move back to origins—and thus visit and revisit such sites of ancient cultures as China, Afghanistan, the Sudan, aboriginal Australia. Chatwin also read massive amounts of mythology, philosophy, science, and religion. His imagination was ignited by the books he read as a child in his grandmothers' and great-aunts' libraries, and he began to see that actually traveling to those once-remote places was a possibility. The relationship between Chatwin's reading and the life of travel he eventually pursued could easily become the rich subject of another book-length study.

The recurring narrative—and thus the key—Chatwin found in both his reading and his travels was the oldest story in the world: the fall of man. He found the clearest illustration of that catastrophe and its consequences not in the story of Adam and Eve but in the story of their children, Cain and Abel. It is in that narrative that one detects the devastating conflict between settlement and nomadism that continues to the present day.

Living with nomads in the Sudan in the late 1960s, Chatwin discovered that the nomadic way of life—traveling along ancient geographical paths in accordance with the cycles of the seasons—harkened back to the original innocence of mankind. Abel was the first shepherd, the first nomad in a genealogy of shepherds that includes Abraham, the father of the Jewish race, and Christ, spiritually the "good shepherd." Cain, on the other hand, after his expulsion from Eden for the murder of his brother, moved "east of Eden" to become a settled agriculturalist and thus to found the first city, Enoch.

Chatwin mythically reconfigures the dynamics of the Fall as "the sins of settlement" and asserts that the origins of human restlessness can be found in the archaic yearnings of the human imagination—a dim remembrance of the original Edenic condition of pastoral nomadism. Another component of the Fall was the transformation of the cyclic time patterns of nomadic tribes into the Western linear pattern of settlers. In short, an apocalyptic time scheme was established by the settled agriculturalists.

Each of Chatwin's five major works demonstrates some aspect of his unique conception of the Fall as the basis of his highly articulated mythopoeic world.

In Patagonia illustrates that European immigrants fled their "fallen" world and moved to Patagonia to regenerate their Edenic agenda but tragically caused the fall—the spiritual and physical ruination—of the native Indians of that region. *The Viceroy of Ouidah* even more ironically shows a European culture righteously enslaving the innocent African natives and utterly destroying their Edenic civilization, all in the name of an ostensibly Christian belief in the redeeming power of what is said to be love. More cogently than any of his other books, *The Songlines* depicts the destruction of another ancient nomadic culture, by colonials who move the natives onto so-called reservations and sacrilegiously violate the very basis of their cosmological relationship to the land. Though *On the Black Hill* does not deal directly with cultural devastation, it shows the hopelessness of trying to evade the life-denying encroachments of mechanization and technology. The twin brothers are damaged even within their own consciously designated Eden, their farm, The Vision. And though *Utz* may reverse the dramatic and sometimes dangerous journeys of Chatwin's early works, Utz's attempts to establish and maintain a completely solipsistic Edenic condition—through his collection of priceless Meissen figurines—is doomed to failure.

Few writers go to such great lengths in pursuing their passionate obsessions as Bruce Chatwin. Believing that what he calls pastoral nomadism was humanity's original and most natural condition, Chatwin journeyed to the most remote and exotic parts of the world to test his cherished theory, and in doing so brought a more precise and multifaceted brand of scholarship to the genre of travel literature. His work documents the brutal consequences that modern industrialized and technological forces imposed on so-called primitive people and simultaneously celebrates the idiosyncratic diversity of the remarkable worlds he explored. There is little question that he was one of England's and America's most brilliant travel writers, novelists, essayists, and journalists in the latter half of the twentieth century.

Acknowledgments

I wish to thank the administrators at the State University of New York, College at Oneonta, for their encouragement throughout the writing of this book. I am especially grateful to Dr. Alan B. Donovan, president of the college, and to Dr. Anne Federlein, vice president and provost of the college, for their unstinting support, particularly when the task seemed overwhelming. Their cheerful attitude and impeccable sense of humor pulled me through many an upstate New York cloudy afternoon. I am also indebted to Dean James Mullen for the many encouraging memos he sent to keep me writing. And no chair of English has ever been more supportive than Professor David Betts.

But of all my friends and colleagues, no one came near to supplying the almost daily support that Dr. Julia Boken did, not only on the phone but in digging up the rarest of scholarly articles throughout the New York City area. Her consistent encouragement and cheerfulness never failed to energize my sometimes flagging spirit. I am also grateful to Elaine and Calvin Bissell for helping me maintain a positive attitude during the writing of the book, and to Dr. Paul Scheele for reminding me to include important details that I had overlooked. Without the assistance of librarians Janet Potter, Mary Lynn Bensen, Christine Bulson, and Andrea Gerberg I simply could not have obtained the necessary materials to complete the book. Last and certainly not least, I wish to thank Mrs. Cheryl Peeters not only for her fast and accurate typing but, more important, her patience and keen editing eyes. And to Professor Yolanda Sharpe, endless thanks for making sure the manuscript was brought to a successful completion.

Chronology

1940   Charles Bruce Chatwin born 13 May in Sheffield, England, the oldest child of Charles and Margharita Chatwin. Spends much of early childhood moving around England because his father is in the Royal Navy during the war.

1946   Attends preparatory school in Birmingham.

1949   First visit to Wales with his father and younger brother.

1953   Spends the summer in Sweden. Attends Marlborough College in Wiltshire, England.

1955   Reads Robert Byron's *The Road to Oxiana,* which influenced him all of his life.

1958   Decides against attending university and begins working for Sotheby and Company of Bond Street as a uniformed porter.

1962   First trip to Afghanistan.

1964   Second trip to Afghanistan.

1965   Marries an American, Elizabeth Chanler, on 12 July. Begins to experience problems with his eyesight. Becomes director of Impressionist Paintings and Antiquities Division at Sotheby's and its youngest partner. Travels to Prague.

1966   Leaves Sotheby's and travels to the Sudan. Begins studies in archaeology at the University of Edinburgh.

1967   Travels to the Soviet Union.

1969   Trip to Kiev, Ukraine, and third trip to Afghanistan.

1970   Publication of essay "The Nomadic Alternative," his first significant piece of writing.

1971   First trip to Dahomey (Benin), Senegal, Mali, and Mauritania.

1973   Begins writing articles for the London *Sunday Times,*
        which he continues to do for three years.

1974   Travels for six months in Patagonia.

1977   Begins writing *The Viceroy of Ouidah.* Publication of
        first book, *In Patagonia.*

1978   Second trip to Benin (the former Dahomey). Wins the
        Hawthornden Prize for *In Patagonia.*

1979   Wins the E. M. Forster Award of the American Acad-
        emy of Arts and Letters for *In Patagonia.*

1980   Publication of second book, *The Viceroy of Ouidah.* Trav-
        els to Wales and begins work on *On the Black Hill.*

1982   Publication of his third book, *On the Black Hill.* Wins
        the Whitbread Award for an author's best first novel
        for *On the Black Hill.* Also wins the James Tait Black
        Prize for best novel.

1984   Visits Australia and travels with Salman Rushdie.

1986   Production of a dramatic adaptation of *On the Black
        Hill* by the Made in Wales Theatre Company in Wales.
        Hospitalized for AIDS.

1987   Filming of *On the Black Hill* by the British Institute's
        Andrew Grieve in Wales. Publication of *The Songlines,*
        Chatwin's fourth book.

1988   Filming of Werner Herzog's *Cobra Verde,* an adaptation
        of *The Viceroy of Ouidah,* in Ghana. Publication of
        Chatwin's fifth book, *Utz,* which is shortlisted for the
        Booker Prize.

1989   Charles Bruce Chatwin dies of pneumonia (caused by
        AIDS) in Nice, France, on 18 January. Posthumous
        publication of a collection of stories, essays, profiles,
        and travelogues entitled *What Am I Doing Here.*

1992   Film of *Utz,* directed by George Sluizer, released.

1993   Publication of *Far Journeys: Photographs and Notebooks.*
        An opera, *L'Homme aux semelles de vent (The Man with
        Footsoles of Wind)*, written in collaboration with Roger
        Clarke and Kevin Volans is produced in both London
        and New York. Nicholas Murray's *Bruce Chatwin,* the

first book-length study on Chatwin, is published by Seren Press.

1994   Argo compact disc of Kevin Volans's *String Quartet No. Three,* entitled "The Songlines: In Memory of Bruce Chatwin," performed by the Balanescu Quartet, is released.

1996   Publication of *Anatomy of Restlessness,* a posthumous collection of stories, travelogues, profiles, and reviews.

Chapter One

The Life of Bruce Chatwin: "A Magnificent Raconteur of Scheherazadean Inexhaustibility"

No writer appreciated the multifaceted talents of Bruce Chatwin better than his friend Salman Rushdie, who labeled him a "magnificent raconteur."[1] As a novelist and one of the twentieth century's most trenchant theorists on the operations of the imagination and its mythmaking potential, Rushdie was never put off by Chatwin's penchant for riding the precarious line between fact and fiction, myth and reality, an objective self and an enhanced self.

The serious scholar encounters the first of many factual confusions about Chatwin when he or she comes upon two different dates for Chatwin's birth. Printed on the first page of his five books is the birthdate 1942, but on his posthumously published books the date is 1940. No one seems to have noted such a small discrepancy or ventured an explanation, so one must assume that Chatwin did what lots of vulnerable human beings do and lied about his age. But one might forgive Chatwin's "mistake"; after all, his life consistently and consciously intermingled—for aesthetic purposes—fact and fiction. It is only in his introduction to *What Am I Doing Here,* a book published shortly after his death, that Chatwin formally distinguishes between fiction and nonfiction; he calls the first three selections "stories" and warns his reader that "however closely the narrative may fit the facts, the fictional process has been at work." As Roger Clarke points out, "Chatwin was making and unravelling myths all his life."[2]

It was not until Nicholas Murray published his highly informative and gracefully written book on Bruce Chatwin in 1993—the first and only full-length book on him besides this work—that the two-year discrepancy of Chatwin's birthdates became obvious. In many of Chatwin's interviews, he was notoriously casual about dates and usually did not even mention them, so a serious scholar of Chatwin's work is deeply indebted to Murray for the almost impossible task of arranging any kind of satisfactory biographical chronology of Chatwin's life. The vast majority of such information used in this book comes from Murray's book. But Murray's last chapter, called "The Chatwin Legend," should serve as a warning to the reader that Chatwin's life story may contain as much fiction as fact.

Charles Bruce Chatwin was born on 13 May 1940 in Sheffield, England. His mother was Margharita Turnell Chatwin, and his father, Charles Leslie Chatwin, was a lawyer in Birmingham. Roger Clarke humorously suggests that Bruce Chatwin used his middle name as his first name because he wanted to avoid being called "Charley Chatwin" ("Wandering Star," 36). The Chatwin family line descended from a Birmingham button maker, and Chatwin was fond of calling the family "Birmingham worthies." Most of the Chatwins, however, had been lawyers and architects. But certain family legends stood out, such as Uncle Charley Milward, whose adventures as a captain on the high seas and whose life in Patagonia motivated Chatwin to write his first book, *In Patagonia*. A piece of mylodon sloth skin that Captain Milward brought to Chatwin's grandmother occupied the central family shrine, her "cabinet of curiosities," and in the young boy's mind the skin took on the dimensions of the Holy Grail.

A lawyer in civilian life, Chatwin's father served on a British minesweeper throughout World War II, which meant that the family was frequently without a permanent residence as they moved among friends and relatives during the first four years of Chatwin's childhood. Two of his favorite residences were that of his maternal grandmother, Turnell, on the seashore in Yorkshire and that of his great-aunts Janie and Gracie (on his father's side) at Stratford-on-Avon. Their house sat directly behind the church where Shakespeare was buried. It was in the libraries of these women that the child Bruce first read books that would influence his imagination all of his life: Joshua Slocum's *Sailing Alone around the World*, a poetry anthology called *The Open Road*, Walt Whitman's poetry, Ernest Thompson Seton's *Lives of the Hunted*, and much Shakespeare. After the war Bruce's father resumed his legal profession and the Chatwins returned to their "grim-gabled" house in Birmingham, where the young boy fell ill with what the family thought might be tuberculosis. However, years later, Chatwin himself diagnosed the condition as *"la grande maladie: horreur de domicile,"* Baudelaire's "horror of home."[3] It is no wonder that Chatwin could never settle in one place for long and that he was obsessed with the idea of settlement, or what he called the "sins of settlement," all of his life. The family's early nomadic wandering, though it provoked anxiety and fear in Chatwin, became for him an unconscious Edenic ideal.

Other of Chatwin's childhood readings were Herman Melville's *Omoo* and *Typee,* and works by John C. Voss, Richard Henry Dana, and Jack London. Chatwin never fell under the spell of Jules Verne, however, finding instead that "the real was always more fantastic than the fantastical" (*Bruce Chatwin,* 22). Chatwin attributed his love for Hemingway's clean, specific prose to his great-aunt Janie, who considered the "cleaner" English of American writers preferable to British English; Chatwin acknowledged that Hemingway's prose was a model for his own lean, lapidary prose. He also pursued a lifelong love affair with world atlases of every sort; the family liked to travel and took summer holidays to Italy, Greece, and the Middle East, and Chatwin spent a summer alone in Sweden when he was 14 years old.

After his elementary school years in Birmingham, young Bruce was sent to one of Britain's more exclusive public schools, Marlborough College, in Wiltshire, when he was 13. There, Murray states, he was considered "a dimwit and a dreamer"—or so Chatwin claimed. He was not a consistently good student and much preferred entertaining his classmates with his finely tuned storytelling and with bicycle tours of the beautiful Wiltshire countryside that included visits to local antique shops and churches (*Bruce Chatwin,* 23). According to Peter Levi, a writer with whom Chatwin later traveled to Afghanistan, Chatwin accumulated large amounts of money at Marlborough "by buying from one antique dealer and selling to another 'until all the local dealers in a body came and protested to the headmaster.' " Chatwin, according to his closest friend at college, Michael Cannon, loved to entertain his classmates not only with his storytelling but by adorning himself in silk dressing gowns and mimicking Noel Coward singing his own songs (p. 24). If the teenage Chatwin didn't learn much from his formal classes at Marlborough, he did fall in love with certain writers who influenced his thinking and writing for the rest of his life. As a gift for his faithful patronage, a local bookseller gave Chatwin Edith Sitwell's unique anthology *Planet and Glowworm,* in which the eager 17-year-old first encountered such spiritual and literary influences as Charles Baudelaire, Gerard de Nerval, and most important, Arthur Rimbaud. He also became interested in Chinese art and poetry, especially the poems of Li Po, and in the visionary poems of William Blake and Christopher Smart. The prose works of both Jeremy Taylor and Sir Thomas Browne influenced not only Chatwin's prose style but also his sense of structure.

After graduating from Marlborough College, Chatwin decided against going on to one of the more prestigious universities, such as Oxford or Cambridge, and chose to go to work at the world-famous art-auction house Sotheby and Company in London's Bond Street. His compulsive love of art and antiquities won out over his desire to follow the traditional path of most upper-middle-class young men: to pursue a university career after their secondary-school years. But Chatwin had always been known as an individual who followed his heart rather than his head, and most of the time he was right by sheer instinct.

Chatwin's first job, in December of 1958, was as a uniformed porter in the ceramics department. His friends who had dutifully gone off to university were envious of his freedom and his association with the prestigious Sotheby's. Michael Cannon tells the amusing story of accompanying Chatwin, during Chatwin's visits to Cambridge, to the Fitzwilliam Museum, where, much to the consternation of the museum's stuffy curators, Chatwin would declaim, "Fake!" "Genuine!" "Fake!" as he blithely passed many of the gallery's venerable pictures. After a short time in the ceramics department at Sotheby's, Chatwin moved into the Impressionist and Antiquities Division, where, six years later, he would become its head. It was while working in this department that an incident occurred that made Chatwin famous in London art circles and contributed to the construction of the Chatwin legend. It seems that young Chatwin, in his gray porter's uniform, casually mentioned that a newly acquired Picasso gouache of a harlequin was actually a fake. After calling in experts, the museum directors found that the young "uneducated" upstart was right—it was a fake. Chatwin was immediately made director of the department, or so the legend contends. Although Murray warns that "Chatwin's habit of vividly enhancing the literal narrative makes verification far from easy" of the fake-Picasso story, he also reports other stories that account for the young man's quick rise to the top. For example, Chatwin's supervisors noticed that he could read ancient Greek and thus decipher the inscriptions on Greek jars, and they began to pay attention to his many other natural abilities. Undoubtedly, Chatwin's eventual rise to the company's top levels had begun in earnest (*Bruce Chatwin*, 26).

In 1965, Chatwin became head of the Impressionist Paintings and Antiquities Division and the youngest partner in the history of Sotheby's. In the same year he also met and became enamored of an American woman, Elizabeth Chanler, who was secretary to the chairman of Sotheby's, Peter Wilson. After a short courtship, they married in August of that same year.

Ms. Chanler was a graduate of Radcliffe College and was the daughter of a retired admiral in the United States Navy. Like Chatwin, she loved to travel, and she made frequent trips with him; he mentions her often in his records of their journey (his third) to Afghanistan. Though Chatwin was obsessively private about his personal life, Paul Theroux, who collaborated with him on the book *Nowhere Is a Place* (1985), claims that many of Chatwin's friends knew that he was a homosexual, and some of them were shocked at his marriage. Theroux states, "Yet it was obvious to anyone who knew him that in speaking tenderly of marital bliss he was always suppressing a secret and more lively belief in homosexuality. That he was homosexual bothered no one; that he never spoke about it was rather disturbing. . . . I wanted to know more about his homosexual life . . . because if I like someone I want to know everything. . . . He never wrote about his sexuality, and some of us have laid our souls bare."[4] Much speculation took place when rumors began to spread in 1987 that Chatwin's mysterious illness was actually AIDS and not the rare Chinese bone disease he claimed to have contracted.

In spite of Chatwin's meteoric rise in the ranks of Sotheby's, he began to have problems with the chairman, Peter Wilson, over some private lucrative deals Chatwin had made with some dealers outside of Sotheby's, a common practice among the poorly paid employees, who, if they were not from wealthy families, were required to supplement their incomes. Though company policy forbade employees to indulge in such private arrangements, many of them did so at their own risk. According to Murray, Peter Wilson himself warned Chatwin to avoid such activities, although Wilson may simply have looked the other way. It was at this time that Chatwin's eye problems began to recur, due mostly to overstrain from examining too closely the art objects he handled daily. One morning he woke up blind, but his sight returned the next day. His ophthalmologist suggested he take a trip to places where the horizons were long and thus might relieve and correct his overworked eyes. Chatwin left London and traveled to the Sudan, where his obsession with nomadic tribes and his concept of pastoral nomadism became firmly entrenched. Shortly after his return, in 1966, he left Sotheby's to take up archaeological studies at the University of Edinburgh.

There are several other theories about the real reasons that Chatwin left his position at one of the world's most prestigious organizations. A close friend of Chatwin's, Kenneth Rose, claimed that Chatwin told him "that Peter Wilson had promised to make him one of the three trusted young directors who would eventually run and control the firm" (*Bruce Chatwin*, 30). He was not appointed and walked out. Peter Levi and

Colin Thubron claimed that Chatwin told them he was both bored and burnt out, though Michael Cannon suggests that Chatwin was "fed up with the people. He just thought they were a bunch of charlatans" (p. 30). He further told Thubron that "combing through the death columns of the *Times* in search of potential pickings . . . ultimately revolted him" (p. 31).

Chatwin's studies at Edinburgh did not satisfy him for long; though he enjoyed learning Sanskrit, he was unimpressed by academic archaeology. He spent his summer vacations on nomadic expeditions in the Central Asian steppes. His interest in the pathways of the nomads who moved eastward from Mongolia to the plains of Hungary involved him in a project for the Asia Society of America. He coedited an impressive book, *"Animal Style" Art from East to West,* with Emma Bunker and Ann Farkas. In the foreword Chatwin is called "an anthropologist at heart" who finds "shamanism the most likely inspiration for the Animal Style in its various manifestations."[5] As Murray explains, "The Animal Style is the name given to the animal motif art of the nomads of the Euro-Asian steppes which flourished from China to Ireland during the Iron Age, and, later, in the barbarian art of the Migrations Period" (*Bruce Chatwin,* 33–34). It is in this book that his first major publication appeared, a 1970 essay called "The Nomadic Alternative" that was to have been the first chapter for his projected magnum opus on pastoral nomadism, a book he would never write. In *The Songlines,* he claims to have burned the manuscript but saved the notes, which became part of the "Notebook" section of that work years later.

Once Chatwin left Sotheby's, he was able to travel to places he had always wanted to visit and to pursue his favorite topic: pastoral nomadism. His visit to the Sudan and the time he spent with an actual nomadic tribe had whetted his appetite for western and northern Africa. In 1971 he traveled to Dahomey, Senegal, Mali, and Mauritania, and it was in Dahomey that he first became fascinated with the Brazilian slave trader Francisco de Souza, who became the subject of his second book, *The Viceroy of Ouidah.* He revisited Dahomey again in 1977 with the intention to do further research into De Souza's life but arrived in the middle of a coup, was arrested for being a mercenary, and decided to leave Dahomey (which had been renamed Benin under its Marxist leaders) and write a novel about De Souza instead.

In 1973 Chatwin, struggling financially, was rescued by an editor at the London *Sunday Times,* Francis Wyndham, who offered him a job as an adviser on art and architectural matters. He became instead a freelance writer on whatever topics he found compelling, thanks to Wyndham's wisdom in letting the young man pursue his own unique interests. It was to Wyndham that Chatwin allegedly sent the now-legendary telegram from Paris—"Gone to Patagonia for six months"—that added to the many myths formulating around Chatwin's life. Wyndham claims he does not remember such a telegram: "It must be a fiction . . . a sort of *Sunday Times* myth" (*Bruce Chatwin,* 39). Out of those six months came Chatwin's first critically acclaimed book, *In Patagonia,* which soared onto the bestseller list. The book was so successful with both the public and the critics that he won two very distinguished awards: the Hawthornden Prize, in 1978, and the E. M. Forster Award of the American Academy of Arts and Letters, in 1979. Though the book purported to be a nonfictional travelogue, several critics spotted some none-too-hidden fictive techniques from time to time, and the question of how to categorize it became problematic. Travel writer and critic Colin Thubron best summarizes all of Chatwin's books' unique formal characteristics: "[F]acts shimmer on the edge of fiction, and fiction reads like facts. They defy category."[6]

It is in *In Patagonia* that Chatwin first presents themes that he would pursue for the rest of his life: nomadic pastoralism versus settlement, the fall of Edenic innocence into the ruins of European technology, and the tragic dependence of one culture's growth on a native culture's diminishment. Though he met any number of interesting characters from Scotland, Wales, Germany, South Africa, and England in Patagonia, he noted that they all unconsciously reconstructed their own cultures in the midst of a thriving native culture that they viewed as benighted and decidedly anti-Christian. It was the European immigrants' unquestioned arrogance and their pragmatic use and abuse of the Araucanian Indians that resulted in the virtual extinction of all native tribes in that area. It is also in this book that Chatwin discovers that great quests for such mythic treasures as the Grail, the Golden Fleece, and the New Jerusalem are actually metaphors for mankind's need for transcendence and are not actual geographical journeys. The great ancient mythic journeys become interiorized epics in the radical works of such writers as Gustave Flaubert, Marcel Proust, and James Joyce. Though Chatwin knew this intellectually from an early age, his own ultimate southern journey to the end of the earth and, in a mythic sense, to hell itself brought home that knowledge with absolute certainty. He also discovered the absurdity of his own quest, to replace his family's grail—the piece of mylodon sloth skin that Uncle Charley Milward brought back to England in the early part of the twentieth century. Chatwin made that most important realization serendipitously; that is, *on his way* to the ancient cave to find a replacement for the family treasure, he realized that the journey itself was the treasure.

The success of *In Patagonia* enabled Chatwin to gather together the research he had done on his two trips to Dahomey (Benin) and to finish his next book, *The Viceroy of Ouidah,* though he continued to publish many travelogues, profiles, and essays for the *Sunday Times* over the next three years. Some of the more notable pieces were his lengthy interviews and profiles of André Malraux and Maria Reiche, the anthropologist working on the Peruvian pampa, and the story of the Soviet Union's greatest art collector, George Costakis. He was also beginning to publish stories and travel essays in *Granta* under its enterprising editor Bill Buford.

In 1980 Chatwin published *The Viceroy of Ouidah,* a book that could not have been more unlike *In Patagonia.* It is unapologetically novelistic, and Chatwin's brilliant characterization of Da Silva (the fictional version of the notorious Brazilian slave trader De Souza) resembles psychological studies by Herman Melville and Joseph Conrad. Chatwin's genius as a fiction writer shows itself in the subtle way he creates an exceptionally evil character who remains compellingly human throughout the book. Chatwin's romantic beliefs in the essential goodness of human nature also come through, in his careful delineation of how the cruel circumstances of Da Silva's childhood brutalized him into one of modern literature's genuine monsters. Like Chatwin's previous book, this novel demonstrates how a Christian European culture corrupts another by engaging one native people in enslaving others of their race. *The Viceroy of Ouidah,* like *In Patagonia,* demonstrates the vicious pattern of building one's Eden on the ruins of another culture but with greater dramatic impact due to the resources that fiction affords.

Chatwin's next book, *On the Black Hill* (1980), which was clearly a novel, reverses completely the direction in which his fiction had been moving for five years. He told Michael Ignatieff, "It always irritated me to be called a travel writer. So I decided to write something about people who never went out. That's how *On the Black Hill* came into being."[7] Such a radical turnabout became a characteristic pattern not only for Chatwin's book topics but also for his rarely predictable lifestyle. For example, Chatwin fell in love with Wales on a childhood visit with his father and on subsequent visits to close English friends who had holiday homes in eastern Wales. Since childhood, he had looked on the borderlands between western England and Wales as a place of great natural beauty, and an important ingredient of that beauty was its remoteness. Mythically, Wales represents for the English imagination the route to the Western Isles of Blessedness, since all quests move in a "westerly" direction—from the familiar to the mysterious and unknown. But in *On the Black Hill* Chatwin takes the opportunity to explore the idea of settlement and to test its human limitations: is it possible for settlers to avoid the inevitable fall into "the sins of settlement"—greed, private property, the corruption of ownership? Can the twin brothers, Benjamin and Lewis, sustain their innocence in the isolation of their Welsh farm, The Vision? Or are even the most remote locations vulnerable to the outside world's corruptions? Chatwin explores those questions and many more in this stunning psychological novel by reworking the Cain and Abel myth with telling insight.

When *On the Black Hill* was published in 1980, it won two major literary awards: the Whitbread Award, for an author's first novel, and the James Tait Black Prize, for best novel. The book was also made into a film seven years later and underwent several dramatic adaptations.

In 1984, Chatwin embarked on an extended journey through the Central Australian desert to gather information for his next book, *The Songlines,* published in 1987, when Chatwin's AIDS was in its first stages. No one expected the phenomenal success, both critical and financial, that *The Songlines* generated; this book is considered Chatwin's masterpiece. Though it is an adventure story of two men exploring the remotest parts of aboriginal Australia, it is also a novel of ideas about the ominous fate of Western civilization. It is also a lengthy meditation on the ruins of a prelogical civilization forced to dwell in the fallen world of time and permanent location—on nomads coerced into settlement. They, like their Patagonian brothers and sisters, are thereafter plagued by depression and alcoholism of epidemic proportions.

The treasure that the narrator uncovers, however, is the infinite distance between a European linear cosmos and the aboriginal cyclic one. He discovers in the aboriginals' concept of the "Songlines" the key to the integral relationship between their spiritual, religious, and geographical worlds—that they are inseparably one. Their spiritual cosmology predicates a world created out of the songs of their ancient ancestors, songs that have established their ancestral territory down to the present time. By naming in song all objects or features of the landscape, they call the world into existence with the musical power of their imaginations. Chatwin found in aboriginal cosmology the final proof that nomadic pastoralism was mankind's original "innocence." As their ancient totemic ancestors traveled nomadically throughout the land, they scattered a trail of words and songs along their footprints known as "Dreaming-tracks," which became paths of communication among the most distant tribes and established a kind of sacramental system in which everyone—past, present, and future—participates equally.

Chatwin published his last novel, *Utz,* in 1988. He intended this novel to be longer than it was, but due to the wasting effects of AIDS it became his shortest work to date. By creating a detailed study of the microcosmic world of postwar Prague, Chatwin once again reversed the literary world's expectations, in the same way that *On the Black Hill*'s domestic world supplanted the earlier exoticisms of Patagonia and Dahomey. An assignment from a magazine editor had occasioned his 1967 visit to Prague to research Emperor Rudolf II's obsession for collecting the rarest kinds of objets d'art. But he found that he wanted to extend that original assignment to examine the nature of collecting—"the psychopathology of the compulsive collector" (*Bruce Chatwin,* 110).

The character of Czech aristocrat Kaspar Utz seems to be an amalgam of the many collectors Chatwin knew throughout his life. The book is also an unapologetic mystery novel in the tradition of Graham Greene or John le Carré, as an unnamed narrator follows one dead-end lead after another in a series of frustrating attempts to discover the fate of Utz's million-dollar collection of rare Meissen figurines after his death. In the narrator's nine-hour interview with Utz, Chatwin juxtaposes the bleak world of Communist bureaucracies with the equally disturbing world of capitalistic greed. The book also explores the bewildering boundaries between appearance and reality and the dangers attending obsessed collectors' ability to confuse those two psychological realms. But *Utz* also continues Chatwin's enduring interest in the nature of the mythopoeic process in the small, solipsistic world of Kaspar Utz.

Though seriously ill, Chatwin managed to visit the movie set of Werner Herzog's adaptation of *The Viceroy of Ouidah* (as *Cobra Verde*) in 1988, an experience he immortalized in one of his most telling and humorous essays, "Werner Herzog in Ghana." He also made a heroic effort to visit the set of Andrew Grieve's production of *On the Black Hill* in Wales in the spring of 1987. It was not until two years after Chatwin's death, however, that George Sluizer directed a critically acclaimed film version of *Utz.*

The facts surrounding Chatwin's death immediately entered the realm of myth and have come down to the present as confusing examples of hearsay, innuendo, impression, and gossip. Chatwin himself claimed that his illness was "a rare fungus of the bone-marrow" he picked up in China that ate up, or prohibited the production of, red blood corpuscles. The fungus, he explained, "had been recorded among 10 healthy peasants in Western China, and in the corpuscles of a killer-whale cast up on the shores of Arabia" (*Bruce Chatwin*, 124). He denied having contracted HIV. Another story was that he fell ill and died "from eating a thousand-year-old egg." All of Chatwin's obituaries mentioned the bone-marrow fungus as the cause of his death. However, three weeks *before* his death, there appeared in the British newspaper *Today* (6 September 1988) a deeply disturbing notice: "Top Author Chatwin Falls Victim to AIDS." When the *Evening Standard* announced Chatwin's death in Nice, France, on 18 May, a reporter stated that Redmond O'Hanlon, one of Chatwin's executors, had claimed that Chatwin had indeed died of "complications arising from AIDS" (*Bruce Chatwin*, 124). No family members are known to have either affirmed or denied the allegation that AIDS was the cause of his death, but there is no question that AIDS killed him.

The battle of sexual politics regarding Chatwin began when Sean French of the *New Statesman and Society* and (at a later date) Duncan Fallowell of the *Guardian* attacked Chatwin for "cowardice in not coming clean about his bisexuality and HIV status" ("Wandering Star," 36). Roger Clarke calls both of these politically correct writers "Puritans from the left" whose language embodies "an almost fascistic enthusiasm for strength and moral probity" (p. 36). Fallowell's criticism opens up new possibilities for alternative interpretations of Chatwin's works, particularly regarding the unconscious sexual agendas beneath Benjamin and Lewis's symbiotic relationship in *On the Black Hill* and Francisco da Silva's covert homosexual life in *The Viceroy of Ouidah*.

Further "evidence" of Chatwin's homosexuality surfaced in July of 1991 when O'Hanlon cited the existence of a secret diary "written in code and deposited with the antiquarian bookseller Bertram Rota in London" (*Bruce Chatwin*, 127). Chatwin's wife, Elizabeth, immediately denied its existence, since her husband never kept a diary—only notebooks. O'Hanlon further insisted that an unnamed "expert" had been hired to break the code. What was revealed, according to the London *Times,* were "detailed records of 'every personal relationship' [that] were 'very explicit about his liaisons' " (p. 127). And Susannah Clapp's comprehensive memoir, published in the *New Yorker* in December 1996, leaves no doubt about Chatwin's homosexual orientation. According to Chatwin's will, however, all his papers were to have been deposited in

the Bodleian Library at Oxford until the year 2009. Other executors
claimed to know nothing whatsoever of the diary's existence, though
David Sexton, an old friend of Chatwin's, insisted that Chatwin wanted
young gay men to know that he had died of AIDS and that when he
first learned of his infection, he had thought seriously about suicide—
leaping off a cliff on the Jungfrau. As history shows, however, he went
ahead and wrote what one critic called his most perfect book, *Utz,* after
he entered the Radcliffe Infirmary (p. 127). Sexton also warned
Chatwin's official biographer, Nicholas Shakespeare, that neither he nor
any other scholar would ever be able to untangle the massive complexities of the man's life. Few biographies are so anxiously awaited.

But it was Chatwin's fellow writer and devoted friend Salman
Rushdie who wrote his most affectionate obituary, in the *Observer;* it is an
obituary that brings to the fore the man's most charming and lovable
virtues: "He was a magnificent raconteur of Scheherazadean inex-
haustibility, a gilt-edged name-dropper, a voracious reader of esoteric
texts, a scholar gypsy, a mimic—his Mrs. Gandhi was perfect—and a
giggler of international class. He was as talkative as he was curious, and
he was curious about everything, from the origins of evil to the question
asked by the Little Suburu. His words about the ex-Chamberlain of
King Zog of Albania are truer of himself: 'People of his kind will never
come again.' What a voice we lost when his fell silent! How much he
still had to say!"[8] What interested Chatwin most was the power of myth
to define reality and not the other way around. John Ryle called him "a
mythomane in the best sense of the term" (*Bruce Chatwin,* 127).

Michael Ignatieff, however, has the last word in his deeply moving
final portrait of Bruce Chatwin, published a few months before his
death; Chatwin was gray haired and emaciated by AIDS "but still incor-
rigibly stylish in a pair of high-altitude sunglasses. He said he had
bought them for his next trip to the Himalayas. He lay there and talked
in a faint whisper, full of cackles and laughter like some grand and unre-
pentant monarch in exile, or like one of the fantastic and touching figures in his own fiction, staring up at the bright blue sky, while the white
clouds scudded across his black glasses."[9]

Chapter Two
In Patagonia:
"The Ultimate Southern Journey"

There are at least three stories surrounding the origins of Bruce Chatwin's momentous journey to Patagonia in 1975. The first concerns a visit he made to the 93-year-old designer and architect Eileen Gray at her Rue de Bonaparte flat in Paris. In her elegant salon hung a map of Patagonia that she had painted in watercolors, a map that Chatwin admired and later inherited. After he told Ms. Gray that he had always wanted to travel there, she said, "So have I. Go there for me" (*Bruce Chatwin*, 40). Nicholas Murray states that this was the decisive moment when Chatwin sent, from Paris, a now-famous telegram to the editor of the London *Sunday Times Magazine* announcing, "Gone to Patagonia for six months."

The "facts" regarding the existence of the telegram are buried in a sea of misunderstandings, doubtful memories, and myth. But this kind of incident was not uncommon in the complex life of Bruce Chatwin, who appeared to thrive on such drama. Two former editors of the *Sunday Times Magazine* claim to know nothing about any such telegram principally because Chatwin was never a member of their editorial staff; he was a freelance contributor who was paid a healthy retainer of £2,000 a year and would not have needed to announce his departure to any editor. A *Times* editor and one of Chatwin's closest friends, Francis Wyndham suggested that "[i]t must be a fiction" and called it "a sort of *Sunday Times* myth" (*Bruce Chatwin*, 39).

However, Chatwin's former editor at the *Sunday Times,* Magnus Linklater, recalls that Chatwin had suggested a piece on the legendary Butch Cassidy and the Sundance Kid and their escape to Patagonia, located on the southern tip of Argentina. Linklater is fairly confident that he commissioned such a piece from Chatwin but lost track of it until *In Patagonia* appeared two years later to worldwide acclaim and jogged his memory.

Much more compelling reasons for Chatwin's trip come out of his childhood memories of his grandmother's cousin, Charley Milward, and

Milward's romantic role as young Chatwin's boyhood hero: "Charley Milward was a captain of a merchant ship that sank at the entrance to the Strait of Magellan. He survived the wreck and settled nearby, at Punta Arenas, where he ran a ship-repairing yard. The Charley Milward of my imagination was a god among men—tall, silent and strong, with black mutton-chop whiskers and fierce blue eyes. He wore his sailor's cap at an angle and the tops of his sea-boots turned down."[1] Chatwin's connection to Captain Milward was made even stronger when Milward brought back to Chatwin's grandmother a piece of brontosaurus skin, which became the family's most sacred relic and was kept in his grand-mother's cabinet of curiosities in Birmingham. That piece of skin became the spiritual center of the Chatwin family history, even though it was later discovered that it was not from a brontosaurus but rather from a mylodon, or giant sloth. The story is that Charley Milward, hav-ing discovered the mylodon in a cave in Tierra del Fuego, had the entire carcass "jointed, salted, packed in barrels, and shipped to the Natural History Museum in South Kensington, London" (*In Patagonia,* 1). Unfortunately, the giant animal went rotten during the trip, and only the bones were eventually displayed. Disaster struck again years later when the young Chatwin asked his grandmother for a piece of the mythic beast's skin and she casually replied that she had thrown it away. That loss then became the call to adventure for young Chatwin for the next 20 years. He simply had to find a way to replace that numinous piece of skin that might somehow restore a kind of sacred center to his family. The skin, with its grail-like qualities, became the object of a holy quest.

Another important but less compelling reason for going to Patago-nia—at least for the child Bruce—was the threatening shadow of Joseph Stalin and Bruce's conviction that Western civilization would soon end in atomic cataclysmic war between the East and the West. It was fairly obvious that Patagonia, located at the very bottom of the world, would be one of the few safe places on the planet in such an event. As Chatwin states, "My interest in Patagonia survived the loss of the skin; for the Cold War woke in me a passion for geography. . . . We started an Emigration Committee and made plans to settle in some far corner of the earth. . . . The war would come in the Northern Hemi-sphere, so we looked to the Southern . . . and we fixed on Patagonia as the safest place on earth" (*In Patagonia,* 3).

A third but equally crucial reason that Chatwin decided to embark on the ultimate journey south was that he wanted to make real the ultimate mythic journey to the earth's literal underworld: "[The journey] did give me the idea for the form of a travel book, for the oldest kind of travel tale is one in which the narrator leaves home and goes to a far country in search of a legendary beast" (*NP,* 35). As the critic Alastair Reid suggests, the tradition of the traveler's tale is "the oldest form of storytelling."[2]

In a lecture Chatwin gave with another formidable travel writer, Paul Theroux, he comments on the mythic resonances that the word *Patagonia* evokes: "The word 'Patagonia,' like Mandalay or Timbuktu, lodged itself in the Western imagination as a metaphor for the Ultimate, to the point beyond which one could not go. Indeed, in the opening chapter of *Moby Dick* Melville uses 'Patagonia' as an adjective for the outlandish, the monstrous and fatally attractive" (*NP,* 21). But he also adds that both he and Theroux always had been "literary travellers" and were interested in how "Patagonia has affected the literary imagination" (p. 21). It is obvious throughout *In Patagonia* that Chatwin is interweaving his own version of his Patagonian journey with those of many previous writers who paved his way, writers such as W. H. Hudson, Thomas Falkner, Samuel Lothrop, Lucas Bridges, Charles Darwin, and even Magellan.

Speaking for both himself and Theroux, Chatwin points out that both travel writers had always been fascinated by exiles: "If the rest of the world blew up tomorrow, you would still find in Patagonia an astonishing cross-section of the world's nationalities, all of whom have drifted towards these 'final capes of exile' for no other apparent reason than the fact that they were there. On any one day in Patagonia, the traveller could expect to encounter a Welshman, an English gentleman farmer, a Haight-Ashbury Flower Child, a Montenegran nationalist, an Afrikaaner, a Persian missionary for the Bahai religion, or the Arch-deacon of Buenos Aires on his round of Anglican baptisms" (*NP,* 21). Chatwin's description is an abbreviated but quite accurate catalog of the variety of people that he encounters throughout *In Patagonia.*

The literary impact of Patagonia on the imaginations of some of English and American literature's greatest writers was another magnet that drew Chatwin to one of the world's most desolate locations. He finds it not at all farfetched that the Tehuelche Indians—a tribe of giants—may very well have been the models for Jonathan Swift's "coarse but amiable inhabitants of Brobdingnan" and that the black albatross that eighteenth-century privateer Captain Shelvocke ominously describes in *A Voyage Round the World* became a defining textual influence on Samuel Taylor

Coleridge's most famous poem, "The Rime of the Ancient Mariner" (*NP,* 25–26). Chatwin cannot resist displaying his immense gift for scholarly documentation and delineates the circuitous journey of that black albatross: "In *The Road to Xanadu,* the American scholar John Livingston Lowes traced the Mariner's victim to a 'disconsolate Black Albatross' shot by one Hatley, the mate of Captain George Shelvocke's privateer in the eighteenth century. Wordsworth had a copy of this voyage and showed it to Coleridge when the two men tried to write the poem together" (*In Patagonia,* 90).

Although documenting the genesis of Chatwin's obsession with Patagonia as a geomythical vortex of literary inspiration is important, he exposes even deeper reasons for his need to identify with earlier exiles and wanderers: "Coleridge himself was a 'night-wandering man' . . . a drifter around rooming houses, unable to sink roots anywhere. He had a bad case of what Baudelaire called 'The Great Malady: Horror of One's Home.' Hence his identification with other blighted wanderers: Cain, The Wandering Jew, or the horizon-struck navigators of the sixteenth century. For the Mariner was himself" (*In Patagonia,* 90). *In Patagonia* is, in effect, Chatwin's first major examination and analysis of what would become one of his lifelong themes. Nicholas Murray succinctly points out that though Chatwin's five books are enormously diverse in both subject matter and theme, they all seem to converge on one major theme: human restlessness. Their diversity "should not prevent us from recognizing the deep continuities between each of them and the way in which they were always the reflection of a brilliant and idiosyncratic inquiring mind that continually revisited a certain set of obsessive ideas about the original restlessness in human nature which he himself so strikingly embodied" (*Bruce Chatwin,* 10). Certainly Chatwin's numerous journeys to write about and live with nomadic tribes and his own nomadic existence attest to his imagination's inability to let go of that idée fixe. And there is little doubt that Chatwin considered himself one of Western civilization's latest "blighted wanderers." He always sided with Abel, the nomadic wanderer, and blamed the Fall of Mankind on Abel's brother, Cain, who not only went in the wrong direction—east— but became the eventual founder of the first city, Enoch. For Chatwin, settlement was the Fall, and he examines even more deeply the cultural repercussions of the "sins of settlement" in his fourth book, *The Songlines* (1987), published some 10 years later.

As if the list of literary masters whose imaginations Patagonia influenced, such as Swift, Coleridge, and Melville, were not impressive enough, Chatwin adds Shakespeare. In both *In Patagonia* and *Nowhere Is a Place* (1985) Chatwin proposes a theory that may seem to more moderate critics a bit farfetched. He unequivocally declares that Caliban, Prospero's deformed, semihuman slave in Shakespeare's *Tempest,* is a Patagonian. But more about that in a later discussion.

The publication of *In Patagonia* brought Bruce Chatwin immediate fame and great praise from most literary critics and journalists. Hilton Kramer, a critic not easily impressed, called *In Patagonia* "a little masterpiece of travel, history and adventure." He also called it "a wonderful read" and added that Chatwin was one of the few writers who could write about both "society and nature with an equally informed and distinguished eye."[3] Critic David Rieff claimed that the book "quite simply revived travel writing from the genteel, philistine slumber in which the genre had reposed since the great days of Lawrence, Waugh, and Robert Byron."[4] It won him two very prestigious awards: the 1978 Hawthornden Prize and, in 1979, the E. M. Forster Award of the American Academy of Arts and Letters.

In addition to the high critical praise for the book, a corollary discussion began concerning the precise genre, or literary form, of this curious best-selling work. Was it merely a travel book, or a novelized travelogue? Hans Magnus Enzensberger notes "Chatwin's sublime disregard for the categories of fiction and non-fiction. *In Patagonia* has been called a 'documentary' and a 'travelogue,' but neither of these odious terms will fit. On the other hand, it showed the hand of a story-teller who did not fall for the illusion of originality."[5] Many travelers treated it as a literal travel guide, the way members of the Beat generation carried Jack Kerouac's *On the Road* in their hip pockets as they hitchhiked across America in the 1950s and 1960s. As James Chatto notes, "I wasn't the only tourist in Tierra del Fuego last year using Chatwin's *In Patagonia* as a Baedecker. His scrupulous honesty . . . lifts him at once above contemporary American travel writers, who cover the same ground but only in order to explore inner, egocentric horizons."[6] Colin Thubron additionally notes that in all five of Chatwin's books "facts shimmer on the edge of fiction, and fiction reads like fact. They defy category" ("Fantastical Tales," G9). Of all commentators, John Lanchester most clearly delineates the exotic nature of Chatwin's baroque imagination and suggests that the book may be so richly textured that it moves beyond any existing literary category: "He has a talent for the off-beat and the out-of-the-way, a kind of archeological talent for the excavation of interesting data—built out of facts and encounters and stories. It is a kind of cubist

travel book, to which the reader comes expecting the familiar exoticism
of travel writing and instead finds a bleaker and more melancholy foreignness, which constantly feeds back into English literary and cultural
history."[7]

There can be little doubt that Chatwin's ability to enhance facts with
fictional techniques raised the level of travel writing from mere
reportage to a serious examination of the spiritual lives of a wide variety
of European and native groups in one of the world's most desolate
regions. What he found in Patagonia confirmed what he had already
suspected about the enormous damage done to both the natives of the
region and the delicate ecological balance between the human, animal,
and plant life forms that cohabit in vital symbiotic relationships.
Chatwin had always been deeply interested in the relationship between
a place's physical geography and the spiritual condition of those who
lived there. *In Patagonia* was his first extensive examination of those relationships, and his findings were worse than he had expected.

Because the book's reach is so ambitious, Chatwin had to employ as
many means of presentation as he could find or invent. *In Patagonia* is,
then, a miscellany of genres that includes biography, autobiography, history, anthropology, myth, geography, religion, character portrait,
strange encounters, family history, and philosophical meditation.
Chatwin uses all of these methods—sometimes simultaneously—not
only to describe the landscape but also to evoke the spirit of the geography and its relationship to the original natives, the Araucanian Indians.
The book celebrates Patagonia's diversity and also, just as vividly,
laments what has been lost as a result of the invasions of the Welsh, the
Scots, the Boers, the Germans, the Afrikaaners—the whole panoply of
European colonizers. Chatwin spends a great deal of time reflecting on
Patagonia as a ruin, sullied by Western materialistic values (i.e., sheep
farming and oil interests). It is the book's meditation on ruins that raises
it into the company of other famous works whose subject matter is
ruins. As Guy Davenport points out, Charles Olson's great poem "The
Kingfishers" broods on the Maya ruins in Yucatan, just as Olson's
model, William Carlos Williams's epic poem *Paterson*, laments the fall of
America as manifested in his hometown in New Jersey. The Chilean
poet Pablo Neruda's long poem *Alturas de Macchu Picchu* and Herman
Melville's *Clarel* both meditate on the ruins of sacred centers.[8]

Although the ostensible reason for Chatwin's journey is to restore the
piece of mylodon skin that Uncle Charley Milward gave Chatwin's grandmother and thus reconstitute his family's mythic center, the quest also

involves Chatwin's attempt to discover his own spiritual resources and, therefore, who he is and what he is capable of. As important, Chatwin wishes to authenticate the findings of his extensive scholarship of this region of the world with a journey to the actual place. He also wants to add oral history to his expanding tapestry of various truths about Patagonia from multiple sources. Only an amalgamation of all these modes of information could satisfy Chatwin's demanding imagination.

As Chatwin arrives in Buenos Aires, he gives the reader an insight into the nature of his hyperactive mind and his research methods by showing how a common object—the telephone book—may contain massive amounts of cultural and historical information. "The history of Buenos Aires is written in its telephone directory. Pompey Romanov, Emilio Rommel, Crespina D. Z. de Rose, Ladislao Radziwil, and Elizabeta Marta Callamn de Rothschild—five names taken at random from among the R's—told a story of exile, disillusion and anxiety behind lace curtains" (*In Patagonia*, 4). What Chatwin is always looking for are patterns of *any* kind, and one of his habitual techniques throughout the book is to describe both the exteriors and interiors of the homes he visits. What he finds is that the majority of the immigrants have re-created, architecturally, the homes they left in Scotland, Wales, Germany, or whatever their country of origin.

Throughout his southern journey, Chatwin often takes trains and buses but also walks or hitches rides with strangers. Sometimes, however, the reader is not sure of how he actually gets from place to place, a flaw that consistently bothered one admirer of the book, Paul Theroux: "But his book was full of gaps. How had he travelled from here to there? How had he met this or that person? Life was never so neat as Bruce made out. . . . I used to look for links between the chapters, and between two conversations or pieces of geography" (*NP*, 14). But once Chatwin begins his journey into Patagonia—which begins at the Rio Negro River—the reader is seduced by the formidable detail that he consistently serves up. He immediately notices the broken condition of the Araucanian Indians—they have become migrant workers—and their sad fall into alcoholic dependence. A hundred years earlier they had been known as a race of fierce bravery, inspiring sixteenth-century poet Alonso de Ercilla to write "an epic poem in their honour and [call] it *Araucana*. Voltaire read it and through him the Araucanians became candidates for the Noble Savage (tough version). The Araucanians are still very tough and would be a lot tougher if they gave up drink" (*In Patagonia*, 14).

Chatwin comments many times throughout the book on the devastating effect that alcohol has had on all of Patagonia's native tribes.
Indeed, the alcoholic demise of the natives is a major theme not only in
this book but in *The Songlines*. Also, by bringing in literary and historical
information about these natives—such as the fact that de Ercilla's poem
influenced Voltaire's formulation of the concept of the Noble Savage—
deepens and enriches Chatwin's book enormously. John Lanchester's
suggestion that *In Patagonia* may be a "cubist travel book" is borne out
in the way Chatwin layers literary, historical, geographical, and mythic
information in one paragraph so that the reader views these Indians
from many perspectives simultaneously. Such great writers as James
Joyce (in *Ulysses*) and T. S. Eliot (in *The Waste Land*) used the same
"mythical" methods to lend historical and literary continuity and weight
to seemingly casual information. The pathetic image of the fall of these
once-noble natives resonates in the reader's mind and recalls instances of
the fall of other indigenous tribes and peoples. Readers of Chatwin's
works should be on the alert for this layering of information and images
because he presents it so artfully and so frequently that one can overlook
its significance.

Another technique Chatwin uses repeatedly is to invoke the presence
of other historical and literary personages on his southern journey.
Charles Darwin's *The Voyage of the Beagle* can be read as a parallel, or
alternative, text because Chatwin so consistently mentions it that he
could have titled *In Patagonia* something like *In the Tracks of Darwin*. The
other book that Chatwin frequently quotes and responds to is the most
famous book ever written on the subject, W. H. Hudson's *Idle Days in
Patagonia* (1893). Samuel Kirkland Lothrop's seminal text, *The Indians of
Tierra del Fuego* (1928), and Magellan's *First Voyage Round the World* surface quite often as Chatwin adds his unique contributions to those of his
historical and literary predecessors. His constant allusions to these writers and the way he brilliantly interweaves their texts with his are perhaps *In Patagonia*'s most impressive stylistic characteristic.

As Chatwin enters the Patagonian desert, he compares it to other
deserts he visited in Arabia but also contrasts his impressions with both
Darwin's and Hudson's. He mentions Darwin's curiosity over why these
"arid wastes" had taken such a strong hold of his imagination. Chatwin
contrasts Hudson's view of the desert and the profound influence it had
on his mind: "Hudson devotes an entire chapter of *Idle Days in Patagonia*
to answering Mr. Darwin's question, and he concludes that desert wanderers discover in themselves a primeval calmness (known also to the

simplest savage), which is perhaps the same as the Peace of God" (*In Patagonia*, 15). It is certainly possible that Chatwin is telling his reader about his own motivations for becoming a desert wanderer and about the rewards and difficulties of that profession. Paul Theroux further expands on Chatwin's speculations about the fertile barrenness of the Patagonian desert in *Nowhere Is a Place:* "Darwin's mistake was that he was looking for something in Patagonia, as in other times people looked for the Andean valley of Trapalanda with its White Indians, or the fabled city of Manoa sought for by Alonzo Pizarro; it is better, Hudson says, to look for nothing at all. Feel it, he says, and be moved by it" (*NP,* 39). What Hudson found there was "emptiness, desolation, the suspension of intellect," and it was those very qualities that brought him satisfaction: "He found in Patagonia an American Eden, a peaceable kingdom" (p. 42).

Though Chatwin considered himself one of history's many wanderers, he was always searching for evidence of the fall of a native people from a condition of Edenic innocence and blissful ignorance into a condition of enslavement in a spiritual and cultural wasteland. He found that evidence everywhere he looked. The irony of his mythic vision confronts him everywhere, however, because the voyage of the European immigrants to Patagonia became, for them, a quest for Avalon, the Isles of the Blessed, or the New Jerusalem. Their attempt to regenerate their Eden—to redeem themselves from the fallen condition of their European past—was, necessarily, built on the ruins of Patagonia's native cultures. The most painful tension throughout this complex narrative is that it witnesses and records the native Indians' fall from Edenic, timeless innocence into the time-bound, linear world of divided consciousness—that European imperative that divides the cosmos into intellectual categories of sacred and profane.

Once Chatwin leaves the great Patagonian desert, he begins a sequence of visits to the "new" citizens: the Welsh, the Germans, the Scots, the Boers, the Russians, and finally the English. The Welsh, like all of the other immigrants, have re-created Wales unconsciously, not only in terms of buildings—churches, cottages, pubs—but also religiously and culturally. What they wanted most to escape was any and all contact with the dreaded English. The Welsh have settled along the Chubat River, a place that earlier belonged to a now virtually extinct tribe of natives called the Tehuelche Indians. Chatwin notices that members of the tribe now work as day laborers and peons and that many of the men are in terrible shape. Chatwin doesn't preach; he merely presents with deadly accuracy. During dinner at a restaurant, he notes, "An Indian came in drunk and drank through three jugs of wine. His eyes were glittering slits in the red leather shield of his face" (*In Patagonia*, 22). Most everywhere Chatwin goes, he is treated decently and given food and a comfortable place to sleep, but he rarely fails to show the reader the natives' abject condition. He never uses the word *genocide*, but it is obvious that that is what is taking place throughout the land. It is a situation that never ceases to bewilder him.

The other narrative that keeps the plot moving throughout the book, besides Chatwin's quest to follow the life and times of Uncle Charley Milward, is the story that Chatwin initially wanted to pursue as a journalist for the London *Sunday Times Magazine*. That story concerns the life and times of two of North America's most lovable hero-outlaws, Butch Cassidy (Robert Leroy Parker) and the Sundance Kid (Harry Longabough). Finding Patagonia one of the world's most remote places, both men fled there to escape arrest and imprisonment by North American authorities. Chatwin makes clear that Butch Cassidy never killed a man; he was merely one of the world's great bank robbers, aided by the Sundance Kid and his woman friend Etta Place. Chatwin spends a great deal of time retelling the adventures of the infamous Wild Bunch, but his real interest is in oral history—that is, in finding and talking to people who may have known these remarkable characters. He even finds a connection between Uncle Charley Milward and Butch Cassidy; they actually met, but under uneventful circumstances. Allusions to Butch Cassidy and the Wild Bunch surface frequently throughout the book and serve to underscore the deep romantic sensibilities that Chatwin cannot resist displaying.

As Chatwin travels deeper into the south, he encounters a Catholic priest—a member of the Salesian order—Father Manuel Palacios. He labels him a "Patagonian Polymath" because he is the first native he has met who, because of his intellectual gifts, has become highly successful in a European religious community. He possesses three earned doctorates (in theology, anthropology, and archeology) and is in the process of writing a comprehensive history of the Salesian order and a treatise on biblical prophecies of the New World. But he is a dying man and so can give Chatwin only a half an hour. After overwhelming Chatwin with massive amounts of information about geography, tribal histories, rock paintings of the South, and other esoteric subjects, Father Palacios stuns him with his passionate conviction that unicorns actually existed in

Patagonia thousands of years ago and is amazed that scientists have not as yet uncovered their bones.

After deciding to search for more information about his uncle Charley and to question some people about the prevalence of the unicorn myths, Chatwin wanders into the town of Puerto Deseado, where he encounters another Salesian House of Study that incorporates "every architectural style from the Monastery of St. Gall to a multi-story car-park; a Gruta de Lourdes; and a railway station in the form and proportion of a big Scottish country house" (*In Patagonia,* 86). During his stay there, he meets and engages in long discussions with a group of scientists, one of whom is an ornithologist studying the migration of Jackass Penguins. During his conversation with this "severe" young man, Chatwin finds compelling support for his theory about the origin of human restlessness: "We talked late into the night, arguing whether or not we, too, have journeys mapped out in our central nervous systems: it seemed the only way to account for our insane restlessness" (*In Patagonia,* 86). Here again is the recurring theme of at least two of Chatwin's books and the subject of his first important anthropological paper, "The Nomadic Alternative." For aeons human beings have been migrating from east to west and from north to south, and virtually all narratives are about journeys of some sort; Chatwin feels compelled to explore even more deeply physiological reasons for these permanent behavioral patterns that humans share with animals.

As Chatwin descends further south nearer Tierra del Fuego, he encounters more English settlers. These settlers are generally more prosperous than others he has encountered because they got into sheep farming at a most advantageous time—in the 1890s. He meets Archie Tuffnell, an old acquaintance of his uncle Charley's, and then travels down to San Julian, where a number of mythic, literary, and historical associations converge. However, Chatwin is generally distrustful of traditional explanations of tribal origins that do not have a linguistic basis to support theoretical positions. For example, he puzzles over the etymological origin of the word *Patagonia* throughout the journey. His presence in a particular geographical locale jogs his memory of other explorers' attempts to understand not only the significance of the word but, as important, to trace the history of the Patagonian figure through the literature and lore of the past. He goes back in memory to the earliest Western accounts of these exotic creatures, found in the text of Magellan's sixteenth-century trip, which was chronicled by Antonio Pigafetta.

Chatwin is convinced that Jonathan Swift's Brobdingnagian giants were Patagonians taken from Pigafetta's accounts. The creatures Pigafetta describes run faster than horses, and Magellan first addresses them as "Patagon!," meaning "big foot," because their moccasins were so huge. Chatwin, however, disputes the translation of the word; even though "pata" in Greek means "foot," "gon" has no meaning. He is convinced that Magellan was familiar with and carried with him an obscure sixteenth-century Castillean medieval romance entitled *Primaleon of Greece* (and this is seven years before Magellan's trip to Patagonia). In the romance, there is a monster called the "Grand Patagon" that has the head of a dog and the feet of a hart but human understanding. Primaleon decides to take the creature back to Polonia, where it becomes a character in a beauty-and-the-beast scenario. Magellan likewise captured two Tehuelche Indians—giants—and intended to take them back to Spain but died before returning home.

What interests Chatwin most is how the same figure of the giant surfaced 90 years later in Shakespeare's *Tempest*. In September of 1521, Magellan saw, near San Julian, a naked, dancing giant. The giant was brought peacefully to Magellan but kept pointing to the sky, thinking that Magellan and his men had come from heaven. Later, when Magellan's men decided to kidnap two of the Tehuelche giants—big-footed ones—the giants cried out to their demonic god, Setebos, to save them. In Shakespeare's *Tempest* there is a very similar scene, in which Caliban asks Stephano, "Hast thou not dropped from heaven?"

> STEPHANO: Out o' the moon, I do assure thee: I was the man in the moon when time was.
>
> CALIBAN: I must obey: his art is of such power
> It would control my dam's god, Setebos,
> And make a vassal of him.

As Paul Theroux notes, "The giants were described by other early explorers: de Weert, Spelbergen and Shelvocke, and they adapted Magellan's term, *Patagones,* 'big feet' " (*NP,* 56). Chatwin, though unconvinced that the word *Patagon* meant "big foot," adds additional lines from *The Tempest:* Stephano says, "If I can recover [Caliban], and keep him tame / and get to Naples with him, he's a present for any / Emperor that ever trod on neat's leather."

He is sure that Shakespeare was familiar with the text; Swift certainly was. But what convinces Chatwin of these writers' knowledge of Pigafetta's chronicle is the image of a dog that emerges regularly in the works of both. Pigafetta mentions that the giant has the "head of a Dogge," and Trunculo says of Caliban, "I shall laugh myself to death at this puppy-headed monster." Here is where the enormous literary and historical resources of Chatwin's memory seem most convincing: "The origin of the 'dog-heads' is to be found in the 'vizzards' or battle masks, such as worn by Genghiz Khan's cavalry or the Tehuelches when they attacked John Davis at Puerto Deseado. Shakespeare could have picked them out of Hakluyt. But either way Caliban has a good claim to Patagonian ancestry" (*In Patagonia,* 97).

Nicholas Murray points out that Chatwin habitually used "a characteristic device" he calls "corroborative anecdote or observation" to support his interpretations and to give them a form of validation (*Bruce Chatwin,* 47). Chatwin's various theories are corroborated by Shakespeare, Magellan, Hakluyt, and, later on, by Swift and then himself. In *Nowhere Is a Place* he offers another discerning comment: "Patagon is a latter-day equivalent of Grendel" (*NP,* 65). He not only brings in historical and literary support for his imaginative assertions but also finds mythic analogues; for example, he identifies Caliban as a recurring type of half-animal, half-human character found in any number of texts. Chatwin summarizes his findings on Caliban's significance and also demonstrates the intricacies of his complex imagination: "I think we have here a situation in which a bad novel [*Primaleon of Greece*] inspired a great explorer to do something shoddy, which, in turn, inspired the greatest playwright to one of his greatest creations" (p. 69).

Chatwin's trip to Rio Gallegos moves him to a lengthy retelling of the fantastic exploits of one of Patagonia's most infamous revolutionary heroes: Antonio Soto. But one of Chatwin's reasons for narrating this complex story is to make the point that Soto survived the barbaric slaughters of many of the striking peasants and unionists and worked in 1945 in the iron foundry of a Mrs. Charles Amherst Milward in Punta Arenas.

It is impossible for Bruce Chatwin to ignore the mythic resonances of his descent into Tierra del Fuego, or "land of fire." And it is equally impossible for the informed reader not to view Chatwin's physical journey also as a mythic journey comparable to that of such literary characters as Ulysses, Aeneas, and Dante—a journey that scholars of mythology call "The Descent into the Underworld" or "The Descent into Hades or Hell." Chatwin reminds us that Tierra del Fuego is also the land of the dead because the Fuegian Indians are all dead, and he cannot resist further explicating the region's name: "Tierra del Fuego—The Land of Fire. The fires were the campfires of the Fuegian Indians. In one version Magellan saw smoke only and called it Tierra del Humo, the Land of Smoke, but Charles V said there was no smoke without fire and changed the name. The Fuegians are dead and all the fires are snuffed out. Only the flares of the oil rigs cast a pall over the night sky" (*In Patagonia,* 111). Though history has changed, mythic patterns remain, and the land of fire continues to be thought of as the bottom of the earth, or the underworld. Dutch cartographers drew Tierra del Fuego as the northern tip of Antarctica and "filled it with suitable monsters: gorgons, mermaids and the Roc, that outsize condor which carried elephants" (p. 111). Similarly, Dante placed the Hill of Purgatory at the center of the Antichthon, or Antarctica: "Fireland then is Satan's land, where flames flicker as fireflies on a summer night, and, in the narrowing circles of Hell, ice holds the shades of traitors as straws in glass" (p. 112).

Chatwin also traces this mythic land back to the ancient Greeks: "Tierra del Fuego was thought to be the tip of the Unknown Continent, the Antichthon or Anti-Earth, whose existence was originally postulated by Pythagoras. The Antichthon was an upside-down country, absolutely not meant for human beings, where snow fell upwards, trees grew downwards, the sun shone black, and its inhabitants were the sixteen-fingered Antipodeans who danced themselves into ecstasy. . . . It was, in other words, some kind of Hell. Small wonder, then, that Magellan refused to land" (*NP,* 85. This land of fire not only spawned Coleridge's albatross but ignited the imaginations of later writers. Edgar Allan Poe's reading of Captain James Weddell's 1822 *Voyage towards the South Pole,* according to Chatwin, was the genesis of Poe's *Narrative of Arthur Gordon Pym,* "his novel of a crazed, self-destructive journey." Pym lands on an island called Tsalal where everything is black, including the natives, and it is obvious that Poe has transformed the Fuegians into Tsalalians. Chatwin further asserts that *Pym* was one of the nineteenth century's most influential books, inspiring Dostoevsky to write one of his few literary essays and, since Charles Baudelaire translated it into French, generating a whole series of French "voyage" poems, from Baudelaire's famous "Voyage" to Arthur Rimbaud's "Drunken Boat" and "Being Beauteous." It is evident from this point on in Chatwin's journey that he unapologetically envisions himself traveling in the illustrious company of Coleridge, Poe, Dante, Ulysses, and even John Donne, whose last poem, "Hymne to God My God, in My Sickness," evoked visionary images of the bottom of the world.

Once Chatwin crosses the threshold and enters the land of fire, he finds validation in his extensive readings of the history of the area's indigenous Indians. The land is now being exploited for its oil reserves, but it was formerly a source of meat for the English. He once again runs into some Salesian priests; these men have become expert taxidermists and flower growers. One of the priests gives him a key to the local museum, where he views artifacts of the now-extinct Indians of Tierra del Fuego: "the Ona and the Haush, who were foot hunters; and the Alakaluf and the Yaghan (or Yamana) who were canoe hunters. All were tireless hunters and owned no more than they could carry" (*In Patagonia,* 114). As in his travels in the Sudan and Afghanistan, Chatwin's attention is drawn to nomadic tribes and to the effect that Western "civilization" had on their destiny. He repostulates the relationship between the natives and the immigrants as "the same old quarrel: of Abel, the wanderer, with Cain, the hoarder of property" (p. 122).

For Chatwin, the entrance into the "fireland" is a dramatic threshold experience rather than simply the logical conclusion to his southern journey, which has indeed become the ultimate journey south. On the shelves of the museum—which seems a mausoleum for the native tribes—the narrator views "their bones and equipment decayed on the glass shelves—bows, quivers, harpoons, baskets, guanaco capes—set alongside the material advances brought by a God, who taught them to disbelieve the spirits of moss and stones and set them to petit-point, crochet and copy-book exercises (examples of which were on display)" (*In Patagonia,* 114).

Chatwin then creates an eerie Dantean scene with overtones of the *Inferno* in which a young Salesian priest "with droopy eyelids" leads him "to some green swellings along the shore. Lansing one of these with a spade, he uncovered a purple pile of mussels, ashes and bones. 'Look,' he cried, 'the mandible of an Ona dog' " (p. 115). Chatwin never becomes strident in his condemnations of the cruel agendas of the European colonizers; rather, he merely presents a scene such as this with vivid accuracy. The images bespeak a kind of arrogant cruelty that overly dramatic rhetoric could never capture. Chatwin, ever the historian, then explains the conflicts between the Fuegian natives and the colonizers in what sounds like the genocidal story of the American pioneers and the Native Americans. The Onas began rustling sheep that the Europeans brought with them, a practice that threatened the big companies' dividends, and in typical European fashion the Onas were accused of Communist tendencies: "[T]he accepted solution was to round them up and civilize them in the Missions—where they died of infected clothing and the despair of captivity" (p. 117).

Chatwin then journeys to the town of Ushuaia, "the southernmost town in the world." The site is also a vortex for all the horrible destruction of another Fuegian tribe, the Yaghans. Chatwin casually but ironically summarizes the process: "For sixteen years Anglicanism, vegetable gardens and the Indians flourished. Then the Argentine Navy came and the Indians died of measles and pneumonia" (*In Patagonia,* 121). The town evolved from a navy base to a convict station and eventually to a military barracks. In *Nowhere Is a Place* there is a diagram showing the pattern of extinction of the Yaghan peoples. In 1843, the year Darwin and *The Beagle* left Tierra del Fuego, there were about 3,000 native Indians. By 1889, after the Argentine government distributed clothing to the freezing and half-starved Yaghans, there were approximately 400. By 1924, according to Samuel Lothrop, there were only 50 remaining. In 1925, a measles epidemic ravaged the rest: " 'With the exception of a few mixed bloods the Indians of Tierra del Fuego are probably extinct. All that is left of them is a monument in the little plaza of Ushuaia, "al Indio" ' " (*NP,* 81–82). Disheartened, Chatwin concludes his visit to the world's southernmost town: "I left Ushuaia as from an unwanted tomb" (*In Patagonia,* 132).

Chatwin retells the adventurous tales of one of Ushuaia's infamous prisoners, Simon Radowitzky, a Russian anarchist, and of Jemmy Button, a kidnapped Fuegian Indian who eventually returned to his home in Tierra del Fuego on *The Beagle* and murdered some missionaries. Charles Darwin, a passenger on *The Beagle,* came to like the young man who had been educated in some of the better English schools. Darwin did not, however, have anything but the most hostile feelings about the rest of the natives of Tierra del Fuego. He called them "the most abject and miserable creatures" and considered their language barely articulate.

It is the language of the Yaghans, however, that gives Chatwin his greatest insights into the deep structure of the natives' culture. After walking the 35 miles along the Beagle Channel, he arrives in Haberton and visits Clarita Goodall, who knew Charley Milward and who gave Chatwin a copy of Thomas Bridges's *Yaghan Dictionary.* Chatwin had actually examined Bridges's original manuscript in the British Museum and knew of the crucial importance of understanding a race through its language. A recurring pattern in Chatwin's research is that he invariably turns to language as the final revelation of a culture's spiritual core. Thomas Bridges, who had come to convert the Yaghans to Christianity in the 1880s, decided he had to construct a dictionary: "To his surprise, he uncovered a complexity of construction and a vocabulary no one had suspected in a 'primitive' people. . . . This gigantic operation was scarcely completed at his death in 1898. He had listed about 32,000 words without having begun to exhaust their reserves of expression" (*In Patagonia,* 135). Chatwin calls Bridges's dictionary a monument to the Yaghan people and suggests that it would have amazed Charles Darwin that a young man or woman of the tribe had a working vocabulary of about 30,000 words, more than even William Shakespeare ever wrote (*NP,* 77). The treasure that Chatwin finds at the bottom of the world becomes the key to his journey: language and etymology.

What Chatwin uncovers in his reading of Thomas Bridges's *Dictionary* becomes one of the major revelations of *In Patagonia,* a serendipitous discovery made possible by a Christian missionary who barely understood what he had happened upon. Long before pioneering linguistic studies by Ferdinand Saussure, Benjamin Lee Whorf, and Alfred Korzybski, Bridges's *Yaghan Dictionary* revealed the profound spiritual riches of so-called primitive peoples. What initially disturbed Bridges was the overwhelming specificity of the language and the complete lack of abstract words to express religious and moral ideas or aesthetic concepts. Everything is particular: "But the concepts of 'good' or 'beautiful,' so essential to Western thought, are meaningless unless they are rooted to things" (*In Patagonia,* 136). The specific richness of the Yaghan language would find its poetic counterpart in William Carlos Williams's later exhortation to his fellow imagist poets: "No ideas but in things!"

The Yaghan language is also tied very much to the local geography: "Named things are fixed points . . . which allow the speaker to plot the next move" (p. 136). Though Yaghan lacks any capacity for abstract, philosophical thought, it is still a highly expressive instrument and has the capacity to be much more subtle than English. For example, the Yaghans define *monotony* as "an absence of male friends"; *adulterous* can be understood only in terms of the hobby, which is "a small hawk that flits here and there, hovering motionless over its next victim" (p. 136). Chatwin also discovers the all-important position of verbs in Yaghan and their enormous capacity to delineate the subtlest distinctions. For example, the verb *īya* can mean only " 'to moor your canoe to a streamer of kelp'; *ōkon* 'to sleep in a floating canoe' (and quite different from sleeping in a hut, on the beach or with your wife); *ukōmona* 'to hurl your spear into a shoal of fish without aiming for a particular one' " (*In Patagonia,* 137).

Chatwin remembers from his earlier research that the Yaghans were inveterate wanderers—nomads who never wandered too far. Fittingly, their language exhibits a mariner's infatuation with space and time. The Yaghans called themselves "Yámana," a word that, when used as a verb, means "to live, breathe, be happy, recover from sickness or be sane" (p. 138). Most interesting, however, is the Yaghan people's religious cosmology: "A tribe's territory, however uncomfortable, was always a paradise that could never be improved on. By contrast, the outside world was Hell and its inhabitants no better than beasts" (p. 138). Once again, Chatwin finds corroboration of his theory about the Edenic condition of nomadic wanderers, and that settlement inevitably leads to a fatal cleavage between the human and the natural—between animal and plant life. Because of the arrogance that comes with settling, humans begin to act as though they were somehow above the laws and obligations of the geography on which they depend. They forget that they are an integral part of it and begin to abuse the land and its resources. The Yaghans are always aware of their connection to the land. Chatwin also suggests that when Jemmy Button—the highly English educated native—returned to Tierra del Fuego and murdered some missionaries, he may have mistaken them "as envoys of the Power of Darkness" (p. 138).

The last leg of the narrator's journey, to Punta Arenas, is also the most dangerous. Chatwin feels he must follow the same track that Lucas Bridges did in his famous book, *The Uttermost Part of the Earth,* one of Chatwin's favorite boyhood books; one of Chatwin's reasons for coming to Patagonia was to walk that very track. His host, Clarita Goodall, warns him not to risk the 25-mile walk because bridges have collapsed and heavy fog has made walking dangerous. There has been widespread flooding because of the beavers, and much of the trip is through dense forest. Indeed, Chatwin not only encounters flooding but is repeatedly attacked by two vicious condors. He refers to his forest journey as one "through a dark wood," a phrase that is unmistakably Dantean, as are many of the images of darkness and danger he uses to describe his trip. He does fall into black mud, as Clarita Goodall predicted he would, and has a very difficult time extricating himself from its dangerous pull. He crosses the same river at least 20 times; river crossings are always threshold experiences in the mythic journeys of young heroes, which Chatwin is obviously reenacting.

He finally arrives exhausted at Punta Arenas, where, once again, he encounters the Salesian fathers and a museum larger than the one he visited earlier at Rio Grande. As he is viewing the museum's contents, he notices with a sinking heart that the Christian sculptor gave the Yaghan Indians apelike features,

> which contrasted with the glucose serenity of the Madonna from the Mission Chapel on Dawson Island. The saddest exhibit was two copy-book exercises and photos of the bright-looking boys who wrote them: THE SAVIOR WAS IN THIS PLACE AND I DID NOT KNOW IT IN THE SWEAT OF THY BROW SHALT THOU EAT BREAD.
> So, the Salesians had noticed the significance of Genesis 3:19. The Golden Age ended when men stopped hunting, settled in houses and began the daily grind. (*In Patagonia*, 144)

The conclusion of the passage from Genesis confirms the ultimate punishment for the fall of Adam and Eve and their dramatic expulsion from the garden of Eden: "Until you return to the ground; for from it you were taken. Dust you are, to dust you shall return."[9] Once again, the recurring thread of Chatwin's pet theory concerning the real nature of the Fall surfaces; that is, the fall of humankind occurred when it settled into one place and stopped its nomadic hunting practices. Cain was the first hoarder and, therefore, founder of the first city, Enoch, which he named after his first son. Abel, with whom Chatwin always identified, was the wanderer-shepherd. The golden age—or Eden—ended when humans moved into settlements.

Bruce Chatwin is anything but a naive, uninformed traveler. He consistently views his journeys against the backdrop of the Bible and countless other books on Patagonia's archaeology, anthropology, and geography. He also cites works on mythology, religion, social and economic history, and local lore and understands and experiences his journey in the company of these previous explorers and authors. In *In Patagonia*, for example, Dante is, in a deeply spiritual way, accompanying Chatwin in another version of *The Inferno*. And since Chatwin believes in a kind of literary synchronicity—that all great works of literature exist and can be accessed in the present—his trip into the land of fire creates resonating parallels with Ulysses, Herman Melville, Edgar Allan Poe, Magellan, Charles Darwin, and every other explorer who literally or spiritually descended into the underworld, or hades.

As Chatwin approaches the fulfillment of his enormously difficult but enriching expedition in Punta Arenas, he catalogs with great detail the many adventures of his uncle Charley Milward. Uncle Charley's story takes up about 20 pages and becomes the central tale around which Chatwin justifies his trip. The culminating novella shows Chatwin at his storytelling best and also illustrates how convincingly he can vivify an already vivid tale. However, for the first time in his full-length work, the question arises of just how much of what he is relating is factual and how much comes from his marvelously fecund imagination. In *An Englishman in Patagonia,* John Pilkington, who followed Chatwin's tracks into Patagonia some 20 years later, suggests that Chatwin had a penchant for "livening up narratives with imagined details." And like Colin Thubron, Pilkington thinks Chatwin's literary model was quite obviously Gustave Flaubert: "Like Flaubert, Chatwin never tired of exploring the Aladdin's Cave of theatrical possibilities which life offered up. He seemed to define the world not by its wisps of reason but by its potential as melodrama."[10] Certainly Uncle Charley's tale is, first and foremost, spectacular melodrama.

The tale of Uncle Charley Milward reads like a Robert Louis Stevenson novella. Chatwin has the same sensitive eye for detail that Stevenson had, and Charley Milward's story contains all the plots that any good sea thriller possesses. Chatwin arrives at Punta Arenas and visits Milward's old home, finding in it a "solid Anglican gloom." The Victorian structure has a tower and resembles both church and castle. But Milward's father was, after all, an Anglican minister. The story begins with Milward's early sailing years on some ships out of Liverpool; Chatwin claims that he got his information from some of his uncle's writings. There are two accounts of his uncle's apprentice voyages: the first is a logbook and the second is a collection of unpublished sea stories he wrote after he retired to Punta Arenas. The writings are full of vivid accounts of near-disasters at sea, visits to various sexual underworlds throughout the world, and meetings with extraordinary characters like those in late-nineteenth-century thrillers. The climax of Charley Milward's 20-year career with the New Zealand Shipping Company came after he was dismissed for losing his ship the *Mataura* as it collided with some rocks near the coast of Desolation Island. Though no one perished (the *Mataura* sank after three days), the company blamed Milward, and he was pensioned off and retired to Punta Arenas, which was the nearest town.

Chatwin relishes conjuring up the details of Milward's second career, as the successful founder of an iron foundry in Punta Arenas. Chatwin's uncle left few writings to help him reconstruct the story of his heroic comeback, but Chatwin reveals to the reader the dynamics of how he creates his compelling stories. This is the first time in *In Patagonia* that he demonstrates the way his creative imagination brings together

diverse materials and formulates them into utterly convincing biographical sketches: "I have had to reconstruct [the stories] from faded sepia
photographs, purple carbons, a few relics and memories in the very old.
The first impressions are of an energetic pioneer, confident in his new
handlebar moustache; hunting seals in South Georgia; salvaging for
Lloyd's; helping a German goldpanner dynamite the Mylodon Cave; or
striding round the foundry with his German partner, Herr Lion, inspect-
ing the water turbines or the lathes they imported from Dortmund and
Göppingen" (*In Patagonia,* 170). The text reads like a Victorian novel;
the details are convincing and the figure of the prosperous businessman
is impeccably drawn. Chatwin develops the portrait even further to
characterize more accurately his uncle's newfound life. But again, the
portrait also shows the reader Chatwin's impressionistic treatment of the
minimal material he had at hand and how deftly he is able to expand it
into a very convincing character sketch: "The second set of images are of
the British Empire's southernmost counsel, a senior citizen of Punta
Arenas and director of its bank. . . . Old members of the British Club
still remember him. And as I sat in the tall rooms . . . I could picture
him on one of the buttoned wash-leather sofas, stretching out his bad
leg and talking of the sea" (p. 170).

   Chatwin tells us again that he had to reconstruct the latter half of his
uncle's life, from some old photos, carbons, and other relics, like a gold
watch. However, the images of "Charley the Sailor home from the sea"
and "Charley the pioneer with the restlessness gone" begin to fade away
when we learn that the foundry failed miserably and he was ruined. The
tale, though, does not end on a tragic note, in spite of photographic evidence: "Photos show a stooping old man in a homburg with huge
whiskers and wounded eyes" (*In Patagonia,* 173). Even though the family fell into disastrous debt, Charley and his faithful wife Belle paid it all
off. And though the story ends on a solemn note, it becomes a morality
tale that would have satisfied the Calvinist sensibilities of the Victorian
reading public and shows the family restoring their honor: "They paid
their debts." Any number of English novelists of both the Victorian and
Edwardian eras wrote about families laboring under the unbearable bur-
den of financial debt; one has only to think of Dickens, Trollope, and
Hardy.

   The tale's final image is of Charley sitting in his tower with his tele-
scope "straining to catch the last of the steamer [his son] took to school
in England. As she headed up eastward and was swallowed into the
night, he said: 'I'll never see the lad again' " (p. 174). Just exactly how

Chatwin knew what those words were is one of many questions surrounding his ability to distinguish between fact and fiction, version and
account, image and reality.

Chatwin begins to feel keenly that the ostensible goal of his trip is
drawing near and that the journey to the cave where his uncle Charley
found the mylodon skin is his last official act, the crowning achievement
of his quest. He finally arrives at Puerto Consuelo, meets and has dinner
with the grandson of Herman Eberhard, the German sheep farmer who
discovered the famous cave. After an exhaustive recounting of the biography of Herman Eberhard, Chatwin brings together all the various
strands of the complicated story of the mythic mylodon sloth. Officially
it was called a "Giant Ground Sloth." Charles Darwin himself had found
evidence of this species and had specimens sent to the Royal College of
Surgeons in the 1840s. There were even rumors that a living sloth had
been spotted in Patagonia in the late nineteenth century. But what
attracts Chatwin to these stories is the effect they had on the popular literature of the early twentieth century. The English public was so taken
by accounts of the sloth that the *Daily Express* financed a trip to the cave
by Hesketh Prichard, who found no trace of the beast. Nonetheless, he
wrote a book about his trip called *Through the Heart of Patagonia*. It sold
very well and was probably the genesis of Arthur Conan Doyle's best-
selling *Lost World,* one of Chatwin's favorite boyhood books.

Charley Milward got involved in the venture through a German gold
panner named Albert Konrad, who stepped in once the archaeologists
had finished their work at the cave. Konrad began dynamiting the
stratigraphy to bits, and Charley gathered large amounts of skin and
piles of bones. Considered valuable, the remains were salable for large
amounts of money; Charley, so conjectures Chatwin, sent a piece of skin
to Chatwin's grandmother as a wedding gift. Once again, the way
Chatwin uncovers the complex strands of the journey, in this case of the
piece of the sloth to his grandmother's house in Birmingham, becomes
the most fascinating part of the tale. It also prepares the reader for the
book's climactic moment—the narrator's actual encounter with the goal
of his long and often dangerous quest. One expects the scene to resemble that culminating moment when Jason takes possession of the
Golden Fleece, or Parsifal, the Holy Grail.

Chatwin actually presents his moment of apotheosis in semicomic
terms. After a great deal of effort, he finds no trace of any skin or bones
of the great giant ground sloth; he finds only bushels full of fecal matter: "The floor was covered with turds, sloth turds, outsize black leath-

ery turds, full of ill-digested grass, that looked as if they had been shat last week" (*In Patagonia,* 194). However, he keeps digging around and finally recognizes some familiar strands of coarse reddish hair: "I eased them out, slid them into an envelope and sat down immensely pleased. I had accomplished the object of this ridiculous journey" (p. 194). At this visionary moment Chatwin hears the ethereal voices of women singing "Maria, Maria, Maria" and thinks he has gone mad. He then discovers seven nuns from the order of the Sisters of Santa Maria Auxiliadora singing before the statue of the Virgin just below the cave. Whether the nuns were there or not, Chatwin's humorous rendition of that sublime moment accompanied by the voices of virgins is a virtual parody of similar visionary scenes from Wagner's *Parsifal* or *Tannhäuser* or from any number of religious films, such as *The Song of Bernadette.* In one of Wallace Stevens's best-known poems, "Sunday Morning," the narrator alludes to the "visionary south" as a place of vision because of its geographical extremity, and Paul Theroux calls the south "the perfect destination" (*NP,* 29). But it is strangely ironic that the Mylodon Cave is situated at Last Hope Sound.

Years later, Chatwin recalls that same scene, and it appears that time has given the whole enterprise a slightly different interpretation, particularly in light of what happened to the replaced relic:

> This spurious quest ended, one stormy afternoon in 1976, when I sat at the back of the cave, after finding a few strands of mylodon hair and a lump of mylodon dung which looked a little like last week's horse (so much so that my cleaning lady took exception to it and, the other day, chucked it out). . . . My piece of dung wasn't exactly the Golden Fleece, but it did give me the idea for the form of a travel book, for the oldest kind of traveller's tale is one in which the narrator leaves home and goes to a far country in search of a legendary beast. (*NP,* 35)

Clearly, Chatwin envisions his quest in mythic terms—that is, one person's Golden Fleece is another person's piece of dung. But what is important is not the end or point of the journey but the journey itself: the authentic treasure is the experience and self-knowledge the quester acquires during the trip. Joseph Campbell suggests that all stories are variations on the theme of the Fall in the Edenic garden and that heroic questers respond to that crisis by venturing forth to find redemptive agents to restore the wasteland to its former Edenic wholeness. The irony of Chatwin's journey is that in his attempt to restore his family's central treasure—the mylodon skin—he discovers that the true treasure is symbolic rather than actual; that on a personal basis concepts of Eden and the wasteland are indexes of spiritual conditions rather than physical journeys.

An even more disturbing find is that one culture's Eden depends on another's fall into a wasteland: European immigrants felt compelled to escape their intolerable conditions (in the wasteland) and journeyed south to redeem their fallen state. However, they invaded and destroyed the indigenous Indians' paradise to fulfill their Edenic agendas. Chatwin's disturbing discovery is little comfort and portends apocalyptic consequences. Though the great Argentine writer Jorge Luis Borges once said, "You will find nothing there. There is nothing in Patagonia" (*NP*, 36), Chatwin found one more tragic instance of the world's oldest story.

Though Chatwin meets a few oddballs at the Ritz Hotel in Punta Arenas—a mad ladies' lingerie salesman from Santiago who quotes pregnant poetic passages from Federico García Lorca—he departs Patagonia a sober and more thoughtful traveler. On board the ship home he meets a young man from the Falklands whose chilling message seems to validate all of Chatwin's worst suspicions about the fate of the southernmost part of the world: " ' 'Bout time the Argentines took us over,' he said. 'We're so bloody inbred' " (*In Patagonia*, 199).

Chapter Three

The Viceroy of Ouidah: "A Clash of Cultural Myths"

Bruce Chatwin's next full-length work, *The Viceroy of Ouidah,* shares similar themes with *In Patagonia* but has strikingly different literary procedures. Though initially intended as a scholarly biography of the notorious Brazilian slave trader Francisco Felix de Souza, Chatwin decided instead to write a fictionalized account of his life, though he studiously avoided calling it a novel. Therefore, the problem of genre once again arises. Though several Patagonian-immigrant readers objected to the liberties Chatwin took in presenting them, their relatives, and friends in *In Patagonia,* the book nonetheless adhered to the literal facts of his trip. The people and places he encountered were all real, and except for the Welsh, he used real names throughout his account. *The Viceroy of Ouidah,* however, posed considerably more complex problems of representation. Though Chatwin had twice visited Dahomey (Benin) and, later, Brazil to collect information for his book, he wrote both history and biography in *Viceroy.* His task, to reconstruct the life of Francisco Felix de Souza in such a way as to clarify the workings of one of the world's most important slave-trading countries, was so daunting that Chatwin eventually abandoned it.

Early African Experience

Chatwin first visited Dahomey in 1971 in the midst of an extensive tour of five West African countries: Dahomey, Niger, Mali, Senegal, and Mauritania. His observations in his notebooks of his visits to the Dahomean cities of Abomey and Cotonou in February—and a passing reference to his next destination, Ouidah—give little indication of what eventually compelled him to write a full-length book on a Dahomean subject. On his visit to Abomey, he remarks that the king of Dahomey is "an important figure in ancient history. The Fon made some of the most remarkable African sculptures of all. . . . The Slaves from the coast were taken largely to Bahia in Brazil and the cultures had much in com-

mon."[1] He was impressed with the refurbished palace of the Kings of
Dahomey and particularly with the polychromed plaques "which served
to instruct the kings in their own history and prowess. The series of
thrones, dating back to 1600, perfectly preserved, was particularly
interesting—also the ceremonial standards of beaten bronze which
didn't change in style over 300 years" (*FJ*, 75). Little escapes Chatwin's
curator's eye, especially cultural artifacts that reveal anthropological and
historical information.

In the 1980 preface to the first edition of *The Viceroy of Ouidah*, however, Chatwin describes his first visit with a novelist's eye and wit:
"When I first went to Dahomey in 1971, it was still called Dahomey
and Cotonou the capital was still a town of belly laughs and French
brasseries. Six years later, a new president had changed its name to the
People's Republic of Benin, and the fetish priests of Ouidah had put pictures of Lenin amid the scarlet paraphernalia of the Thunder Pantheon.
I had come a second time to collect material for a life of the white
Brazilian slave-trader, Francisco Felix de Souza."[2]

Chatwin then presents a two-paragraph summary of the notorious
life of De Souza, who came from Brazil and settled at the Portuguese
port of Ouidah in the early nineteenth century. Ouidah had become the
major source of manpower—slaves—for Brazil's mines and plantations,
and the slave trade was an enterprise in which De Souza desperately
wanted to participate. Though he ran into severe difficulties with the
brutal Dahomean King Adandozan, he was rescued by a young prince of
the court who later became King Gezo. After swearing a blood pact
with Gezo, De Souza acquired the necessary firearms to help him overthrow the mad King Adandozan, and together they became the richest
and most powerful slave traders in the world. Gezo's reward to De
Souza was a virtual monopoly on the sale of slaves. By the 1830s De
Souza "was the richest man in West Africa and the bugbear of the
British Abolitionists. He died a ruined man" (*VO*, 2). The story of his fall
from riches to ruin constitutes *The Viceroy of Ouidah*'s basic plot.

Chatwin's 1978 visit to gather more material for the life of Francisco
Felix de Souza, however, was marred by a frightening incident that dis-
couraged him from pursuing any further research in Benin. As he was
riding in a taxi in Cotonou, he was stopped, arrested as a mercenary, and
detained in jail for two very tense days. It so happened that the Beninian
Army was undergoing one of its perennial political realignments.
Chatwin tells this fascinating story in *Viceroy*—presumably adding some
fictional elements—in "A Coup," which appeared first in the British

magazine *Granta* and later in his collection of essays and stories, entitled *What Am I Doing Here*. As in *In Patagonia,* the reader is given an opportunity to hear several versions of Chatwin's story, in this case in the preface to *Viceroy* and in "A Coup." "A Coup" tells of possible firing squads, though the character—who is Chatwin—escapes with minor scars, thanks to the influence of the German counsel. Within a week he is safely conducting research on De Souza and the slave trade in Rio de Janeiro "to follow the Brazilian aspects of my story." Though he decides that he will by no means return to Benin, he has obtained valuable material nonetheless: "I did come away with the bones of the story and a number of vivid impressions. . . . Such is the background to this book. But such was the patchiness of my material that I decided to change the names of the principal characters—and went on to write a work of the imagination" (*VO,* 2–3). He renames De Souza Francisco Manoel da Silva.

Curiously, the full preface to *The Viceroy of Ouidah* appears only in the first edition; Nicholas Murray suggests that its later omission was "presumably to encourage [the book's] focus on its fictionality" (*Bruce Chatwin,* 54). But that omission also deprives the reader of the valuable knowledge of Chatwin's sources, and Chatwin was a consistently reliable researcher and genuine scholar. For example, he admits to reading, as a boy, about King Gezo and to studying accounts of human sacrifice by such Victorian travel writers as John Duncan, F. E. Forbes, Richard Burton, and J. A. Skertchly; he also met Pierre Verger, the master of Afro-Brazilian studies. Further, he discloses in the preface that he came into contact with many of De Souza's descendants and actually called on King Gezo's grandson, Sagbadjou. In later editions of *Viceroy,* the editors included only the first two paragraphs of the preface—without calling it a preface. Without the remaining nine paragraphs—the autobiographical section—the book begins like a novel.

Historical Background of Ouidah

The actual historical figures of *The Viceroy of Ouidah* are presented in rather objective terms in Samuel Decaldo's 1976 *Historical Dictionary of Dahomey (People's Republic of Benin)*. Decaldo calls De Souza a "drifter or political refugee who arrived in Whydah [the British spelling of Ouidah] from Brazil around 1788. Of humble origins De Souza started off as a minor trader in a variety of commodities, including slaves, eventually prospering."[3] Decaldo goes on to detail De Souza's imprisonment

by King Adandozan when he tried to collect on a debt and the beginning of De Souza's 30-year relationship with the next king of Dahomey,
Gezo. King Gezo appointed De Souza "Chacha," or chief customs collector, and Viceroy of Ouidah, a powerful position that made him the
personal representative of the monarchy and director of the Fort at
Ouidah. The effect of these powerful appointments was that De Souza
exercised a monopoly on all trade—including the slave trade—in the
port. He was also able to reorganize Ouidah's customs systems by convincing the king "to channel slave labor into the development of the
royal palm tree plantations which later on became one of Dahomey's
principal exports. De Souza was also King Gezo's chief supplier of arma-
ments from Europe. He prospered enormously and upon his death (May
8, 1849) human sacrifices were offered for him in Whydah" (HDD, 52).
By contrast, although Chatwin's recording of the facts of De Souza's life
is fairly accurate, he fashions a dramatically different ending for De
Souza's life and omits the human sacrifices: he shows a suicidally
depressed De Souza trying to drown himself repeatedly in the sea and
finally dying a broken man covered with scabs and vermin.

Chatwin's portrayal of the historical King Gezo is fairly accurate up
to a point. Decaldo claims that King Gezo (whom he calls "Ghezo") was
responsible for greatly expanding Dahomey's power during his reign:
"Ghezo succeeded to the throne after a dynastic upheaval in which King
Adandozan was deposed. One of his first acts was to throw off the
restraining and humiliating tributary relationship with the Oyo Empire
[present-day Nigeria], greatly weakened by now" (HDD, 65). He also
restructured the military and created the famous female forces, the elite
Amazon units. The king greatly strengthened his country, which
became the preeminent power between Ghana and Nigeria. What
Decaldo does not mention is that the money for Gezo's establishment of
such power came directly from the slave and gun trade that De Souza
facilitated.

As expected, critics—though they generally praised Viceroy for its
vivid presentation and superb characterization—could not comfortably
place it within any traditional genre. One of Chatwin's best critics,
Michael Ignatieff, calls it "a surreal fable" ("On Bruce Chatwin," 4).
Andrew Harvey calls it "a baleful, mock-historical fantasy,"[4] and Mary
Hope labels it an "extraordinary fictional treatment of the life of a
Brazilian slave-trader."[5] Chatwin himself called it a "work of the imagination." Richard Hall considers it "a superb, impressionistic piece of his-
torical reconstruction." Hall cautions readers, however, not to waste

time on unnecessary genre labeling: "So the way to approach this brief, splendid book is to put aside any agonizing about truth (even the Aristotelean sort) and treat it as an 'entertainment,' in Graham Greene's use of the word."[6]

More important than critical appraisals that quibble over formalistic labels are those that delineate the book's brilliant style. In comparing the high critical acclaim of *In Patagonia* with that of *Viceroy,* Nicholas Murray states, "The chorus was once again unanimous in its praise. Reviewers noted the book's brevity, its stylistic brilliance, and the vividness of its imagery. . . . With references back to his brilliant debut, reviewers now started to place Chatwin. Graham Greene, Joseph Conrad and Malcolm Lowry were mentioned as precursors in a tradition of English imagining of exotic excess" (*Bruce Chatwin,* 54). Murray disagrees, though, with comparisons to Conrad because "Chatwin's book . . . lacks the brooding metaphysical depth of Conrad's novel [*Heart of Darkness*] and avoids, scrupulously, any authorial interventions or oblique commentaries that would attempt to draw out its significance . . . the resulting picture is intended to speak for itself. There is no moral revulsion at the slave trade, only vivid portrayal of the decadent splendor of Dahomey and the life-style of the slavers" (pp. 54–55). Murray alludes to some negative comments on Chatwin's writing because of his refusal to take a moral position on the slave trade generally. He calls the author's technique "brilliantly amoral" and points out "its aesthetic relish in rendering barbarism beautiful" (p. 55).

Another reliable Chatwin critic, John Lanchester, attributes the byzantine brilliance of the book's style to Chatwin's need to depict accurately the main character's byzantine lifestyle: "In *The Viceroy of Ouidah,* it's as if the exoticism Chatwin repressed to such effect in *In Patagonia* all at once erupts. Francisco Manoel da Silva's life embraced sensual extremes . . . and much spectacular violence. . . . At no point in the book is there any comment on the morality of the slave trade" ("A Pom," 10). Lanchester, though, finds Chatwin's model to be Gustave Flaubert's detached, objective aesthetic, particularly as embodied in Flaubert's African novel, *Salammbô.*

The key, however, to Chatwin's aesthetic and methodological approach to his material in *Viceroy* can be found in his story "A Coup." Just after having escaped the dangers of a Beninian jail during his 1978 visit there but nonetheless having found the life of De Souza "a story worth telling," he explains his dilemma: "After this interruption I lost the stamina to pursue my researches, though I had acquired ripe material for a novel. Since it was impossible to fathom the alien mentality of my characters, my only hope was to advance the narrative in a sequence of cinematographic images, and here I was strongly influenced by the films of Werner Herzog. I remember saying, 'If this were ever made into a movie, only Herzog could do it.' But that was a pipe dream."[7] Amazingly enough, Herzog eventually made the book into a film in 1987 entitled *Cobra Verde*. Herzog sought Chatwin out after reading the book and invited him to participate in the filming, which was done in Ghana due to the same uncongenial political climate in Benin that Chatwin had found nine years earlier. The key, then, to understanding the novel's structure is to view it as "a sequence of cinematographic images." *In Patagonia*'s structure is built on an actual journey Chatwin took, though he included a number of historical overlays as the book evolved into a kind of hypertext that accommodates excerpts from journals, novels, and travel books, as well as personal anecdotes and simple narrative. His methods allowed a multidimensional text to develop in 97 chapters and produced a narrative that fluctuates from the present to the past and back to the present with a minimum of intrusion to the reader.

The striking structural difference between the two books is that whereas the narrative of *In Patagonia* is linear and chronological, Chatwin begins *Viceroy* in the present and then very adroitly moves back, incrementally, to the distant past. The book then concludes in the present, thus completing a satisfying narrative circle. The novel's form is really an extension of its content; that is, the highly colorful opening scenes that commemorate the death of Francisco Manoel da Silva and its portrayal of various races and religious traditions combine in a vividly predictive tableau that presents the entire novel's subject matter comprehensively. Further, somewhat like *In Patagonia*, the novel is arranged in 87 cinematic scenes, although they are generally more exotically delineated than those in *In Patagonia*. Chatwin uses an additional structural device in *Viceroy*: he divides the narrative into six major sections, or, as Nicholas Murray calls them, "movements." Murray characterizes the opening scene: "The first six sections or movements which make up the book thus establishes the scene: the sense of decline in this extraordinary clan, the weight of its history, and the bizarre but static splendor of its rituals and processions which contrast with the absurd present day Marxist-Leninist rhetoric crackling out of the public radios" (*Bruce Chatwin*, 55). Murray further defines Chatwin's narrative technique as one of "reanimating the past." Its vividness, though, is expressed through the concentrated use of specific imagery, and it is Chatwin's specificity that makes the book's imagery so remarkably cinematographic. As Richard Hall points out, "[T]he prose coruscates, so that many images from this African horror story linger disturbingly in the mind" ("Nightmare," 4).

The themes that Chatwin articulates in *Viceroy* are very close to those in *In Patagonia,* with a few modifications. This novel examines the results of the fall of native peoples from their pristine Edenic innocence into the degradation of European (i.e., Portuguese) colonization, just as *In Patagonia* traced a similar fall of native tribes into economic enslavement, drunkenness, and eventual extinction by European powers. Chatwin characterizes the colonizers as the Tribe of Cain, engaged in the politics of settlement and opposing the people of Abel, the innocent nomadic wanderers who avoid any impulse to settle into anything remotely suggestive of private property—which would be the ultimate sacrilege against their nature religions. Both novels are brilliantly delineated examples of the white race's relentless exploitation and enslavement of the darker races. And both novels perceptively compare the devastating clashes of four competing mythologies: Christianity, capitalism, Marxism-Leninism, and animism, or native religion. Both novels also divide their characters into victims and/or victimizers. However, the consequences for the victims in *Viceroy* are immediately violent and, in the long run, more deeply tragic. The Portuguese—as embodied in Francisco Manoel da Silva—supplied the king of Dahomey and his people with guns for the express purpose of subjugating people of their race and selling them as slaves to Brazil. Though the Dahomeans looked upon other African tribes as their enemies and apparently felt little or no remorse in plundering them, the long-term moral consequences were traumatic for West African culture as a whole. The critic Victoria Glendinning acutely summarizes the major theme of *Viceroy* in terms of the conflicts that run throughout the work: "The overriding impression is of clashing cultural myths, all of them with death at their center, that lie rotting one on top of another in a dreadful, comic compost—and not only . . . in Dahomey."[8]

There is little doubt that Chatwin, working this time as a novelist, evolved more sophisticated literary strategies in developing his characters in *Viceroy* than he had in *In Patagonia.* Though Francisco Manoel da Silva is based on a real person, Chatwin fashions a fictional character who embodies perfectly the conflicts of two diverse cultures. The story of Da Silva's fall into the lowest forms of moral degradation is a personalized version of the fall of capitalist Europe into a maelstrom of greed, exploitation, and enslavement. Additionally, Chatwin probes the complex psychological dynamics of how victims become victimizers—an old story—in depicting the child Francisco's brutal upbringing as an illustration of why people become what they are. In fact, one of the questions that drives the novel is how much more evil Da Silva can become before we lose interest in him as a human being and therefore as a literary character. But one of the miracles that Chatwin brings off in *Viceroy* is to portray a hateful, sadistic sociopath who remains an intriguing human being until the novel's end; even the vilest of literary characters—if artfully rendered—begs for some kind of human response and understanding. All of *Viceroy*'s major characters, and many of the minor ones, remain interesting throughout the novel and never become mere stereotypes of wicked or virtuous people.

Another recurring theme that Chatwin carries over from *In Patagonia* is the symbiotic relationship between Eden and the wasteland. Just as the European immigrants in *In Patagonia* find their native country an unbearable wasteland and journey to Patagonia to generate a new Eden, so too did the Portuguese and Brazilians invade Africa and enslave African natives in order to regenerate their Eden, both economically and politically. Both European cultures used Christianity's privileged position to justify their atrocities. The establishment of one group's Eden depends on the destruction of another group's Eden, and the victimized group's Eden is then transformed into a wasteland: the Dahomean heaven becomes a hell. On a personal level, Francisco da Silva's childhood wasteland is transformed, once he attains power in Dahomey, into his personal Eden, or heaven.

The Celestial Python versus the Last Supper

Chatwin's evolving novelistic powers are never more impressive than in his fashioning of the two major symbols that recur throughout the book: the Celestial Python and the Last Supper. These symbols embody precisely the cultural and mythic crises that drive the narrative backward—not forward—and illustrate mutually exclusive value systems. The book opens with the image of Ouidah as a wasteland: "today a forgotten town memorable only for the ruins of three European forts and its temple of Dagbé, the Celestial Python who opened the eyes of Man" (*VO*, 1). Throughout the book, the image of the serpent is intricately interwoven with a major Christian image, that of the Last Supper. Francisco da Silva first sees the portable oratory, or shrine, at the chapel on the Brazilian slave plantation of his friend and eventual business partner, Joaquim

Coutinho: "It was a glass-fronted vitrine, the size of a small doll's house and made by the nuns of the Soledade in Bahia. . . . Wooden figures of Christ and the Apostles were sitting down to a meal of plaster-of-Paris chicken. The eyes of Our Lord were the color of turquoise and his hair bristled with real red hair" (p. 45). After Da Silva becomes wealthy, he decides to build himself and his family a *simbodji*—a big house—and uses as a model Tapuitapera, the house of Joaquim Coutinho, in northeast Brazil. He asks Joaquim to send him a replica of the piece but instead is sent the original. Da Silva makes the oratory the centerpiece of his household for many years, and his daughter, Eugenia, keeps it for 60 years after his death. The shrine then appears decades later, after her death, along with her house in a wasteland condition: "Spiders had turned the parrot cage into a grey tent. The pictures were peeling, and all Twelve Apostles eaten away to leprous stumps. Yet, from the head of Christ, like the periscopic eyes of certain fish, two blue glass beads stood out on stalks" (p. 46). Chatwin brilliantly combines the Christian image with the natural one to show the inevitable course of natural evolution.

Interspersed among images of the Last Supper and of many other Christian icons are images of the sacred serpent, the Celestial Python. Chatwin juxtaposes that image with the Christian ones to show how Da Silva eventually succumbs to the pull of nature in Africa: "Gradually Africa swamped him and drew him under . . . he slipped into the habits of the natives. . . . He wore amulets against the Evil Eye. Taparica [the majordomo of his estate] taught him to shuffle his feet at the phallus of Papa Legba and, together, they went to diviners. . . . Some evenings they went to the Python Temple to watch the novices sink their teeth into the necks of living goats. The spectators screamed with laughter as boys somersaulted on one another's backs and mimicked the motions of sodomy. . . . He never knew what drew him to the mysteries. The blood? The god? The smell of sweat or the wet glinting bodies?" (p. 93)

Ironically, one of the taboos for the king of Dahomey is that he must never be exposed to the dangers of the coastal snake cults or the white man's friendship or look upon the sea. The fact that Da Silva becomes the king's representative on the coast in Ouidah and succumbs to the cult of the serpent suggests the wisdom of the native religion. The great Western scholar of the Dahomean people, Melville Herskovits, explains that the Dahomeans, including the people of Ouidah, worshiped three types of gods: "the snake, some lofty high trees, and the sea."[9] He further explains that the snake cult was not simply a phallic cult. Rather, it embodied all of the qualities that are in direct opposition to Christian

practices and dogma. The quality of the snake "incarnates the quality of
dynamics in life—it is movement, flexibility, sinuousness, fortune. It
manifests itself as serpent, as rainbow, as plant roots, as the nerves of
animal forms, as the gaseous emanations that issue from mountains"
(*Dahomey*, 245). Christianity, on the other hand, is not built on natural
processes; there is no room for nature in any form of Christian belief. St.
Francis of Assisi was one of the few saints who was able to communicate
with animals, so it is both ironic and fortuitous that Chatwin did not
have to find another name for his character, Francisco da Silva, who
comes to Ouidah as a Christian conqueror and eventually falls into an
animistic view of a cyclic world. The point is that Da Silva never understands why he is so drawn to the mysteries of the Python Cult and thus
never comes into any authentic knowledge about his place in the world.

Though there are similarities between the structures of *In Patagonia*
and *Viceroy,* the latter is more obviously novelistic. One way to understand the novel's six-part structure is to view it as six movements of a
symphony or six acts in an opera. The first movement initiates the reanimation process as the action begins its retrograde motion from present
to past. The book opens with a highly elaborate Catholic requiem mass
to celebrate the 117th anniversary of the death of Francisco Manoel da
Silva, the family's great patriarch: "At his death in 1857, he left sixty-
three mulatto sons and an unknown quantity of daughters whose ever-
darkening progeny, now numberless as grasshoppers, were spread from
Luanda to the Latin Quarter. . . . The lives of the older Da Silvas were
empty and sad. They mourned the Slave Trade as a lost Golden Age
when their family was rich, famous, and white. . . . They called themselves 'Brazilians' though they had lost their Portuguese. People slightly
blacker than themselves they called 'Blacks'. They called Dahomey
'Dahomey' long after the head of state had changed its name to Benin.
Each hung Dom Francisco's picture among their chromolithographs of
saints and the Virgin: through him they felt linked to Eternity" (*VO*,
8–9). As in the exposition of a symphony or the overture of an opera,
Chatwin presents the major motifs that the rest of the novel will
develop: the fall of the Da Silva family, the loss of a Portuguese-Brazilian
cultural center, the yearning for the Edenic days of yesteryear with Dom
Francisco as their central icon, and the lament over the Marxist-Leninist
takeover that denies the efficacy of any and all spiritual and cultural traditions. There is a continual counterpointing of lament and celebration
throughout the entire first chapter, which is composed of seven separate
sections. The third section contains the central image—a very cinemato-

graphic one—of Dom Francisco's elaborately baroque tomb. He is buried beneath his own giant Goanese four-poster bed in a barrel of wine with the heads of a young boy and girl. Next to the bed is a statue of St. Francis of Assisi and an open bottle of Gordon's gin in case he awakens from the dead. Hidden beneath the bed covers is "a rusty iron object resembling an umbrella, clotted with blood and feathers, and stuck into the floor. This was an Asin, the Dahomean Altar of the dead" (p. 18). As Father Olimpio da Silva announces several hours later, this shrine is an example of what anthropologists call cultural syncretism, that is, the fusion of differing belief systems. That syncretist pattern surfaces throughout the rest of the novel to show how tightly intertwined the elements of Christianity, animism, and European culture became.

The last section of chapter 1 concludes with a magnificent counterpointing of the voices of the Da Silva family and the Marxist-Leninist rhetoric of the president of Benin blaring from the radio. Chatwin comically contrasts formalist political assertions with the dinner guests' tipsy comments:

> "Revolution or Death!"
> "So when they passed the law, there were no more cowries [the medium of exchange of Dahomey]."
> "Marxist-Leninism is our only philosophical guide!"
> ". . . and that's how Dom Francisco was ruined!" (p. 24)

Chapter 2 begins with the stark image of Francisco Manoel da Silva's ancient daughter, Eugenia da Silva, refusing to participate in the feast. She won't eat. For years the family has called her Mama Wéwé—the White One—to prove that Dom Francisco was white. She is well over 100 years old and resembles "a skeleton who happened to breathe, [who] lay dying on an etruscan couch of jacaranda wood. . . . Her tongue had locked to the roof of her mouth" (*VO*, 27). Chatwin then immediately moves back in time through reanimation to when the young and attractive Eugenia fell in love 98 years earlier: "She was tall and beautiful. Her skin was golden and her black hair streaked with auburn. She had eyes of greenish amber, the color of a troubled sea. The corners of her mouth lifted in a perpetual smile from pronouncing the slushed, suggestive consonants of Brazilian Portuguese. At the sight of her swaying walk men had to hold themselves—yet, at the time, she was a virgin" (p. 29). The luscious prose style is more sensuous than Chatwin's austere but vivid language in *In Patagonia*.

All of the 16 sections of chapter 2 are devoted to Mama Wéwé's difficult life. Her first tragedy results from falling in love with a handsome
English lieutenant who has come with an English agent to Dahomey.
Though she resists his seductive advances at first, she later gives in and
makes love to him after he promises to take her with him. Of course, he
leaves and never returns. While waiting for him, she learns how to make
lace and to read and takes long walks on the beach alone. Two years
later she discovers that the "tall, freckle-faced lieutenant with the red
moustache and blue eyes" has left the military, married, and settled in
Somerset, England. (Her story is, of course, a modified version of David
Belasco's *Madame Butterfly*, which Giacomo Puccini transformed into
one of the world's most popular and poignant operas.) Eugenia da Silva
does not, however, become pregnant. Embittered by her first amorous
experience, she becomes increasingly more introspective. Chatwin draws
her as a character who has the capacity to experience life on several
planes: "One by one, her acquaintance narrowed to her maid, her Mahi
slave-boy, her father and the red-haired stranger. Unable to make the
distinction between the real and the supernatural, she made none
between the living, the absent and the dead" (p. 35).

After several devastating raids on her *simbodji* (big house) by Dahomean Amazons warning her not to sell land to any prospective colonizers, she takes in one of her irresponsible relatives' homeless children. His
name is Cesário and he becomes her adopted son. Her life brightens considerably as she devotes herself to educating and loving the young boy.
Tragically, a crew ship brings a cholera epidemic to Ouidah and Cesário
dies an agonizing death. Stunned again, Eugenia turns to her religious
practices for consolation and transforms her father's bedroom into a
shrine. But when the White Fathers of Our Lady of Africa see the syncretist shrine she has built, they are outraged: "They saw the head of
Holophernes, the head of the Baptist, the silver chains, a toilet mirror
and the nails and bloodstained feathers. Father Zerringer, who was an
amateur zoologist, looked over the reliquaries and identified a vulture's
claw, a python vertebra, a fragment of baboon skull and the eardrum of a
lion" (p. 44). She also has put a statue of St. Francis at the shrine's center
along with statues of Santa Marta and Santa Luzia and "improvised a
Holy Ghost from a Pirevitte teapot in the form of a chicken" (p. 43). Her
response to the priest's outrage is to fall into a hysterical fit and disappear
into the jungle. When Mother Agathe of the Little Sisters of the Poor
comes to comfort her two days later and forces her way into her room,
she emerges quickly, "her face scratched to ribbons and her habit a mas-

sacre of carmine" (p. 44). After that final outrage, Eugenia becomes a recluse and for 60 years stares enigmatically at her father's portable oratory of the Last Supper. The concluding section of chapter 2 depicts the death of Eugenia da Silva—or Mama Wéwé—as Father Olimpio da Silva administers the sacrament of extreme unction to the ancient woman. A member of her family, Papa Agostinho, can hear her speaking her last words, but unfortunately she is speaking Portuguese and none of the now thoroughly African ancestors can understand that language.

The Life of Da Silva

Chapter 3, which is made up of 17 sections, begins with the introduction of Eugenia's father, Francisco Manoel da Silva—the actual subject of *Viceroy*—as he lands in Ouidah in 1812 at the age of 27. Chatwin then provides the reader with important information about Brazilians from the northeast part of the country; throughout the book, Chatwin provides similar pertinent information in his consistent attempt to uncover and expose those influences that shaped Da Silva's character and personality. Certainly one of the main forces that carries the reader through the book is Chatwin's tracing of the moral and psychological evolution of this highly complex man. Chatwin's greatest novelistic accomplishment in *Viceroy* is perhaps the masterfully psychoanalytic way he illustrates Da Silva's troubled journey into himself. Each major section of the book delves more deeply into the agonizing maelstrom that makes up one of modern literature's most enigmatic historical and literary characters. Few characters have been so convincingly drawn as both victim and victimizer.

Da Silva was born "near Jaicos in the Sertao, the dry scrubby cattle country of the Brazilian North-East. The Sertanistas are wild and poor. They have tight faces, sleek hair and sometimes the green eyes of a Dutch or Celtic ancestor. They hate negroes. They believe in miraculous cures. . . . Like all people born in thorny places, they dream of green fields and a life of ease. Sometimes, with light hearts, they set out south for San Salvador da Bahia, but when they see the sea and the city, they panic and turn back to the badlands" (p. 51). The city of Bahia eventually becomes for the young Da Silva the mythic Eden, or New Jerusalem, that he always desired. But it is also in Bahia that he completes his descent into the depths of depravity.

Maintaining the reanimation process by moving backward in time, Chatwin describes Francisco's miserable childhood; his father dies when he is a year old. His widowed mother is full of anger: "Years of drought had set her mouth in an expression of rage" (p. 51). They live in a mud-brick hut of three rooms. Shortly after Francisco's father's death, his mother takes up with an Indian half-breed, Manuelzinho, who "had a hare-lip and teeth like bits of rusty metal. . . . He killed snakes for a living and sold the flaky white flesh at market" (p. 52). The only activity that cheers his dour mother is strenuous sexual activity with Manuelzinho, usually in Francisco's presence. Those awkward unions make the young boy feel completely isolated: "He never knew a time when he was not a stranger" (p. 52). In a very literal sense, the young Francisco felt, from the cradle, alienated, isolated, and alone, all compelling reasons for his wandering during much of his youth. So, too, is Manuelzinho a born wanderer, and he serves as the young boy's only paternal role model.

After the death of his mother during a drought, Francisco finds his way to Bahia, on the Atlantic coast, where he is taken in by a pederastic Portuguese priest who kisses him at night, teaches him some rudimentary Latin, and "made him play the role of St. Sebastian at Corpus Christi processions. He called him 'my green-eyed angel' yet made him grovel and confess the blackness of his soul" (p. 57). Young Francisco experiments sexually with a black boy, Pepeu, and they try, unsuccessfully, to crucify a cat. Both love to hang around slaughterhouses and watch obedient cows get brutally massacred: " 'Like the saints,' said Francisco Manoel: He knew, far better than any priest, the meaning of Christ's martyrdom, and the liturgy of thorns and blood and nails. He knew God made men to rack them in the wilderness, yet his own sufferings had hardened him to the suffering of others. . . . By the age of thirteen . . . he showed not a trace of squeamishness when he went to watch a flogging at the pillory" (p. 57). Early on, young Francisco acquires a ravenous taste for blood, a craving that will be satisfied only in the slave trade. Chatwin brilliantly shows the complex connection between suffering and character formation. Sometimes suffering ennobles human beings and makes them compassionate, but in Da Silva's case it does just the opposite: he is brutalized into propagating brutality.

When Francisco hears that his mother's old lover, Manuelzinho, is dying, he goes to him and is given the dying man's traveling clothes. Francisco then decides to leave the Portuguese priest and his few acquaintances and take to the road. For the next seven years he wanders, working as a butcher's apprentice, a mule driver, and a gold panner, thus beginning a career of drifting to which he will repeatedly return whenever his life gets too complicated or whenever there is any danger of getting too close to another person. He abhors genuine human contact of any kind: "Faces he forgot, but he remembered the sensations: the taste of armadillo meat roasted in clay; the shock of aguardiente on the tongue; the pleasures of hot blood spurting over his hands" (p. 59).

He comes into intimate contact with large numbers of black slaves while working at a diamond camp: "It astounded him to find their fetor so exciting." He also finds that killing another man means nothing to him and merely leaves him feeling empty. He does happen to meet a legendary character, the bandit Cobra Verde, "who robbed only rich women and only for their finery."

Francisco unexpectedly meets a woman, marries her, and settles down. He begins working on the land of some absentee landlords named Coutinho and becomes especially adept at working with cattle. His favorite activities are castrating young bulls and branding them: "They slavered and moaned as the iron sizzled into their flanks: it gave him pleasure to rub the hot tallow into his own initials" (p. 61). After a while, he can no longer stand to live in a house with his pregnant wife and sleeps in the woods, where he brutally kills a frog and then a friendly cat. After his wife gives birth to a healthy baby and its crying annoys him, he almost murders it but decides to begin another round of aimless wandering. It is after his brutal murder of the cat, though, that Francisco experiences massive existential emptiness: "Then he stood for hours, hopelessly alone, in the cloudbursts" (p. 63).

Francisco begins to see any kind of domestic situation as a tomb or prison and continues to wander in search of a self that continually eludes him. During one of his travels, he encounters a crippled man who takes him to a church and uncovers a sculpted cadaver of the dead body of Christ. The sight of the figure and of the penitential pilgrims at the church makes him feel a part of something and also brings about a need to unburden himself of his remorse. He is stunned to find himself bursting into tears as he actually touches the hunched shoulder of the pathetic cripple. The experience seems to temporarily relieve his sorrow over his empty, brutal life and to lift his fear of becoming a killer. Though he becomes able to drink and gamble at bars, he still cannot trust any woman. As he wanders toward the cities on the sea, he meets Joaquim Coutinho, the son of one of the most powerful plantation owners in northeast Brazil. The two young men become friends—and possibly lovers—as Francisco teaches the awkward Joaquim to lasso cattle, braid whips, and break colts. Joaquim's incessant talk of the glories of his 200-year-old palatial home at Tapuitapera succeeds in luring Fran-

cisco to work for his family. Long after Francisco leaves Tapuitapera, he
yearns for its order and luxury, and the place becomes his Edenic paradise.

True to its Edenic status, Tapuitapera excites in Francisco Manoel a
desire for a kind of wealth and power he has never imagined. He learns
from Joaquim's father, Colonel Coutinho, the rudiments of manipulation and acquisition. His hunger for the slave trade grows as he works
on the vast sugar plantation. The slaves' blood and sweat cause him to
look further into their African background. The drumbeats of the slaves
at night "calling their gods across the Atlantic" brings about a friendship with a Yoruba freeman named Jeronimo, and he discovers the
power of their animistic religions: "Nothing gave Francisco Manoel
greater pleasure than to sit with the androgynous bachelor and hear him
sing the songs of the Kingdom of Ketou in a voice that suggested, not
the gulfs between continents, but planets" (p. 71). Jeronimo tells him
stories of his ancestral home, Dahomey, where there is "a Holy Snake
that was also a rainbow, and kings with testicles the size of avocados" (p.
71). Francisco's experiences on the sugar plantation and listening to the
wondrous myths of Dahomey become his call to adventure and engen-
der his need to leave his temporary paradise, Tapuitapera.

Simultaneously, relationships begin to collapse. Joaquim's mother,
who calls Francisco "the Catamite," wants him off the estate, and many
of the other workers begin calling him "the Brute." Once, again, he
takes up his old profession, that of a wanderer. He drifts again toward
Bahia, where "his principal amusement was to follow funeral processions. . . . He lodged in a tenement in the Lower City and got a job with
a man who sold the equipment of slavery—whips, flails, yokes, neck-
chains, branding irons and metal masks" (p. 73). He also begins to have
sexual liaisons with both men and women: "he performed the mechanics
of love in planked rooms. They left him with the sensation of having
brushed with death: none came back a second time" (p. 73). And
though his anger seems to leave him, his remorse does not, a detail that
Chatwin sets forth as vital in understanding the man's complex nature.
Along with this partial resolution comes a deep desire to go to Africa.

The Life of a Slaver Begins

He begins to hang around the slave quays and watch the slaves be
tested for their strengths and weaknesses. If they are defective, they are
sold cheaply to gypsies. He learns from one of the gypsies ways in which

to cover physical defects from prospective buyers: "how to hide bloody dysentery with an oakum plug, or a skin disease by smearing it with castor oil. . . . But when he talked to old African hands, every one of them shuddered at the mention of Dahomey" (p. 74). Few writers have so deftly shown the detailed formation of a character as complicated as Francisco da Silva. But all of his emerging traits derive from a few consistent behavioral demands: his inability to settle in one place, his unslackable taste for blood and cruelty, and his sadomasochistic sexual impulses. All of these pathologies are, ironically, part of what makes him a genius and, eventually, one of the world's most renowned slave traders. His brutal life experiences never allow him to connect love with sex. Indeed, sex is simply another means of control, power, and manipulation, even though he fathers hundreds of children after he becomes the infamous viceroy of Ouidah. He also becomes an outstanding businessman who seeks out only quality merchandise: "The most valuable slaves came from Ouidah—and Ouidah . . . was the only port north of the Equator where it was legal to trade: the only problem was the King of Dahomey, who was mad" (p. 75).

Though Da Silva's relationship with the Coutinho family has soured, the family fortunes have dwindled since the colonel's death, and Joaquim brings Francisco back into the family business because he recognizes his peculiar kind of genius. The Coutinho family and the city fathers of Capitania, Brazil, commission Francisco Manoel a lieutenant, which gives him the "privilege" of trading in slaves in Dahomey. Chatwin's description of the colonel's farewell mass staggers the imagination with its irony as the hushed crowd prays to the patron of slavers, St. José the Redeemed: "The captain and sailors sat in the front pews. . . . All were men with blood on their hands; yet all gazed lovingly at the milk-white body of Our Dying Lord, identifying His Agony with their agony and calling on Him to pacify the sea" (p. 76). Chatwin allows himself the rare editorial comment in this passage—"with blood on their hands"—although his portrayal of the sadistic treatment of African slaves is otherwise steadily objective. He found it necessary to maintain such objectivity to show, as clinically as possible, the profound irony of Christianity's ability to absorb every conceivable activity into its system of the "sacred." The fact that a patron saint of slavers, St. José, existed speaks volumes.

But when Chatwin points out that the "milk-white body" of the pietà is a mirror image of the churchgoers' own—all-white—suffering, the irony reaches almost unbearable proportions. Added to the growing

ironies is the name of the ship, *Pistola,* that will carry Lt. Francisco da
Silva to his new duties. The etymology of the word *pistola* reveals multiple connotations. *Pistola* in Spanish, Italian, and Portuguese means both
a gun that is fired in one hand and also a great dagger or wooden knife.
The word is derived from the Czech word *pistola,* meaning pipe or shepherd's pipe; the phallic connection—indicating male power—is unmis-
takable. By intermixing the Christian elements with the Freudian and
blessing the *Pistola* on its savage quest, Chatwin allows the facts to
speak for themselves in all of their brutal significance.

Chapter 4 is divided into 18 sections and opens with Francisco da
Silva's dramatic entrance into the forbidden precincts of Dahomey. This
chapter also begins the major narrative of Da Silva in his official capacity
as a slave trader. When he arrives Dahomey is a wasteland because it has
been looted by the king's soldiers: "The flagstaff was broken, the Royal
Arms defaced. Walls were roofless and smoke-blackened . . . turkey
buzzards flapped off as he stepped into the yard. A pig was teasing the
rind off a jackfruit. A dog pissed against a tree and started howling"
(p. 82). Da Silva meets the lone survivor, a Yoruba freeman named
Taparica the Tambour, who becomes Da Silva's truest friend and, eventually, the majordomo of his household. Da Silva's entrance into the Fort
of Ouidah is, mythically, a major threshold experience; the pissing dog is
a Cerberus figure and Taparica is his new wise guide into an inferno
ruled by a mad Hades-like king.

After two years and the imposition of Da Silva's administrative
genius, Ouidah becomes the most financially successful slave-trading
post in Africa. The business is so prosperous that the Coutinho family
gives him a place in the syndicate. As a result of his enormous success,
Da Silva becomes a "respectable" man of property and no longer thinks
of himself as an aimless wanderer. His faithful Taparica carefully guides
him through the dangerous intrigues of the Dahomean court: "He slept
on a mat outside the master's room. He cooked and tasted his food, con-
trolled his drinking habits and emptied the slop pail. He found girls for
his bed, aphrodisiacs if the weather was exceptionally sticky, and warned
him not to make lasting attachments. Francisco Manoel would use the
same girl for a night or two, then send her home with a present for her
family" (p. 87). Da Silva also gains a reputation for being an "honest"
businessman with both veterans of the trade and the king himself,
though he has not yet met the king because of the Dahomean taboo
that warns the king not to look upon the sea or come into contact with
either the coastal serpent cults or the white man.

One of the ironies of Da Silva's character is found in the reasons he objects to the slaves' cruel and inhuman treatment by the king's warriors who capture them: "The Dahomeans' mindless cruelty offended Da Silva's sense of economy. Time and again, he complained . . . that the guards were ruining valuable property" (p. 88). However, he still insists on performing certain specialized tasks himself: "Francisco Manoel preferred to do the branding himself, taking care to dip the red-hot iron in palm-oil to stop it sticking to the flesh" (p. 89).

After five years, however, Da Silva feels the need for some form of recognition—he wants to become governor of the fort; the huge wealth he has accumulated does not satisfy him enough. Da Silva then experiences a decisive spiritual transformation. He begins to participate in the Africans' native habits and starts going to the Python Temple to observe animal sacrifices. But he never understands what, exactly, draws him to the mysteries of the Dahomean serpent cults. As a result of his shift from a European to an African sensibility, he decides to take an African bride, a 16-year-old named Jijibou. After a short while they have a son, Isidoro, whose name means "gift of God."

Meanwhile, the mad king begins to have serious financial problems and finds foreigners to be convenient scapegoats. Da Silva is arrested and brought before the king after suffering horrible humiliations and physical injuries. Chatwin's description of the king—who in real life was the infamous King Adandozan—attests to his novelistic powers to create vivid cinematographic images: "He was a tall sinewy man with dry eyes, automatic gestures and the bonhomie of the seasoned slaughterer. The rising sun shone on his chest. . . . At his feet were the heads of a boy and girl, sent half an hour earlier to tell the Dead Kings that their descendant had woken up. He glared at the Brazilian and spat" (p. 99). He lies lounging on a throne surrounded by naked women who fan him with ostrich feathers and wipe the sweat from his forehead. The description is almost a parody of scenes out of so-called jungle movies of the 1940s and 1950s.

Da Silva so charms the king that by the end of the interview the king decides not to execute him. Furthermore, the king is unable to execute Da Silva because there is no precedent for beheading a white man, so he tries to dye him black in a torturous series of indigo dips and decides to let him starve to death naturally. During Da Silva's hallucinations, typical of those that accompany starvation, he revisits his childhood in Brazil and the happy life at the Coutinhos' estate, Tapuitapera. Throughout his tortures, a young man named Kankpé follows his every move. Kankpé,

who happens to be the king's mad half-brother, sees Da Silva's release as
a way of gaining the throne. He cleverly smuggles him out of the king's
prison and meets him in the forest, and the two hunt together for five
days. On the fifth day they swear a pact, drinking blood from a skull
and spitting it into each other's face as Kankpé murmurs, "[B]lood-
brothers live together and together they must die. Francisco Manoel
drank with the light heartedness of the man who had skipped from certain death. It took another thirty years for him to realize the extent of
his obligations" (p. 107).

Chapter 5, the longest in the book, is divided into 31 sections of various length and traces the spectacular rise and fall of Francisco Manoel
da Silva. To attain complete control, Da Silva realizes that he must
somehow rid the country of the king and find a way to elevate Kankpé
to the throne. In letters to Joaquim Coutinho—Chatwin uses the episto-
lary device throughout the book—Da Silva asks the family for help, and
they gladly send "muskets, rum, and tobacco" to prepare an army to
overthrow the king. The coup is a peaceful one: two of the king's chief
ministers—at the behest of Kankpé—announce to him that "The Dead
Kings have deposed you!" The king immediately abdicates and volun-
tarily goes to prison, "where he would linger on for another forty years,
ordering imaginary executions and slumped in a torpor of compulsive
eating" (p. 112). As a reward for helping the new king of Dahomey—
King Gezo in real life—King Kankpé invests Da Silva with the regalia
of a Dahomean chief and within the year makes him the official viceroy
of Ouidah. From then on all address him as Dom Francisco, a title that
has always been reserved for members of the Portuguese royal family.

One of the first actions that the king and his viceroy take is to reform
the flabby Dahomean army by creating a wing of female soldiers, called
Amazons, who are far more fierce than their male counterparts. They
are known as " '[t]he King's Leopard Wives.' They ate raw meat, shaved
their heads and filed their teeth to sharp points. . . . [T]he Amazons
would be parading before the King swinging severed heads like dumb-
bells. . . . Dom Francisco greeted each fresh atrocity with a glassy smile.
He felt no trace of pity for the mother who pleaded for her child" (pp.
116–17). Though there are some indications that Da Silva is gradually
becoming less savage, his involvement with King Kankpé's renewed
atrocities merely reawakens any residual sadism that may have faded
from the dom's memory. Unfortunately, King Kankpé, over the years,
becomes more ferocious than any of his ancestors, and Dom Francisco
gradually tires of the bloodshed, especially when the king's Amazons

begin gratuitously garroting small boys for their skulls. But it is the king's obsessive need to collect skulls that finally turns Dom Francisco away from unnecessary bloodshed. The king's motive for skull collecting is a classic existential one: "The skulls of his enemies assured him that he was alive in the world of real things" (pp. 117–18).

Eventually the king and the dom communicate only through gifts, and by 1835 the size of Da Silva's family has outgrown the fort. He decides to construct a *simbodji* and to build his version of Tapuitapera. In fact, his *simbodji* turns out to be an exact replica of that mythic Camelot. After importing expensive European and Asian furniture, he receives the vitrine oratory of the Last Supper from the Coutinho family in gratitude for the wealth he has brought them. But they also want to avoid the embarrassment of having him return to Brazil.

Da Silva's return to Brazil would be unpalatable to the Coutinho family for several reasons. Though married to Jijibou, Da Silva contin- ues to find other avenues of sexual release from his chronic state of bore- dom, paranoia, and fear of the passing of time: "on the bad nights, the game of breaking virgins was his only hope of consolation" (p. 122). He has sent his son, Isidoro, to live with and be educated by the Coutinho family, but the boy has become a drunken, whoring brat. He is so out of control that the Coutinhos have sent him to a seminary, and Joaquim uses the boy's outrageous behavior to break up his business partnership with the dom. Also, it is now 1838, and slave trading has become not only an occupation that no civilized Brazilian gentleman would partici- pate in but also a criminal offense; there was a significant slave revolt in Bahia in 1835. Joaquim Coutinho's reward for turning away from such barbaric activities is a royal title; he becomes the baron of Paraíba.

Because slave trading has become illegal in most civilized countries, the dom needs to move into some other, "clean" business, so when Isidoro returns from France with a scheme to go into the palm-oil trade, Dom Francisco embraces it. The scheme goes bad, though, and prob- lems arise with the British Navy, who attack Ouidah after King Kankpé insults Queen Victoria. After 5,000 Dahomeans are slaughtered, Dom Francisco is blamed for the debacle and, once again, becomes a scape- goat.

Da Silva's Fall Begins

Da Silva's troubles could certainly be seen to result from the conse- quences of what Chatwin calls "the sins of settlement," and there is little doubt that once he localizes his occupation, stops wandering, and builds his "big house" his life becomes a curse. One of the insidious results of settlement is that from it emerges the concept of private property—that one owns land and the people who live on it. The very concept of slavery derives from ideas of private property, authority, and social privilege. Freedom, particularly freedom of movement, is the antithesis of slavery.

The pathological effects of Da Silva's sense of isolation and alienation are profound. His insistent feeling that he is outside the community is transformed, once he gains property, into a feeling of being above it and, therefore, in charge of it. The dom's personal-wasteland condition of isolation and communal rejection is relieved only when he controls the entire community. His wasteland is then transformed into his New Jerusalem, or Eden. In short, the consistent patterns in the dom's life are dramatized by his movement from isolation to joining the community, or leaving the community and returning to isolation.

Once King Kankpé scapegoats the dom, the dom's movement toward isolation becomes inevitable. But other elements add to that downward motion. Ironically, many ex-slaves begin to return to Ouidah, which becomes known as "Little Brazil." Along with the ex-slaves come a young doctor and his wife, Dona Luciana, both from the badlands in Brazil where Dom Francisco was born and raised. Dona Luciana takes one look at the dom and swears she sees the devil. The dom then makes the fatal error of marrying off one of his native assistant's daughters, a Christianized Dahomean, to King Kankpé because the king feels he needs a Christian wife. The daughter, Venossa das Chagas, outraged over the way Da Silva has used her, will become the major instrument in the eventual downfall of the Da Silva family years later.

Meanwhile, Venossa's father betrays Da Silva and gives the king reasons to take all of the dom's gold and silver. Not only are the resources of Da Silva's fiefdom partially collapsing, but his beloved majordomo, Taparica, is dying because he has been poisoned by Jijibou, Francisco's vengeful Dahomean wife. What saves Da Silva's empire temporarily from total collapse is an outbreak of yellow fever. Ten Da Silvas die in addition to many mulattos and blacks, but the whites are spared.

Though Dona Luciana becomes very ill, she miraculously regains her health and attributes it, for some reason, to Dom Francisco: "Then suddenly, overnight, the man who had been the Devil was transfigured into her Guardian Angel" (p. 140). Since her husband has died of yellow fever, they then marry and live in a celibate union for a short while. His legal wife, Jijibou, vows revenge and gets her wish: after Dona Luciana gives birth to Eugenia, and after she valiantly tries to smuggle the dom, Eugenia, and herself out of Dahomey and back to Bahia, she becomes violently ill and dies. It is fairly obvious that she has been poisoned by Jijibou. Once the dom's attempt to sneak out of Dahomey becomes public knowledge, he is stripped of his wealth and privileges and given a small room to live in for the rest of his life. Because he is King Kankpé's blood brother, however, no one is allowed to harm him in any way.

Da Silva's fall is complete, and bereft of family (except for his daughter Eugenia), friends, and business associates, he lingers on in disgraced isolation. Two of his beloved daughters are forced to become prostitutes to support themselves. A desperate letter for financial help to Joaquim Coutinho goes unanswered, and Da Silva's creditors foreclose on his mortgages and the bailiffs carry away everything. He spends his remaining time wandering around Ouidah a lost and pathetic soul, covered with sores, weeping and begging. He confronts his successful son, Isidoro, at a lavish banquet but is ignored and forced back to his tiny room: "He opened his mouth to speak, but his lower lip hung slack, and the music whirred, round and round his skull, as he reeled from the room, out into the light and dust and hawks and dark and nothing" (p. 150).

Return to the Present

Chapter 6—divided into two short sections—returns to the deathbed of Mama Wéwé, or Eugenia da Silva, who remembers with great sorrow her father's terrible fall from his high position to that of a beggar. As she herself is dying, she recalls details of her father's funeral and the deep sorrow of King Kankpé, his blood brother, who would die barely a year later. Her last image is that of her father welcoming her to a celestial banquet.

The final section of chapter 6, which frames the entire book, depicts a stark scene in the headquarters of Lieutenant Colonel Zossoungbo, the Marxist-Leninist chief of police in the People's Republic of Benin. The book also returns to its beginning. The voice of Benin's president is coming to the end of the same broadcast that Chatwin interwove with the voices of the Da Silva celebrants at the book's beginning: "Voices to the People! / Glory to the People! / Power to the People! (p. 154). *Viceroy* concludes with an alarmingly vivid image—a masterful cinematographic collage of the social and economic icons that represent Benin's new political and cultural powers and that have replaced the Catholic crucifix and the Portuguese flag: "Fixed to the wall were a pair of handcuffs and a broken guitar. There was also a stuffed civet cat, nailed, in mockery of the Crucifixion, with its hind legs and tail together and its forelegs stretched apart. Above the desk hung the scarified face of the President" (p. 154).

In *The Viceroy of Ouidah* Chatwin uses many of the literary techniques that he used to structure *In Patagonia,* but his principal method of development is to reanimate the past by starting the book in the present. As he moves backward in time, the reader gains a sense of how the past creates the present and the future and, additionally, a foreboding sense of fate and destiny that Francisco da Silva could never have avoided. Chatwin's most striking novelistic accomplishment, however, is that Francisco remains a completely believable human being in spite of his sociopathic behavior. We clearly understand the dom as both oppressor and oppressed, as both victim and victimizer. Chatwin also shows us how he transforms Da Silva's Edenic agendas into wastelands—his heaven into his hell. Da Silva's rise and fall can be seen as particularized versions of the rise and fall of the Portuguese and Brazilian colonizers and slave traders because they all shared the same Christian and capitalist racist attitudes that not only allowed but rewarded and encouraged them to save the darker races from their benighted "savagery." The novel's principal theme is, as Victoria Glendinning asserts, "a clashing of cultural myths," which are comprised of the Marxist-Leninist, the Christian, the capitalist, and the animist Python Cult. Bruce Chatwin's deft interweaving of the complicated threads of these clashing myths demonstrates his genius as both a novelist and a cultural historian.

Chapter Four

On the Black Hill:
"Simpletons, Saints, and Grotesques"

Bruce Chatwin was anything but predictable, so it should come as no surprise that his third book, *On the Black Hill,* shares very little with his earlier works. As Michael Ignatieff states in his preface to a lengthy interview with Chatwin in *Granta,* "Each of his books escapes the last one: *In Patagonia,* a travel narrative and voyage of self-discovery; *The Viceroy of Ouidah,* a lushly coloured miniature about a Brazilian slaver in Dahomey; *On the Black Hill,* his only novel set in Britain, about the lives of two Welsh hill-farmer brothers" ("Interview," 23). Chatwin confesses in the same interview that his principal reason for writing this book was to reverse a growing critical assumption that pigeonholed him too narrowly: "It always irritated me to be called a travel writer. So I decided to write something about people who never went out. That's how *On the Black Hill* came into being" (p. 27).

Nicholas Murray excerpts another interview Chatwin had, with Melvyn Bragg on a popular London television program called *The South Bank Show* on 7 November 1982:

> I was told a story, it doesn't matter which one, which does not appear in the book, about two bachelor brothers, and I wanted to write a short story. And so I started out writing a few paragraphs and then, suddenly, I wrote that the brothers were identical twins. I don't know why I wrote it, but it just occurred to me that they might be. And having written that line, which is a separate paragraph to itself, I suddenly realized that this was a novel and not a short story and that what I'd done sort of predicated a book of about 450 pages instead of 30. And so one just had to carry on till the end." (*Bruce Chatwin,* 63)

He adds in the same interview that the geography of the borderlands between eastern Wales and western England was one that he was quite familiar with: "The areas that I know are the Black Mountains and the Radnor Forest. [The story] can in fact happen anywhere between South Shropshire and Monmouthshire, in theory, because it's all the same board and it's all got the same character" (p. 63). He confessed to Bragg that this section of the Welsh borders became for him "a sort of metaphorical homebase if you like and it's the place I love" (p. 60).

Early Visits to Wales

Chatwin's first visit to the area was with his father, Charles, in 1949; the family had just bought a new car, and his father took him and his brother Hugh for a ride into Wales, where they spent the night (*Bruce Chatwin*, 22). He later visited Wales when he was a student at Marlborough College, which sponsored a youth-club summer-camp project that brought together young people of diverse social classes. Later, as a young adult, he stayed at Llanthony Abbey, which was once owned by the English poet Walter Savage Landor. He told one of his best friends, the poet Hugo Williams, that his grandparents used to take bicycling tours there as teenagers and remarked that very little had changed from those days.

Chatwin also stayed with several friends who lived in that particularly beautiful locale. As Murray points out, he regularly visited Penelope Chetwode (Lady Betjeman) at Hay; Diana Melly, who lived in a lovely Norman tower near Brecon, Wales; and one of his closest friends, Martin Wilkinson, who had a home near Clun. It was at Clun that Chatwin began writing the book. During many of his trips to Wales and the Radnor Hills, he absorbed much from conversations he had in local pubs and inns, where he unobtrusively questioned the natives at length but always with respectful consideration. One of the book's enthusiastic Welsh readers, Nancy Powell, says that she recognized many of the stories, particularly the more bloody murders and suicides (attempted and successful). Regarding the likeliness of twin brothers living together and refusing to marry, Powell claims that the practice was not all that uncommon because twins were often fearful of losing part of their farm to the other's widow and her family. (*Bruce Chatwin*, 60–61).

Murray also talked with several natives of the region, who vividly remembered Chatwin during the time he was writing the book. Roger Fry, who worked at the Blue Boar Inn in Hay, recalls Chatwin frequently coming in for lunch: "He was always watching people, how they spoke, and their mannerisms. . . . No one really knew him" (*Bruce Chatwin*, 60).

Fry also remembers that when Chatwin wanted to impress his audience, he was fully capable of putting on a good show: "He had quite a theatrical way about him. . . . He had a face you really wanted to look at. His eyes really glittered. If he had been born in the twelfth century he would have been a wizard" (p. 60). Murray warns, however, that readers must not assume that the geographical areas in which the novel takes place are literal representations. Chatwin synthesized several towns into one. The town Rhulen, Chatwin insisted, could have been "any one of the border towns (he mentioned specifically Kington or Knighton). . . . Certainly, an identification of the topography of the novel with the Llanthony valley seems reasonable enough, although Chatwin was drawing on explorations and researches up and down the border, even as far north as Clun" (p. 60). Murray also points out that there is "a Rhulen on the Ordnance Survey map and there is a Vision farmhouse but these were raided for their names only and are not the ones in the book" (p. 62). Chatwin also sometimes uses geographical fact to add a comic twist. For example, the book contains a character named Mr. Evenjobb; those familiar with the local geography recognize Evenjobb as the name of a village in the Radnor Valley.

Murray is quick to warn, though, that *On the Black Hill* is not a work of "social anthropology but a novel. . . . Whatever the documentary sources or echoes it is an imaginative reordering of experience" (*Bruce Chatwin,* 62). He also suggests that we keep the work's fictional intent in mind and not overplay the literal. Regarding the identical twins Benjamin and Lewis Jones, for example, Chatwin insisted that they "were an amalgam of at least three sets of twins" (p. 62). The critic Karl Miller even suggests that Chatwin found the idea for this subject encoded in his own name: *Chatwin*.[1] Chatwin was not averse to discussing his working methods or the way his imagination experimented with possibilities. During the *South Bank* interview with Melvyn Bragg, he clearly states, "I've done the usual novelist thing of combining two, three, four characters and then the character has a life of its own. . . . It has the same tenuous dividing line between fact and fiction and real people and something invented. And I quite honestly used them. If you're off on a journey, you meet somebody, they go into the book in one form or another" (p. 63).

Twins are a natural corollary subtopic of Chatwin's enduring obsession with the biblical twins Abel (the wanderer) and Cain (the settler), who appear figuratively throughout his works. As Murray succinctly asserts, "Chatwin was obsessed with the Biblical story of Cain and Abel which he saw as a fundamental paradigm of the nomad and the settler, of the two great human impulses that were in conflict: to settle and acquire the habits of civilization, and to wander" (*Bruce Chatwin,* 68). Even in so spatially limited a novel as *On the Black Hill,* it is clear that the Cain/Abel archetype operates throughout; Benjamin may be viewed as a Cain figure, and Lewis, an Abel figure. Chatwin, whose final proof of documentation was always etymological , researched the roots of both names with impressive results. Chatwin revealed to Bragg that the names of both Abel (the martyr) and Cain (the settled agriculturist) bespoke their identity and their destiny: "[T]he word Abel means motion, transitoriness, breath, and therefore life, whereas the word Cain comes from a verbal root, meaning to accumulate and acquire, making the agriculturalist a property owner" (p. 68). There is little question that Lewis more closely resembles Abel—even though he physically runs the farm—because of his consistent desire to move about the world and because of the few times that he actually leaves the protection of The Vision. Benjamin is a devoted and ultimately successful farm manager and property owner and, ironically, buys his brother a tractor, which inadvertently causes Lewis's death.

Obsession with Twins

Chatwin also told Bragg that he became so obsessed with the idea of twins that he went to the British Museum to study the Freudian and psychoanalytical literature on the topic but came up with nothing very revealing. As a last resort, he read the work of Professor René Zazzo, one of the world's authorities on the topic. Zazzo's book contained 1,500 case histories, each of which to Chatwin was like "a tiny little short story." He interviewed Professor Zazzo in Paris and told him about his idea for a novel on twins; the professor then made a number of suggestions, which became the basic structure of the book (p. 65). It is clear why John Updike labeled Chatwin "a demon researcher" in his 1983 *New Yorker* review of *On the Black Hill.*[2]

Although there is little question that *On the Black Hill* is and was intended to be a novel, critics are once again divided as to how to define the book's genre. Nicholas Murray, who has written the only full-length book on Bruce Chatwin and whose critical assessments are both reliable and cogent, plays down, correctly, the importance of literal "documentary sources" (p. 62). That Chatwin possessed one of the most fecund imaginations in modern British literature is unquestionable. Karl Miller, an academic critic whose Freudian analyses enhance *On the Black Hill*'s interpretative possibilities, calls the work "a Christian romance—the exemplum without the sermon, so to speak" (*Doubles*, 404). Miller considers Chatwin's treatment of the "lore of twinship"—normally a romantic topic—"a religious one" in *On the Black Hill* (p. 403). Another critic, Andrew Harvey, labels the book "a brooding pastoral tale full of tender grandeur" ("Footprints," 1). The novel certainly can be considered a pastoral because it deals with rustics and their difficult—not glamorous—lives. The great English fiction writer and critic V. S. Pritchett calls the novel "a plotless chronicle, the mixing of outward and inner life," and points out its most obvious link to *In Patagonia*'s similar subject matter, sheep farming. Pritchett adds, "The people of *On the Black Hill* are part of the sturdy remnant who toiled and haggled at home."[3]

Pritchett also suggests that Chatwin's ability to "make it strange"—a penchant he learned from his favorite writers, the Russians—is key to understanding the tone of this very strange work. John Updike, who describes the book's form as "a mosaic of wonderfully sharp and knowing small scenes" ("The Jones Boys," 126), also uses words like "allegorical" and "slightly fabulous" to characterize the theme and the Welsh setting. He states that the book's style "touches on the epic" (p. 130). *On the Black Hill*'s clear arrangement in a series of closely interconnected episodes is much more convincing than the loosely episodic structure of *The Viceroy of Ouidah* and shows that Chatwin has substantively refined his novelistic technique.

Karl Miller, in his scholarly book *Doubles*, seems to support Updike's use of such mythic terms as "allegorical," "fabulous," and "epic" when he plainly asserts, "Then again there is a literature and fairy-tale of twins, and it is to this category that *On the Black Hill* belongs" (*Doubles*, 403). Miller also invents a new mythopoeic term, "Chatwinshire," to characterize the author's uniquely personal cosmos and agrees with V. S. Pritchett's assessment of the book's Russian "strangeness": "The Chatwinshire we read about in the novel is apt to look apocryphal, like some Kamchatka—Russia's Patagonia, which figured, during the Romantic period, in the inventory of the remote, as part of the fairyland of the traveller's tale. . . . This is the strangeness of the traveller's tale and of the fairy-tale, and of a mode of writing to which Mr. Chatwin has always been drawn" (p. 403). Miller also asserts that the characters in the novel fall into three categories: "simpletons, saints, and grotesques" (p. 406).

Questions also arise about Chatwin's important literary influences in
On the Black Hill, since most critics agree that this work was Chatwin's
first genuine novel. Indeed, Chatwin won the Whitbread Award, a prize
given only for an author's first novel. Updike finds evidence of D. H.
Lawrence's "inspired swiftness" and Ernest Hemingway's "chiselled
bleakness" ("The Jones Boys," 130); he also finds Flaubert's influence in
the grotesque peace celebrations in Lurkenhope. V. S. Pritchett detects
some Thomas Hardy but has serious reservations about Chatwin's spiritual reach: "*On the Black Hill* has been compared to works like Thomas
Hardy's *The Woodlanders* or *Tess of the D'Urbervilles,* because it comes so
close to the skin of its peoples, but the comparison is misleading.
Chatwin dispenses with grand tragic plot and the theatrical use of coincidence. Above all there is no classical President of the Immortals, indif-
ferent to fate; there is no Victorian pessimism."[4] Francis King, one of
Chatwin's keenest critics, finds the novel's theme and setting akin to
Mary Webb's novels (especially *Precious Bane*) about the emotionally
stultifying and claustrophobic lives of Shropshire farmers in the late
nineteenth and early twentieth centuries. King specifically points out
that though Chatwin is a more "fastidious writer" than Webb, they both
share "an ability to evoke country lives . . . [and] a poetic sensitivity to
landscape."[5] Miller, however, finds traces of a very popular satiric work,
Stella Gibbons's *Cold Comfort Farm* (1932), which was a parody of novels
like *Precious Bane.* Gibbons's brilliant satire of Hardy-like novels about
rustic pessimism and doomed farmers brought an end to that particular
genre of popular literature. Obviously, Karl Miller and Francis King
interpret *On the Black Hill* from widely different critical perspectives.
John Lanchester, like Updike, finds Flaubert's influence throughout *On
the Black Hill* because the novel's predominantly cinematic technique
carries the story along and makes it an apt vehicle—like *The Viceroy of
Ouidah*—for Andrew Grieve's critically acclaimed 1987 film of the work
("A Pom," 10).

Thematically, *On the Black Hill* appears to bear little relationship to
Chatwin's earlier books. It is certainly true that there are few important
trips in *On the Black Hill.* Its subject matter is stasis, and mythically
speaking, the Joneses' farm The Vision is viewed as Eden from the
beginning, so there is no reason to leave it. The idea of an Eden is, in
fact, a "vision" that the twins' father, Amos Jones, strives for and finally
attains before his death and that Mary maintains for her children. Like
In Patagonia and *The Viceroy of Ouidah,* however, *On the Black Hill* does
share a spiritual vision of the local geography as Edenic. In *In Patagonia,*

Chatwin feels he must restore his family's Edenic center by bringing home the fabled sloth skin, and Francisco Manoel da Silva, who constantly yearns to return to Tapuitapera, his personal paradise, instead replicates it in Ouidah. The Vision is the Edenic center that is constantly threatened by both exterior and interior forces—its fall is often imminent. So it is the constant mission of Amos and Mary Jones, the twins' parents, and later of the twins themselves to cleanse, restore, and keep sacred the hearth of innocence. All three books, then, share the theme of the fall from innocence.

Critic Lorna Sage connects the theme of innocence with that of survival: "Chatwin . . . is interested in the way his characters' insulated and conventionally crazy existence is, against all odds, a good recipe for survival. Lewis and Benjamin preserve an innocence that satirizes the outside world. By the original accident of their twinship they've never learned to be 'individuals,' never tried to take possession of their destinies."[6] John Updike quite bluntly calls the relationship of Benjamin and Lewis "a homosexual marriage, with Benjamin the feminine partner and Lewis the masculine" ("The Jones Boys," 129). Presumably, the "marriage" is a chaste one, since Benjamin's primary duty is to keep Lewis, like himself, a virgin for life. Benjamin is devastated by Lewis's few sexual encounters because Benjamin experiences them as intensely painful *as they occur*. What the twins have, after their parents' death, is The Vision—their remote farm—but more important, their childhood innocence, which The Vision embodies and preserves. They can maintain their Edenic condition only as long as they remain together on the farm, or metaphorically, within The Vision. When the brothers do venture out into the world, they are brutally ridiculed and abused, and as Karl Miller asserts, they find that "This world is contemptible . . . here is a world from which it is right to retire" (*Doubles*, 405–6). Miller goes on to point out that *On the Black Hill* expresses one of English literature's perennial themes, at least since the romantics—that "The country is better than the town . . . but the country is terrible" (p. 406). From the evidence in this book, though, the country is less terrible than the town and can be tolerated if your neighbors are halfway decent and if you're living with someone you love or can tolerate. There can be little argument that this book is an updated version of an old and respected English literary form, the pastoral, but it is a pastoral with a heavily Freudian message that also makes it an authentic contemporary psychological novel. As important as the novel's Freudian overtones, though, are its mythic resonances.

V. S. Pritchett makes the brilliant observation that the "imagination of the Border people is mythical and Biblical. . . . The Bible people see themselves as descendants of Abraham—the man of flocks—and look upon the money-making English cities across the Border as examples of the corruption of Sodom. They see themselves as travellers to the 'Abiding City' of God" (*Lasting Impressions,* 43). It is clear to Benjamin and Lewis that staying in The Vision is the only way—the narrow path—to that heavenly city. The broad path leads to the dangerous temptations of the ever-threatening earthly city.

The Country and the City

Pritchett is the only scholar-critic to connect the novel's themes to its local geography and to Christian and Celtic mythology. He points out that the twins' farm was originally called (in Welsh) "Ty-Cradoc—the name of Caractacus, the Welsh hero who fought the Roman invaders, [which] is still evocative in the Border country—but [is] now known as The Vision because a country girl saw the Virgin there in the eighteenth century" (p. 43). It seems that Chatwin is once again using one of his favorite anthropological techniques, syncretism, in somewhat the same way he used it throughout *The Viceroy of Ouidah.* The twins, in unconscious imitation of their predecessors (who originally named the farm Ty-Cradoc; then renamed it The Vision, which recalls the visionary virgin), are also engaged, mythically, in rebuffing the barbaric invading hordes: the Romans, Satan, and destructive English materialism. As Pritchett points out, "The modern world comes slowly in with the trippers and its weekenders, its washing machines, its cheating antique dealers who try to strip the old farmers of their treasures; but the Bible is the ruling consolation. The mythical world lives side by side with reality. The Border people live by their imagination" (p. 46). Most important, though, is Pritchett's conclusion about *On the Black Hill*'s proper subject matter, mythically speaking, and his interpretation of the twins' principal mission: "They are carrying with them the inner life of their race" (p. 42).

The outlines of the principal conflicts that illustrate the twins' struggles can be found in the recurring metaphors of the country and the city. The city represents corruption, temptation, and possible damnation, whereas the country symbolizes the possibilities of hope, virtue, and natural piety in the Wordsworthian sense. Since Benjamin's greatest skill is delivering lambs—figures of innocence and sacrifice—his character is defined by his brutal innocence and arrogant sexual abstinence. The name Benjamin means "son of the right hand" or "the righteous one." In the Old Testament, Benjamin is the youngest son of Jacob and Rachel and is also his father's favorite. The tribe of Israel actually descends from the line of Benjamin. It is fairly obvious that Chatwin uses the biblical references to Benjamin ironically, since Benjamin never marries, is without issue, and is his mother's favorite, not his father's. The name Lewis, on the other hand, derives from the Indo-European root *weik,* which according to the *American Heritage Dictionary* means "to conquer, to be able in battle and famous in war." Again ironically, Lewis is exempted from war but is physically more aggressive and powerful than Benjamin, since he performs the farm's day-to-day chores. The twins have a sister named Rebecca, who in the Old Testament is Benjamin's grandmother, so Chatwin attaches the modern figure to the ancient one. The twins' mother, Mary, is quite clearly named after the mother of Christ. Their father is named Amos, who in the Old Testament is a prophet and is renowned as a shepherd and herdsman. The biblical Amos is also a visionary who prophesies (in five visions) the destruction and rebuilding of Jerusalem.

The other two symbols of opposites—or twins—that appear throughout the novel are The Vision and The Rock. The Rock is an adjoining farm that represents everything that The Vision is not. Its closest literary equivalent could be Erskine Caldwell's *Tobacco Road.* The Rock is the natural, or vegetable, equivalent of The Vision's anagogic, or spiritual, condition. Its longtime resident, Meg, is actually—and comically—mistaken, at one point, for a large clump of earth. There is little question that Meg's half-wit brother Jim (who returns from World War I as a heroic mule driver), resembles, in his drunken dissipation, one of Dionysus's favorite companions, the satyrlike Silenus, an ancient drunken mule driver. Both characters may remind some readers of John Steinbeck's rarely sober Danny in *Tortilla Flat,* who returns from World War II a hero because of his masterful handling of mules. *On the Black Hill*'s earthly city and heavenly city are analogous to The Vision and The Rock. *The Viceroy of Ouidah* uses the same kind of metaphors—the Celestial Python and the Last Supper—to represent similar spiritual conflicts.

Another recurring image in *On the Black Hill* is the famous painting *The Broad and Narrow Path,* which graphically represents the temptations of the pagan, non-Christian world as the broad path and contrasts it to the narrow path, one of penitential sacrifice amid natural beauty. The sign on the threshold of the broad path quite bluntly reads "Death and Damnation," whereas the narrow path's much smaller door announces, "Life and Salvation." This famous picture is the centerpiece of the Jones family household. The painting, which is also Benjamin's most inspiring religious object and embodies his beliefs, is cinemato-graphically one of the major images that provides coherence and struc-ture to the book's plotless chronicle. Nicholas Murray, in talking with Chatwin's friends, discovered that the writer actually kept a reproduc-tion of "The Broad and the Narrow Path" over his desk as he worked on the book's early chapters at the Shropshire home of his friend Martin Wilkinson in Clun in 1980: "The simplicity and austerity of the non-conformist chapel culture fascinated Chatwin and he would often pay visits to a chapel at Hay-on-Wye during his researches" (*Bruce Chatwin*, 66). Chatwin wrote the bulk of the book, however, at the Brecon, Wales, home of one of the book's dedicatees, Diana Melly.

Another important image that appears throughout the novel and that is always associated with Lewis is an oleograph that Amos Jones's brother, Eddie, sent to the family from Canada. It is this picture, "with its Red Indian, its birchbark, its pines and a crimson sky . . . that first woke in Lewis a yearning for far-off places."[7] Once again, Chatwin uses a pair of symbols, or twin symbols, the painting and the oleograph, to structure the brothers' emotional and spiritual paths as they begin to understand their place in the world. Another notable instance of twin symbols of romantic duality is found later in the novel, when the wandering South African Buddhist-hippie Theo the Tent becomes involved with the recluse Meg the Rock; critic Karl Miller cannot resist calling the relationship a form of "Meg-magical" and "Theo-centric" exoticism. (*Doubles*, 406).

Reanimation Once More

The novel's structure is much simpler than that of either *In Patagonia* or *The Viceroy of Ouidah,* though it is divided into 50 short chapters. *On the Black Hill* begins as the twins approach their 80th birthday and as they prepare to turn over The Vision to their nephew, Kevin. Chapter 2, though, moves back in time to the 1899 wedding of Amos Jones to Mary Latimer, Benjamin's and Lewis's parents. The remainder of the work is, in true Chatwin fashion, a reanimation of the past and makes a full circle back to the twins' 80th birthday and beyond, to Lewis's death.

Chatwin opens the novel with a solemn quotation from Jeremy Tay-lor, one of the seventeenth century's most popular religious and devo-tional writers. Taylor was most famous for two books, *Holy Living* and

Holy Dying, both of which offer the hope of true happiness only in the life to come. These books are meditations on the transitory nature of human existence: "We must look somewhere else for an abiding city, a place in another country to fix our house in" (*OBH,* 5). A similar theme runs throughout *On the Black Hill.*

Chatwin wastes no time in presenting the novel's subjects: "For forty-two years, Lewis and Benjamin Jones slept side by side in their parents' bed, at their farm which was known as 'The Vision' " (p. 9). Chatwin then offers a summary of the twins' daily lives as hardworking sheep farmers and describes them physically: "Lewis was tall and stringy, with shoulders set square and a steady long-limbed stride. Even at eighty he could walk over the hills all day, or wield an axe all day, and not get tired. . . . Benjamin was shorter, pinker, neater and sharper-tongued. His chin fell into his neck, but he still possessed the full stretch of his nose, which he would use in conversation as a weapon. He had less hair. He did all the cooking, the darning and the ironing" (p. 10). It is clear from the division of labor that Lewis occupies the masculine role of the husband, and Benjamin, that of the wife. Benjamin does perform one role—that of delivering the lambs—that may seem to qualify him as an Abel figure, but it is Lewis who does the actual shepherding of the sheep; Benjamin acts as the agriculturalist—property owner—and thereby plays the role of Cain. The twins' spiritual core is maternal because they "lived for the memory of their mother" (p. 11).

Not only are Benjamin and Lewis identical twins, they share emotional and psychological habits as well: "Because they knew each other's thoughts, they even quarrelled without speaking" (p. 11). What brings them back together after their silent quarrels is the memory of their mother, evoked by some detail of her patchwork quilt or her apron. Most important, the twins keep everything in the house exactly the way it was on the day their mother died many years before. They also rigidly keep to her schedule—Friday had been her baking day, and it remains Benjamin's. The centerpiece of the household is the devotional picture *The Broad and Narrow Path,* which rests in the same kind of gothic frame that their father carved for all the other pictures and family photographs that hang on the wall. Benjamin's most beloved picture is *The Broad and Narrow Path,* an image that defines his austere Christian adherence to the gospel. Lewis's favorite is an oleograph of a Red Indian, which has awakened in him a deep desire for far-off places.

The day on which the novel opens is a few months before the twins' 80th birthday, the same day that their nephew, Kevin, will inherit the farm. As they survey the pictures on the wall, they are especially moved by their mother's sweet smile, which reminds them of Kevin's smile, and they experience a redemptive epiphany: "they knew that their lives had not been wasted and that time, in its healing circle, had wiped away the pain and the anger, the shame and the sterility, and had broken into the future with the promise of new things" (p. 14). It is this tone—sad but hopeful of the future—that separates Chatwin from the great English pastoral novelist Thomas Hardy, whose themes tend toward ultimate hopelessness.

The next chapter begins with the marriage of Amos Jones to Mary Latimer, the twins' parents, and then moves back in time to Amos's childhood with an embittered mother, Hannah, and a fun-loving but irresponsible alcoholic father, Sam the Waggon. Amos is thrown out of the house as a teenager and works on farms in the area. At 28 he marries a dull-witted woman named Rachel, who gives birth to a baby who dies. Rachel stops eating and dies shortly thereafter. From the day of her funeral, Amos Jones becomes a regular churchgoer. He then meets Mary Latimer, the daughter of a highly educated Anglican minister who has spent many years in India, and marries her after her father's sudden death. Mary then sells the contents of her father's library—he was a classical scholar—and the couple have enough money to rent a farm on the side of Black Hill called The Vision. Amos's mother, Hannah, visits the couple and makes life difficult for Mary. She resents Mary for her education and refined manners and is obviously jealous of her relationship with Amos. Mary becomes pregnant and gives birth to Benjamin and Lewis, and Hannah dies three days later.

The first evidence of the twins' hypersensitivity to each other becomes their first memory. Lewis is being fed by Mary when Benjamin, in a jealous fit, waves his hand and strikes a wasp. The wasp stings Benjamin, but it is Lewis who begins whimpering and stroking his left hand, as though he had been stung. Benjamin does not even cry. They also develop, in early childhood, a secret language that only they can understand, and they like to pretend they are little lambs, habits that annoy Amos greatly. Their earliest shared traumatic experience comes when their father decides to kill their favorite pig, Hoggage, because it is the runt of the litter. Their alienation from their father and from Rebecca, their sister and Amos's favorite, begins with Hoggage's murder.

Another instance of Benjamin's jealousy occurs when Lewis meets and begins to flirt innocently with one of their neighbors, Rosie Fifield. This crucial pattern of Benjamin's jealousy continues throughout the rest of the twins' youth right up into their thirties. Though they attend school for a while, Amos decides that nothing of much value can be learned in an environment where they waste time memorizing the poems of Shelley and Tennyson, and he insists that they start working on the farm. Benjamin comes down with a severe case of pneumonia and almost dies, but he slowly recovers. From then on he is obsessed with death and begins to bury dead animals and to perform Christian rituals over their graves. Mary uses Benjamin's illness as an opportunity to tutor him in such classical writers as Shakespeare and Dickens, and even some Latin authors, like Caesar and Cicero. At about the same time, Lewis becomes obsessed with airplanes because of the French pilot Louis Blériot's recent famous flight across the English Channel. A friend of Lewis's not only saw Blériot at an air show but also witnessed an actual plane crash. Lewis starts to cut out newspaper articles on any and all air disasters, a practice he will continue for the rest of his life.

It is about this time that Amos's estrangement from his sons deepens, and Mary tries to defend them from their father's brutality. Amos also begins to beat Mary, which further alienates the twins. Disaster then strikes when a wing of the barn burns down and Amos suspects arson because of a long-standing conflict with a neighboring family, the Watkinses—Amos's nemeses in every way.

Because of Amos's rage over the local constabulary's failure to punish Watkins's obvious arson and because he is frustrated and depressed over the death of his father, Sam, Amos joins a fundamentalist nonconformist Congregational church that has recently come under the influence of Owen Gomer Davies, a preacher whose sermons are full of literal interpretations of the Bible and hellfire and damnation. Amos has finally found someone who agrees with his views, and leaves the Church of England; he makes the twins work from 10 to 12 hours a day on the farm. He also forbids them to share the same bed. Mary knows that her protests will only bring more beatings and recalls the practices of nonconformist missionaries in India with disgust: "for her the word 'Chapel' represented all that was harsh and cramped and intolerant. Yet she masked her feelings and consented to go" (p. 84). With the passing of time, though, Mary admits to her Anglican friends that "The Chapel gives me great comfort" with its simple and intimate rituals (p. 85). Amos's physical and mental sufferings seem to increase, however, and his religious fanaticism grows more destructive.

Chatwin's delineation of the novel's characters clearly fits a pattern found in the works of Thomas Hardy and D. H. Lawrence. Mary Amos

resembles Paul Morel's mother in Lawrence's *Sons and Lovers;* both
women come from sophisticated and educated middle-class back-
grounds and marry oafish, lower-class men who resent learning and cultural refinement. Although Paul Morel's father does not physically
abuse his wife, as Amos Jones does, the effect of the men's psychological
abuse is the same. The twins, especially Benjamin, are driven into
deeper emotional dependence on their mother, a dependence that borders on the pathological. There appears to be an unspoken conspiracy
between Benjamin and Mary to protect Lewis from any woman who
might lure him away from the family: "Benjamin loved his mother and
his brother, and he did not like girls. When Lewis left the room, his eyes
would linger in the doorway, and his irises cloud to a denser shade of
grey: when Lewis came back, his pupils glistened" (p. 88). It is clear that
Benjamin is homosexual and in love with Lewis.

However, there is no evidence that Benjamin ever acts on his homosexual proclivities. His fiercely religious beliefs protect him from the
danger of recognizing his true nature: "He would spend long hours pat-
terning his ideas of sin and retribution into a vast theological system
that would, one day, save the world. . . . [H]e would pour over Amos's
colour print of 'The Broad and the Narrow Path' " (p. 89). For Benjamin
the road to hell is the road to Hereford, and the heavenly road leads to
the Radnor Hills. Lewis, on the other hand, "still dreamed of faraway
voyages but his interest had shifted to airships. And when a picture of a
Zeppelin appeared in the newspaper—or the mention of Count Zeppelin's name—he would cut out the article and paste it in his scrapbook.
Benjamin said that Zeppelins looked like cucumbers" (p. 88).

With the coming of the Great War, the twins enter the most emotionally devastating phase of their entire lives: their fall from innocence
begins.

A fall from innocence, in the mythic sense, is a fall from an Edenic
condition of harmony and happiness into one of separation and isolation. The Vision is aptly named because it embodies life on the farm as a
visionary fulfillment—a dream actualized. However, the preservation of
the visionary condition depends on its permanence—it must never
change. Any family member's separation from its precincts is the beginning of a fall from that visionary state—timeless and permanent—into
the realm of time, experience, and death. William Blake's *Songs of Innocence* and *Songs of Experience* dramatically demonstrate the fall from innocence (timelessness) to experience (time and death). Joseph Campbell, in
The Hero With a Thousand Faces, presents a brilliant schema of the

mythological journey of the hero. He proposes three phases of the hero's fall from innocence, which may be understood as rites of passage: separation, initiation, return. With the advent of World War I, Benjamin and Lewis begin the first and most painful phase of their fall: they are separated from one another, and their visionary existence, their heaven, becomes their hell. Chatwin's naming the farm The Vision could not make the twins' mythic rite of passage any clearer, nor could it define the pain of their separation more effectively.

World War I

In spite of the support for the 1914 war by Gomer Davies, Amos Jones's minister, Amos refuses to register his sons in the British Army because he hates both war and the British. As a result of his refusal, the novel's villain appears, the aptly named Mr. Arkwright, and humiliates the Jones family by asking for the twins' national identity cards. The very next day Amos takes Lewis to a local farmer who agrees to employ him as a ploughman, an occupation that could exempt him from military service. Lewis's departure is traumatic for Benjamin—they have never been away from each other for more than a day or two—and Benjamin begins to pine for him. He refuses food, stops washing, and revisits places where they played together as children in an attempt to regenerate the innocence of childhood. But a strange kind of anger also surfaces in Benjamin's depression, accompanied by an existential terror of vanishing: "He hated Lewis for leaving and suspected him of stealing his soul. One day, staring into the shaving mirror, he watched his face grow fainter and fainter, as if the glass were eating his reflection until he vanished altogether in a crystalline mist. This was the first time he thought of killing himself" (p. 99). Indeed, Benjamin unconsciously attempts suicide by walking out into the snow, ostensibly to gather some sheep off a hill. Instead he gets lost, but Lewis's voice directs him to seek shelter in one of their old childhood haunts, where he will be protected from the freezing snow. When Lewis finds him, Benjamin says accusingly, "You left me" (p. 104).

The twins are then brought before a tribunal, presided over by the most powerful landowner in the area, Colonel Bickerton. Bickerton owns The Vision and represents, along with Mr. Arkwright, the arrogant power of British landowners over the Welsh. Colonel Bickerton and his committee decide the fate of all the young men who are requesting exemption from military service. In a scene similar to the biblical one in which Christ is judged by Pontius Pilate, Benjamin and Lewis become victims of Bickerton's capricious judgment. Lewis, whose physique would obviously make him an excellent soldier, is immediately exempted. Benjamin, whose gentleness and emotional delicacy would normally exempt him, challenges the tribunal by asking them if they have ever heard of the sixth commandment—"Thou shalt not kill!" (Actually, "Thou shalt not kill" is the fifth commandment.) As a result of Benjamin's perceived insolence, he is immediately ordered to the Hereford Barracks to begin his basic training. How correct Benjamin was in earlier designating Hereford the "broad path," or the road to hell.

Readers of *On the Black Hill* can best understand the twins' plight by examining the biblical imaginations of Welsh farmers. Benjamin must undergo scourging at the pillar and crucifixion during his confinement in the Hereford Barracks. Once again, Lewis experiences the sufferings his brother is undergoing: "From the ache in his coccyx, Lewis knew when the N.C.O.s were frog-marching Benjamin round the parade-grounds; from the pain in his wrists, when they lashed him to the bed-frame; from a patch of eczema on his chest, when they rubbed his nipples with caustic. One morning, Lewis's nose began to bleed and went on bleeding till sundown: that was the day when they stood Benjamin in a boxing ring and slammed straight-lefts into his face" (p. 109). (There are echoes here of Alexander Dumas's [*père*] famous novel about twins, *The Corsican Brothers* [1845], in which Lucien de Franchi feels the pain of his twin brother, Louis, from many miles away. The name Lewis is derived from the French Louis, a fact that Chatwin was undoubtedly aware of.) For both brothers, nothing they undergo for the rest of their lives will approach the trauma of the war years. Their fall from innocence is complete and their joint project will be to generate another Edenic realm—an "Abiding City," in Jeremy Taylor's words—that will somehow restore The Vision to its former efficacy.

At the end of the war, Benjamin is released from the barracks with a "dishonourable discharge," and his experiences as a soldier have been so emotionally damaging that he is unable to leave The Vision for three months. He exhibits many of the marks of a victim of war: facial ticks, agoraphobia, and a reversion to childhood behavior. To make matters worse, Lewis is becoming interested in an old acquaintance, Rosie Fifield. Benjamin, knowing there is nothing he can do to forestall the affair, suffers in silence but "knows" everything that transpires between Rosie and his brother.

Chapter 24, one of the book's longest, constitutes one of the novel's principal dramatic climaxes. There can be little doubt that John Updike's suspicion of Flaubert's influence—especially the agricultural fair scene from *Madame Bovary*—is correct here. Benjamin and Lewis decide to attend the national peace celebrations in Rhulen, though Benjamin doubts that their presence will go unnoticed. And he is right. The colorful festivities quickly turn into a nightmare for the twins; the sadistic Mr. Arkwright ridicules them and calls them "shirkers." To his horror, Benjamin notices one of his torturers from the Hereford Barracks eyeing him and tries to get his brother to leave the celebration. As a storm erupts, Mr. Arkwright's patriotic rhetoric reaches its climax. But the worst is yet to come: Rosie Fifield, who agreed to meet the twins at the celebration, is swept into the patriotic hysteria and confronts Lewis and Benjamin in front of the crowd. She hands Lewis a white feather—a symbol of cowardice—and he thanks her, not realizing the significance of the object. Rosie also jeers the twins, calling them "[s]hirkers!" as had Mr. Arkwright. The twins barely escape a mob beating and somehow make it back to The Vision. As a result of this renewed torment, the brothers decide to avoid any journeys outside their immediate locale: "Since the day of the peace celebrations, the twins' world had contracted to a few square miles, bounded on one side by Maesyfelin Chapel and on the other by the Black Hill: both Rhulen and Lurkenhope now lay on enemy soil" (p. 131). At the age of only 22, they begin to behave, according to their mother, like "crabby old bachelors."

Meanwhile, the twins' sister Rebecca—their father's favorite—becomes pregnant. Amos's enraged response is to give her her dowry and throw her out of the house. The family never sees her again, but her son, Kevin, enters the story toward the end of the novel and inherits the farm. Ironically, the Bickertons go bankrupt and Rosie Fifield moves into an adjoining farm, The Tump. Rosie has become pregnant by the alcoholic Reggie Bickerton and been given the house as a payoff. Chatwin's portrait of Reggie is one of many throughout the book that demonstrate the writer's growing skill at developing complex characters: "In 1914, Reggie had gone to war with a head full of chivalric notions of duty to caste and country. He had come home a cripple, with a receding hairline, three fingers missing from his right hand, and the watery eyes of a secret drinker" (p. 134). Because of Chatwin's growing sophistication as a novelist, most of his characters are believable, sympathetic, and genuine human beings, whether virtuous or wicked. Reggie Bickerton, for example, though a coward off the battlefield, is drawn as a complex but wounded human being.

Amos wants more than anything to buy The Vision from the Bickertons, who have fallen on hard times financially. In an auction run by the

truly awful Mr. Arkwright, Amos gets into a monetary duel with his
nemesis, Mr. Watkins; he wins the farm but at an astronomical price that
he will never be able to pay. Mary uses her skills as a diplomat and writes
the matriarch, Mrs. Bickerton, in France, who agrees to sell The Vision at
a much lower and affordable price. Amos's unbelievable response is anger
and resentment at his wife's use of her middle-class privileges, and he
hysterically blames Mary for everything that has gone wrong in his life.
All of his long-standing resentments toward her come gushing forth: "It
had been *her* connections that got them the lease. *Her* money that
stocked the farm. *Her* furniture furnished the house. Because of *her*, his
daughter had run off with the Irishman. It was *her* fault that his sons
were idiots. And now, when everything had gone to whinders, it was *her*
class and her clever clever letter that had saved all that he, Amos Jones—
man, farmer, Welshman—had worked for, saved for, ruined his health
for—and now did not want!" (pp. 146–47). Again, Chatwin's ear for the
authentic rings true in the outrageous but convincing portrait of how an
aggressive man's nature is not ameliorated by the love and dedication of
a devoted wife and mother. Indeed, such love and devotion seemed to
elicit the very worst qualities from the brutalized soul of Amos Jones. It is
to Chatwin's credit that Amos Jones leaves the novel a believably complex but sympathetic character. Shortly after this outburst, Amos has a
stroke but dies from a horse kick to the head.

   Even more disturbing than Amos's irrational ingratitude is Mary's
response to his death. Though she is unable to cry—Amos's beatings
and brutality have cured her of that capacity long ago—she nonetheless
buys into and accepts his judgment of her. A week after his funeral,
Mary descends into black despair: "First, she blamed herself for Amos's
stroke. Then she assumed those aspects of his character which had once
annoyed her most. . . . She lost her sense of humour, no longer laughing
at the little absurdities that had lightened her existence; she even
remembered his mother, old Hannah, with affection" (p. 153). Like
Mama Wéwé in *The Viceroy of Ouidah,* she treats Amos as though he is
not dead and continues to set a place for him at the table. She still darns
his socks and "converses" with him three times a week. She will not
make any major decisions without his assent. Again like Mama Wéwé,
she keeps the house exactly as it was when he was alive: "Nothing—not
even a teacup—was replaced; and the house began to look like a
museum. The twins never ventured out, rather from force of habit than
fear of the outside world" (p. 154).

Another disturbing event takes place, at The Rock—the farm next to The Vision. A child is born, the result of Jim the Rock's incestuous union with his sister Ethel. The boy, Alfie, "grew up simple" and one day drowns in a boggy pool. Ethel immediately accuses Benjamin of murdering Alfie—and of molesting him. The police interrogation of Benjamin brings back the horror of his days at the Hereford Barracks. Though Mary, as usual, straightens out the whole affair, relations between the Rock and The Vision are damaged for years.

Mary then begins to pressure Lewis into looking for a woman so that she may have grandchildren, and Lewis and Benjamin venture forth to a fair in Rhulen. Benjamin does everything he can to dissuade his brother from meeting women or attending licentious sideshows. Lewis finally convinces his brother to go on the Wall of Death, a circular ride in which the bottom falls out and riders are suspended against a wall. To Benjamin's horror, at the ride's conclusion, "the girls slithered down and their frocks concertina-ed above their hips, so that gaps of bare flesh showed between their stockings and suspender-belts. Benjamin staggered on to the street and vomited into the gutter" (p. 160). As the boys retire to their bed that night, "Mary brushed her cheek against Benjamin's and, with a sly smile, thanked him for bringing his brother home" (p. 160). An oedipal conspiracy is obvious.

Recognizing that the twins need to brighten up their lives with activities other than farming, Mary buys them Hercules bicycles for their 31st birthday. The brothers begin extensive tours of the Welsh countryside, which compel Benjamin to examine the historical background of many of the places they visit. Benjamin shares his books with Lewis, and the two find there cultural and spiritual riches that were not available to them before. They have arrived at an age at which history begins to mean something to them because they can see themselves moving in both historical and familial contexts. As they read such classics as *The Chronicles of Jean Froissart* and Adam of Usk, they envision themselves as romantic figures during the time of the Crusades, an era that becomes more real than their own, uneventful lives: "Benjamin vowed himself to chastity; Lewis to the memory of a fair damsel" (p. 161). The early Celtic saints appeal to their sense of spiritual austerity, and they seriously consider "taking up the life of anchorites—an ivy bower, a babbling brook, a diet of berries and wild leek and, for music, the chatter of blackbirds" (p. 163). Chatwin shows that for many who live far from cultural centers, there is sustenance available in the rich possibilities of the imagination and in the local culture. The brothers also discover that other kinds of Edenic settings surround The Vision and are available to those who seek them.

The concluding section of chapter 35 deals with Mary Amos's sense of impending death. One of the ways in which she exhibits this premonition is that she begins to assemble a patchwork quilt that brings together crucial phases of her life on The Vision. Lewis later remembers her working diligently on the quilt as she combines materials of all kinds: "Her scissors sliced the skirt into strips. Next, she cut into the dresses of gaily-coloured calico—all reeking of camphor after forty years in a trunk. Then she stitched together the two halves of her life—the early days in India, and her days on the Black Hill" (p. 172). But Lewis has also become more than vaguely conscious of the conspiracy of his mother and Benjamin against him: "the fact that he was womanless was all part of their plan. He resented the way they kept him in ignorance of the farm's finances. . . . He resented, too, their stinginess. . . . She and Benjamin bought land with a passion, as if with each new acre they could push back the frontier of the hostile world" (pp. 172–73). Though these revelations might have caused a family breach, Lewis takes them in stride and seeks what pleasures he can.

One possibility that presents itself for the relief of Lewis's long-standing sexual frustration is the arrival of a decadent English couple, Joy and Nigel Lambert. Nigel is an artist, and though he and his wife enjoy swilling gin together they do not share a bed. The aptly named Joy immediately begins her project of seducing handsome Lewis, and Benjamin, who feels comfortable with Nigel, a homosexual, shares intimate secrets with him about his vicious treatment at the Hereford Barracks years earlier: "things the guards made him do; dirty, shameful things; things he had never told Lewis, which now he could get off his chest. 'Yes, they often do that,' Nigel said, eyeing him up and down, and then looking at the ground" (p. 177). Joy successfully seduces Lewis in a hollow. When she returns to Nigel, she announces victoriously,

> "You lost the bet, duckie. You owe me a bottle of Gordon's."
> "You had him?"
> "Under an ancient pine! Very romantic! Rather damp!" (p. 179)

As soon as Lewis returns to the farm after his sexual adventure, Benjamin knows immediately what took place. When he confronts Lewis with blatant questions regarding the lipstick on his cheek, Lewis smashes him in the face and flees the farm: "Benjamin's love for Lewis was murderous." It is only Mary's imminent death that brings Lewis back home to be at her bedside; she dies from a fatal coronary. The day after Mary's funeral, the brothers move into their parents' bedroom and climb into bed together: "United at last by the memory of their mother, they forgot that all of Europe was in flames" (p. 183).

World War II

There is little recognition on the brothers' part of the devastation going on throughout World War II, and air disasters so frequently appear in the newspapers that Lewis gives up trying to record them in his bulging scrapbook. They do, however, encounter a black American soldier on leave, and a German prisoner of war, Manfred Kluge, is assigned to help them on the farm. Lewis visits Rosie Fifield and asks about her daughter Meg, whose father was Reggie Bickerton. As Lewis leaves Rosie's pathetic farm, Rosie recalls their romance many years ago, when they were young and attractive. V. S. Pritchett points out the poignant beauty of Chatwin's description of the scene of Lewis's departure: "She watched him from the bedroom window walking away along the line of hawthorns, with the sunlight passing through his legs. Five times, she wiped the condensation from the pane until the black speck vanished from view. 'It's no good,' she said out loud. 'I hate men—all of them!' " (p. 186). Pritchett expresses his appreciation of Chatwin's phrasing: " '[W]ith the sunlight passing through his legs' is an example of Mr. Chatwin's ability to catch the evanescent detail that lights not simply the act of parting but a moment in the life of the heart. He is a master of catching the day itself passing through his people. He is not a professional sorrower at the toils of the peasantry" (*Lasting,* 46). Perhaps Chatwin's greatest and most consistent literary accomplishment is his ability to illuminate profound moments "in the life of the heart," and he performs this daunting task with such ease that the reader is left breathless by such moments' sudden and unexpected appearance. Their seeming casualness makes them deeply affecting.

Just after the war, a Viennese psychotherapist, Lotte Zons, appears at The Vision's door to interview the twins. She is conducting research on twins who have never separated and asks them if they will answer some questions. The name Zons and her interest in twins might be particularly unsubtle allusions to Professor René Zazzo, the French expert on twins, since both names start with Z and contain the same number of letters. Lotte relates Benjamin and Lewis to the mythological twins Castor and Pollux, who were the sons of Zeus and Leda, a swan, and popped out of the same egg "'like you two!' 'Fancy!' They sat up" (p. 192).

Chatwin uses the figure of Lotte Zons to probe into some of the inarticulated yearnings and motivations of the very unselfconscious Benjamin and Lewis. Because of their simplicity and the austerity of their country lives, there is little opportunity for them to understand themselves or to be understood by the reader without the aid of the almost comic Viennese psychotherapist. But it is her very foreignness that wins the brothers over and helps them open up to her: "Neither was accustomed to making confessions; but her warm understanding and harsh guttural accent struck a proper balance of proximity and distance" (p. 193). Lotte is amazed that the reason Benjamin attends the chapel is not to enter heaven or avoid hell—his concept of the afterlife is "a blank and hopeless void"—but rather because of his mother.

Lotte's interview with Lewis is one of the book's most emotional moments because of Lewis's searing honesty. Though he confesses his deep love for Benjamin, he says that he always felt left out, that his mother loved Benjamin more because he was smarter. He admits doubts about his isolated life on the farm: "Sometimes I lie awake and wonder what'd happen if him weren't there. If him gone off . . . was dead even. Then I'd have had my own life, like? Had kids?" (p. 194). Lewis's admission that he has, in a very real sense, missed the riches of life engenders a similar response in the lonely Lotte: "[f]or suddenly all the loneliness of her life came back to stifle her—the narrow spinster's bed, the guilt of leaving Austria, and the bitterness of the squabbles in the clinic" (p. 195).

On their 60th birthday, the twins become quite conscious of the emptiness of their lives: "Each time they tore a page from the calendar, they had forebodings of a miserable old age. They would turn to the wall of family photos—row on row of smiling faces, all of them dead or gone. How was it possible, they wondered, that they had come to be alone? Their wrangles were over. They were inseparable now as they had been before Benjamin's childhood illness" (p. 203). It is obvious that they are concerned with an heir. Coincidentally, in December of 1965 a Mrs. Redpath appears and announces that she is the daughter of their sister, Rebecca Jones; she also tells them that she has a son named Kevin. The twins' prayers have been answered, and the last phase of their lives begins on a happy and hopeful note. Young Kevin comes to visit his uncles often and they grow to love him deeply and unconditionally. When Kevin turns 17, the brothers decide to give him The Vision in five years' time, when they will be 80. Such a bequeathal will exempt him from paying "death-duties," or inheritance taxes.

Once the legal arrangements are in place, Mrs. Redpath's true nature emerges. Her anger at being left out of the family community and her sense of grievance grows by the year. After Jim the Rock dies, Meg inherits The Rock and lives in great poverty; however, she meets Theo the Tent, a South African Buddhist hippie who has been roaming the Radnor Hills for years. Theo has studied with a renowned Tibetan rinpoche but decided to live the life of a wanderer after seeing the "Kalahari Bushmen trekking through the desert, the mothers laughing, with their children on their backs. And he had come to believe that all men were meant to be wanderers, like them, like St. Francis; and that by joining the Way of the Universe, you could find the great spirit everywhere—in the smell of bracken after rain, the buzz of a bee in the ear of a foxglove, or in the eyes of a mule, looking with love on the blundering movements of his master" (p. 229). Chatwin has rarely been clearer about expressing his sympathy for Abel, the wanderer, and about identifying himself with his Christian counterpart, St. Francis of Assisi. Theo the Tent's words are a comprehensive adumbration of the theme of Chatwin's next and greatest book, *The Songlines,* since the Australian aboriginals' deepest beliefs are embodied in the concept that the way of the universe (living as a wanderer) is the key to finding the great spirit *everywhere.* Meg the Rock and Theo the Tent recognize in each other the other half of their souls and find consolation in each other's company. Theo—whose name is Greek for "god"—helps the twins and Meg with their farm work but, being a devout Luddite, refuses to have anything to do with machinery of any kind. For him, technology is to blame for most of the woes of the world.

In the meantime, Kevin has gotten an ambitious young girl pregnant, and the couple marry in the Anglican church and move into a bungalow that the twins have built for them on their property. He has also begun to disappoint Benjamin and Lewis with his questionable judgment: "He had a snake tattooed on his arm, and he had bad friends" (p. 214).

Theo invites the brothers to visit him in the yurt he built himself, and it is clear through Chatwin's description of Theo that he intends him to greatly resemble the Greek god Dionysus, who is often pictured with leaves and flowers entwined in his hair and who is frequently associated with mules and donkeys: "He was waiting to greet them, in his homespun jerkin and leggings. His hat was crowned with honeysuckle, and he looked like Ancient Man. Lewis had crammed his pockets with sugarlumps to give to the mule and donkey" (p. 233). The name Meg comes from the Greek word for "pearl." And Pearl, the name of the nature child in Hawthorne's *Scarlet Letter,* can be viewed as the feminine counterpart to the nature god, Dionysus. Indeed, Meg is mistaken for a tree stump as she feeds birds: "Her skin was plastered with reddish mud. Her breeches were the colour of mud. Her hat *was* a rotting stump. And the tattered green jerseys, tacked one to the other, were the mosses, and creepers, and ferns" (p. 210). Kevin refers to her from then on as "Bird Lady." The appearance and pairing of Meg and Theo disturb such critics as Karl Miller, who finds the couple contrived and heavy-handedly archetypal. Miller calls the novel "a *tour de force* of doorstep exoticism which, so far as it can be accounted Meg-magical or Theocentric, fails" (*Doubles,* 406).

The Beginning of the End

The celebration of the twins' 80th birthday constitutes the emotional climax of the novel and, symbolically, a successful regeneration of Edenic redemption on several levels. Chatwin's language intimates the joy of a visionary event, as the twins awaken to "the sound of music. . . . The sun was up. Kevin was strumming at his guitar. Theo played the flute. Eileen, in maternity clothes, was clinging to her Jack Russell terrier, and the mule munched a rose bush in the garden. Parked outside the barn was a red car" (*OBH,* 236). Kevin has arranged "a mystery tour," an old English custom in which a couple is taken on a journey but remain ignorant of its destination. After riding for many miles, Kevin and his uncles arrive at an airfield for a ride in a Cessna piloted by Kevin's friend, Alex Pitt. Benjamin is terrified and Lewis is stupefied at the prospect. Once the plane is in the air, however, Benjamin begins to relax when he and Lewis look down on The Vision and see Theo. Then, after instructing him in how to maneuver the plane, Alex turns the plane over to Lewis:

> "You're on your own now," said Alex calmly, and Lewis made the same maneuvers, on his own. And suddenly he felt—even if the engine failed, even if the plane took a nosedive and their souls flew up to heaven—that all the frustrations of his cramped and frugal life now counted for nothing, because, for ten magnificent minutes, he had done what he wanted to do. (p. 240)

The great mythologist Joseph Campbell designates the hero's highest and most profound experience an apotheosis—that is, an elevation into a visionary realm in which the hero-quester participates in both a divine and a human consciousness. For Lewis, his flying experience is a quasi-apotheosis insofar as he realizes that his attenuated and remote life has been a form of preparation for the complete freedom of doing exactly "what he wanted to do" for once in his life. Alex Pitt then talks Lewis through some complex maneuvers; Lewis realizes only after the fact that they have traced the number 80. Chatwin concludes chapter 48 in his best cinematographic fashion by depicting the twins trying to find an appropriate place for the color photograph of The Vision that Kevin commissioned several weeks earlier. Lewis finds the solution: "by shifting Uncle Eddie and the grizzly *up* one, and by shifting Hannah and Old Sam *along* one, there was just enough space for it to fit beside their parents' wedding-group" (p. 241).

Murray mentions that the novel's climactic moment bears a slight resemblance to a scene in another novel: "It is also, in truth, a denouement disturbingly congruent with that of *Cold Comfort Farm* where an aeroplane flight performs a related function!" (*Bruce Chatwin*, 81). There is a similar scene also in Georges Bernanos's great novel *Diary of a Country Priest* in which the sick and dying Curé of Ambricourt can recall only one exhilarating moment of freedom from his youth, when he rode on a motorcycle with a French Legionner. As the French landscape flew by it was the only time he ever noticed its grandeur, and the experience revealed a love of life he had never before felt. Chatwin was thoroughly familiar with French literature and no doubt knew Bernanos's greatest novel.

The last major scene before Lewis's sudden death on the tractor takes place during a Thanksgiving ceremony at the Harvest Festival. Chatwin's sense of context is masterful: he embeds the lives of the twins and their family and friends—alive and dead—in the Welsh biblical and mythical traditions. As V. S. Pritchett asserts, "[T]he Bible is the ruling consolation. The mythical world lives side by side with reality. The Border people live by their imagination" (*Lasting Impressions*, 46). The nonconformist preacher Isaac Lewis powerfully interweaves the thunder of the Old Testament and the serene hope of the promised land with the rhetorical tonalities of Jeremy Taylor:

"For the city we seek is an Abiding City. . . . Our life is a bubble. We are born. We float upwards. We are carried hither and thither by the

breezes. We glitter in the sunshine. Then all of a sudden, the bubble
bursts and we fall to the earth as specks of moisture. We are as these
dahlias, cut down by the first frosts of autumn." (p. 246)

In the last scene, after Lewis's sudden death, Benjamin haunts the
Maesyfelin graveyard, waiting for death.

On the Black Hill won several prestigious awards when it appeared in
1982, including the previously mentioned Whitbread Award, for an
author's best first novel, and the following spring, the James Tait Black
prize for the best novel of the year. It sold very well and because of the
effectiveness of its episodic structure was successfully adapted for both
stage and screen. A stage version by Charles Way was presented by the
Made in Wales Theatre Company in 1986 and revived in 1988 by Theatre Clwyd. Chatwin was very supportive of the stage versions and actually visited Way at his home in Abergavenny, Wales. Murray mentions
that the novel itself became something of a "cult book" in the Welsh
border region and was enormously popular (*Bruce Chatwin*, 84). The
director Andrew Grieve made a film of the novel in the spring of 1987
in Wales and used two Welsh actors, Mike and Robert Gwilym, as the
twins. The film, which opened in April of 1988 at the Lumière cinema
in London and at the Chapter cinema in Cardiff, Wales, pushed the
novel onto the bestseller list (p. 85). At the time of the premieres,
Chatwin was very ill with the disease that would kill him the following
year, and no one had any idea that his greatest work, *The Songlines,* was
about to be published.

Chapter Five
The Songlines: "A Seething Gallimaufry of a Book"

No book of Bruce Chatwin's has been scrutinized more closely than *The Songlines,* nor have critical opinions been more divided on its literary merits. The respected travel writer and literary critic Colin Thubron unequivocally states that *The Songlines* is "his masterpiece, the culmination of an obsession of more than twenty years" ("Fantastical Tales," G9). Certainly the circumstances of Chatwin's trip to Australia differ little from those of his travels to Patagonia or Benin to collect materials for *In Patagonia* and *The Viceroy of Ouidah.* Further, V. S. Pritchett's term "plotless chronicle" could apply equally to *In Patagonia* and *The Songlines,* both of which explore Chatwin's enduring topics: nomadism and the nature of human restlessness. However, *The Songlines* brings together, once and for all, Chatwin's conclusions—spiritual, philosophical, and anthropological—into one grand collage. In attempting to categorize the sprawling character and reach of *The Songlines,* critic Andrew Harvey explicates both the themes and the various forms that constitute its kaleidoscopic structure: "Part adventure-story, part novel-of-ideas, part satire on the follies of 'progress,' part spiritual autobiography, part passionate plea for a return to simplicity of being and behaving, *The Songlines* is a seething gallimaufry of a book, a great Burtonian galimatias of anecdote and speculation and description, fascinating, moving, infuriating, incoherent, all at once. . . . No one will put it down unmoved, however rickety they may in the end find its form and conclusions" ("Footprints," 1).

Fortunately, the author himself answered important questions about the book's genesis and purpose in the lengthy 1987 interview with Michael Ignatieff in *Granta.* Ignatieff begins his questions with his own insightful opinion about the book's formal composition:

IGNATIEFF: *"Songlines* is a bit of everything: autobiography, fiction, anthropology and archeology. How would you describe it?"

CHATWIN: "It has to be called a novel because I invented huge
                chunks of it in order to tell the story that I wanted to
                tell. But I suppose as a category it's indefinable." ("Inter-
                view," 23)

A short time later, Chatwin explains the advantages of fictionalizing:
"To write [a true story] as a fiction gives you a greater flexibility" (p.
24). Ignatieff then proceeds to ask him a question that becomes crucial
in understanding early influences on Chatwin's imagination:

IGNATIEFF: "Were there any books that served as models?"

CHATWIN: "I'm interested in an eighteenth-century form, the
                dialogue novel, I mean particularly Diderot's *Jacques
                Le Fataliste*. The *philosophes* of the eighteenth century
                had a way of expressing serious concepts very lightly
                indeed. That was one of the things I was trying."

IGNATIEFF: "Where in your work is the division between fiction
                and non-fiction?"

CHATWIN: "I don't think there *is* one. There definitely should be,
                but I don't know where it is. I've always written very
                close to the line. I've tried applying fiction techniques
                to actual bits of travel. I once made the experiment of
                counting up the lies in the book I wrote about Patago-
                nia. It wasn't, in fact, too bad: there weren't too many.
                But with *Songlines*, if I had to tot up the inventions,
                there would be no question in my mind that the whole
                thing added up to a fictional work." (p. 24)

After answering some other questions about his job at Sotheby's and
about his trauma of going temporarily blind, Chatwin admits that the
subject he has pursued throughout his life has been the nature of human
restlessness and that theories about restlessness became a persistent
obsession "particularly after I left the art world. It was at the time of the
Vietnam War, and I was having to think for the first time. . . . I was
extremely successful [in the art world] and smarmy, and I suddenly realized at the age of twenty-five or so that I was hating every minute of it.
I had to change" (p. 26). What had to change was Chatwin's lifestyle as
a highly successful English businessman working in the art world at the
prestigious Sotheby's in London. His temporary blindness would be
relieved by taking a trip. His doctor advised, "You've been looking too
closely at pictures. Why don't you swap them for some long horizons?"
Chatwin then traveled to the Sudan, where he accidentally

"spent time with a very extreme nomad people called the Beja. They alerted me to certain things which were obviously close to me but which I hadn't realized before. They started my quest to know the secret of their irreverent and timeless vitality: why was it that nomad peoples have this amazing capacity to continue under the most adverse circumstances, while the empires come crashing down? It seemed to me an immensely interesting subject to tackle. But the literature of the nomad peoples is very difficult to handle, and the more I delved into it, the less wise I became. So this is why I did a lot of travelling and why I left a conventional job at the age of twenty-six." ("Interview," 25)

Chatwin's quest to find the origins of human restlessness led him to write both *In Patagonia* and *The Songlines* and, Ignatieff suggests, to an examination of his own restlessness:

IGNATIEFF: "In *Songlines* you put together a narrative of your voyage in search of aboriginal wisdom in the Australian Outback, and interspersed it with some extraordinary passages of theorizing and quotation culled from twenty years of your notebooks. These gave the impression of being put down just as you thought of them, but in fact they struck me as the most heavily worked, the most fictional parts of the book."

CHATWIN: "The juxtapositions are artful—I hope not arty—a collage of disparate things, whether it's a description of a bus journey in downtown Miami or a quotation from the ancient Greek. I was impressed by that essay of Walter Benjamin in which he says the ideal book would be a book of quotations, and then there's a wonderful commonplace book by Hofmannsthal, which is a sort of dialogue of quotations and his own thoughts as well, all jammed in. I also had the remains of an essay about nomads ["The Nomadic Alternative"], about the metaphysics of walking, and it struck me that the only way to use it was to graft it on to a narrative of a journey to Australia." (pp. 26–27)

Chatwin's grafting technique has caused endless critical discussions regarding his strengths and weaknesses as a novelist and travel writer. What appear to be structural flaws to one critic are postmodern collage to another.

Ignatieff then directly confronts Chatwin with the crucial question "What does travel mean to you?"

CHATWIN: "The word travel is the same as the French *travail*. It
             means hard work, penance and finally a journey. There
             was an idea, particularly in the Middle Ages, that by
             going on pilgrimage, as Muslim pilgrims do, you were
             reinstating the original condition of man. The act of
             walking through a wilderness was thought to bring
             you back to God." . . .

IGNATIEFF: "But is it true that you yourself can't write unless you
             travel?"

CHATWIN: "That's very true."

IGNATIEFF: "Then the question is why?"

CHATWIN: "I wish I knew. I do find it quite interesting that in
             one form or another all the great early epics—whether
             it's the *Odyssey* or *Beowulf*—are traveller's tales. Why
             should it be that the metaphor of the voyage is at the
             heart of all story-telling? It's not simply that most sto-
             ries are traveller's tales, it's actually the way these
             epics are patterned into a voyage structure. Lord
             Raglan, a British folklorist, took the great myths and
             showed they have a common paradigm. The story
             begins with a young man, who is often a foundling,
             who goes on a journey and finds a population men-
             aced by some kind of monster or wild beast. He saves
             the population, rescues the damsel in distress and
             receives a reward, usually of the damsel in marriage,
             the kingdom and treasure. In his maturity he rules
             people who are strangers to him, and then in old age
             the forces of destruction close in, restlessness strikes
             again, and he departs to do battle with another mon-
             ster, and then vanishes. I once mapped Che Guevara's
             life against this paradigm and it fitted pretty well.
             (Laughter.) The point is that the classical hero cycle is
             an idealized programme for the human life cycle. Each
             stage corresponds to a biological event in human life."
             ("Interview," 27–28)

   It's at this point in the interview that Ignatieff gets Chatwin to clarify, theoretically, the precise nature of his Jungian stance: "You think
that most fictions replay archetypal, universal stories," he asserts.
Although Chatwin admits that Ignatieff's suggestion constitutes "tricky
ground," he concedes the point. Then Ignatieff pushes even further:
"But doesn't that go against the idea of the modern writer as the inventor, the originator of his stories, the creator of something new?"

CHATWIN: "I'm unimpressed by the idea of the new. Most advances in literature usually strike me as being advances into a *cul-de-sac.*"

IGNATIEFF: "And so a good writer ought to be in touch with the recurring character of certain story forms?"

CHATWIN: "He may be in touch with them although he doesn't realize it. There's a strong instinctive bias in human behavior, a template into which we slot. I don't believe *all* behavior is learned. We're not a blank slate." ("Interview," 28–29)

Ignatieff continues to press his point when he paraphrases Chatwin's views on the connections between narrative utterance and genetic coding: "And you think some story-telling is instinctive?" Chatwin hesitates to answer the question directly, but he does elaborate on anthropologist Konrad Lorenz's findings concerning various stages, or "calls," in animals' lives. The animal may or may not take up a call for a variety of reasons, but Chatwin finds in these Lorenzian "behavioral chains" similarities to "the structure of myths. If myths have a sort of spontaneous activity in the human psyche, then a section of that myth corresponds to a certain section of the human life cycle. I would say tentatively that there is a connection between instinct and story-telling" (p. 29).

Ignatieff then summarizes Chatwin's theories: human beings had their origin on the desert plains of Africa more than three million years ago and gradually acquired a set of instinctual behaviors that enabled them to survive and overcome their natural predators. And "as they acquire a set of instinctual nomadic patterns of behavior they also acquire a meaning system, a set of myths which are imprinted on the brain over millions of years . . . and these are story patterns that keep recurring even in the modern day. . . . An example of this kind of eternal story would be the young man who leaves home, goes off into the wilderness to find himself. Bruce Chatwin, archetypal hero, goes out into the desert in search of . . ." (p. 30). After Chatwin objects that Ignatieff's summary makes him sound "very pretentious," the interviewer clarifies:

IGNATIEFF: "I'm just taking seriously the idea that *Songlines* itself works through a certain mythic story form. . . . In your version of the myth, the callow young man travels into the Australian desert in search of enlightenment and finds Aboriginal peoples engaged in precisely the same quest." . . .

CHATWIN: "Exactly." (p. 30)

Once the autobiographical pattern is firmly established—that the archetypal is the personal in this book—the fractured narrative seems an appropriate form for a kind of belated bildungsroman in which a naive young man comes into contact with philosophical and spiritual profundities he has never before encountered. Chatwin also admits using Denis Diderot's dialogic novel, *Jacques Le Fataliste*, as his model, since dialogue is what carries both the narrative and the thematic concerns throughout the book. Though *The Songlines* documents a difficult journey to one of the strangest locations on earth, the dialogue between Bruce and his guide, Arkady Volchok, records their continuously developing relationship. Their relationship is very different, however, from that between Diderot's Jacques and his master in *Jacques Le Fataliste*. As Nicholas Murray suggests, "[T]here is nothing in the Arkady/Bruce relationship equivalent to the wily antagonism and witty subversion of Jacques towards his master that itself helps to construct the philosophical meaning of Diderot's book; Bruce and Arkady tend to agree with each other" (*Bruce Chatwin*, 93).

The Songlines opens with a short but detailed sketch of the narrative's main character, Arkady Volchok: "In Alice Springs—a grid of scorching streets where men in white socks were forever getting in and out of Land Cruisers—I met a Russian who was mapping the sacred sites of the Aboriginals. His name was Arkady Volchok. He was an Australian citizen. He was thirty-three years old."[1] The name Chatwin chose for the main character is significant since Arkady refers, quite obviously, to the word *arcadia*, which is a term for a rustic, simple, pastoral, Edenic location. Outside of the word's mythic resonances, Arkadia is a mountainous region in central Greece whose name was used frequently by ancient Greek poets to epitomize rustic contentment and an idealized life. Since Bruce Chatwin's lifetime quest was an investigation of pastoral nomadism, he could have hardly found a more appropriate name. Indeed, his journey, with Arkady Volchok as his wise guide, is a journey into the heart of the aboriginal concept of Eden. Arkady's surname, Volchok, is a diminutive of the Russian word for "wolf" and also means "a rotating or spinning top," certainly apt images for Arkady's relentless journeys throughout central and western Australia. Since all of the native aboriginals are connected to their geographical cosmology through totemic animals, Volchok has one too, the wolf, a nomadic animal.

After a lengthy description of Arkady Volchok's background—his father was a cossack (the cossacks were considered nomadic) and his mother, a Ukrainian from Kiev. After a failed marriage, Arkady found solitude preferable to domestic strife and was drawn to the mysteries of the Australian aboriginals. He was "a tireless bushwalker." After he returned from a hundred-mile walk, he "would play the music of Buxtehude and Bach on the harpsichord. Their orderly progressions, he said, conformed to the contours of the Central Australian landscape" (*The Songlines*, 2). He earned an honors degree in history and philosophy at Adelaide University and became a teacher on an aboriginal settlement in the Walbiri country to the north of Alice Springs:

> He liked the Aboriginals. He liked their grit and tenacity, and their artful ways of dealing with the white man . . . and had come away astonished by their . . . feats of memory and their capacity and their will to survive. . . . It was during his time as a school-teacher that Arkady learned of the labyrinth of invisible pathways which meander all over Australia and are known to Europeans as "Dreaming-tracks" or "Songlines"; to the Aboriginals as the "Footprints of the Ancestors" or the "Way of the Law.". . . Aboriginal Creation myths tell of the legendary totemic beings who had wandered over the continent in the Dreamtime, singing out the name of everything that crossed their path—birds, animals, plants, rocks, waterholes—and so singing the world into existence. (p. 2)

It is the beauty of this poetic cosmology that drew both Arkady and Bruce Chatwin to their involvement with the aboriginals.

Arkady came to know the Walbiri tribe, who shared certain secret information with him because they learned to trust him, even though an anthropologist from Canberra who came to look into Walbiri systems of land tenure, had betrayed one of their secrets. There was such a row after that betrayal that Arkady decided to travel abroad and visited Java, India, Kabul, Israel, and Greece. In Greece, he married a Greek girl from Sydney. They both moved back to Australia, but after a year the marriage fell apart. It was then that Arkady invented a profession for himself, which was to interpret " 'tribal law' into the language of the Law of the Crown" (*The Songlines,* 3). Arkady's job became a necessity after "[t]he Land Rights Act gave Aboriginal 'owners' the title to their country, providing it lay untenanted" (p. 3). Arkady knew that the aboriginals' arcadian-idyllic days of wandering and hunting were over and attempted to preserve their basic liberties: "the liberty to remain poor [and] . . . the space to be poor if they wished to be poor" (p. 3).

His job as an interpreter grew into one in which he helped map a new 300-mile railroad route from Alice Springs north to Darwin. One hun-

dred and fifty miles of that route had already been surveyed by a sur-
veyor who was sensitive to the aboriginals' sacred beliefs: "He was especially concerned to avoid the kind of rumpus that broke out whenever a
mining company moved its machinery into Aboriginal land. So, promis-
ing not to destroy a single one of their sacred sites, he had asked their
representatives to supply him with a survey. Arkady's job was to identify
the 'traditional landowners'; to drive them over their old hunting
grounds, even if these now belonged to a cattle company; and to get
them to reveal which rock or soak or ghost-gum was the work of a
Dreamtime hero. He had already mapped the 150-mile stretch from
Alice to Middle Bore Station. He had a hundred and fifty to go" (p. 4).

The following dialogue owes much to Diderot's dialogic technique,
which Chatwin uses throughout the book. Arkady warned the engineer
that

> "he was being a bit rash . . ."
> "Why rash?" I asked.
> "Well, if you look at it their way," he grinned, "the whole of bloody
> Australia's a sacred site."
> "Explain," I said (p. 4).

That explanation constitutes the book's major thematic thrust.

Chapter 2, in typical Chatwin fashion, moves back in time to
Chatwin's childhood and concentrates on the genesis of the young boy's
interest in and love of Australia. Chatwin uses the same pattern of reanimating the past that he used in *In Patagonia, The Viceroy of Ouidah,* and
On the Black Hill, and for the same reason: to establish a thematic bond
between his own sense of homelessness and that of the wandering aboriginals. His family fluctuates between periods of settlement and wandering because his father was in the British Navy in World War II. One
of his most vivid childhood memories is of a book about Australia that
belonged to his great-aunt Ruth, who lives in Stratford, England:

> She had a book in her library about the continent, and I would gaze in
> wonder at pictures of the koala and kookaburra, the platypus and the
> Tasmanian bush-devil, Old Man Kangaroo and the Yellow Dog Dingo,
> and Sydney Harbour Bridge.
>   But the picture I liked best showed an Aboriginal family on the move.
> They were lean, angular people, and they went about naked. . . . The
> man had a long forked beard and carried a spear or two, and a spear-

thrower. The woman carried a dilly-bag and a baby at her breast. A
small boy strolled beside her—I identified myself with him.
I remember the fantastic homelessness of my first five years. (p. 5)

The picture he describes is, of course, the one that some enterprising
editor at Viking-Penguin put on the cover of the American edition of
the book, except that in Chatwin's description of the aboriginal family,
the mother is nursing her baby, and in the actual picture she is carrying
it on her head and shoulders—an instructive example of how Chatwin
sometimes unconsciously alters the facts to conform more accurately to
his emotional and aesthetic needs. The point is that he identifies with
the young boy in the sketch, an image that grows into a controlling
metaphor of the relationship of the book to his own life experiences.

After a survey of the influential books in his great-aunt Ruth's
library—especially the Shakespearean ones—Chatwin zeroes in on a
popular anthology of verses for children called *The Open Road,* "an
anthology of verse especially chosen for travellers" (p. 9). But it is Great-
aunt Ruth's explanation of the origin of his surname that interests
young Bruce the most: "One day, Aunt Ruth told me our surname had
once been 'Chettewynde,' which meant 'the winding path' in Anglo-
Saxon; and the suggestion took root in my head that poetry, my own
name and the road were, all three, mysteriously connected" (p. 9). By an
almost magical set of linguistic circumstances, Bruce Chatwin's very
name becomes his own Anglo-Saxon Songline that leads him all over the
world.

In chapter 3 Bruce and Arkady discuss, over cappuccinos in Alice
Springs, aboriginal philosophy. Though *The Songlines* is a narrative about
a journey, significant developments in the novel take place as Bruce
enters new and deeper understandings of the complex cosmology of
aboriginal belief systems. The work's structural development depends,
then, on the process of Bruce's emerging epiphanies and not necessarily
on any geographical journey, though new knowledge seems to come to
him while he is on the road. His function is to find analogies for himself
(and for us, the readers) that connect and clarify those aboriginal complexities into understandable European concepts. Arkady fills the
mythic role of the wise guide, or go-between, who educates Bruce
because he knows the language of both sides. Bruce's role is, as Arkady's
scribe, to ask the right questions, to translate Arkady's answers into an
understandable European idiom, and to find equivalent texts. Bruce also

serves as a kind of Greek chorus insofar as he records the cultural damage done to the sacred aboriginal systems by "a Europe of mindless
materialism" (p. 3).

During Bruce and Arkady's Diderot-like dialogue Bruce marvels at
the comprehensiveness of Arkady's mind and at the sophistication of his
intellectual references:

> "The Aboriginals had an earthbound philosophy. The earth gave life
> to man; man gave his food, language and intelligence; and the earth took
> him back when he died. A man's 'own country,' even an empty stretch of
> spinifex, was itself a sacred ikon that must remain unscarred."
> "Unscarred, you mean, by roads or mines or railways?"
> "To wound the earth," he answered earnestly, "is to wound yourself,
> and if others wound the earth, they are wounding you. The land should
> be left untouched: as it was in the Dreamtime when the Ancestors sang
> the world into existence."
> "Rilke," I said, "had a similar intuition. He also said song was exis-
> tence."
> "I know," said Arkady, resting his chin on his hands. "Third Sonnet to
> Orpheus" (p. 11)

Chatwin finally admits why he came to Australia: "My reason for
coming to Australia was to try to learn for myself, and not from other
men's books, what a Songline was—and how it worked" (p. 12). His
discussion with Arkady delves deeper into the conceptual components of
what constitutes a Songline. Arkady tells Bruce that to understand the
concept of a Songline, you have to understand what Dreamtime is
about. And to understand Dreamtime you need to think of it as the
equivalent of the first two chapters of Genesis, but with a distinction:

> "In *Genesis* God first created the 'living things' and then fashioned
> father Adam from clay [the name Adam in Hebrew means "clay"]. Here
> in Australia, the Ancestors created themselves from clay, hundreds and
> thousands of them, one for each totemic species.
> "So when an Aboriginal tells you, 'I have a Wallaby Dreaming,' he
> means, 'My totem is Wallaby. I am a member of the Wallaby clan.' "
> "So a Dreaming is a clan emblem? A badge to distinguish 'us' from
> 'them'? 'Our country' from 'their country'?"
> "Much more than that," he said. (p. 12)

Arkady goes on to elucidate the complex strands of this cosmology.
Every Wallaby man comes down from a universal Wallaby father who

was the ancestor of all other Wallaby men and animals. If you killed a Wallaby, members of your entire clan were committing fratricide and cannibalism. Bruce then tries to clarify the totemic relationships by comparing them to other iconic emblems, like the Russian bear, the British lion, and the American eagle. Arkady expands the concept even further:

> "any species can be a Dreaming. A virus can be a Dreaming. You can have a chickenpox Dreaming, a rain Dreaming, a desert-orange Dreaming, a lice Dreaming. In the Kimberleys they've now got a money Dreaming."
>
> "And the Welsh have leeks, the Scots thistles, and Daphne was changed into a laurel."
>
> "Same old story," he said. (p. 13)

Arkady goes on to explain how each totemic ancestor, while traveling through the country, was thought to have scattered a trail of words and musical notes along the line of his footprints, and how these Dreaming-tracks lay over the land as communications between the most far-flung tribes.

> "A song", he said, "was both map and direction finder. Providing you knew the song, you could always find your way across the country."
>
> "And would a man on 'Walkabout' always be travelling down one of the Songlines?"
>
> "In the old days, yes," he agreed. "Nowadays, they go by train or car."
>
> "Suppose the man strayed from his Songline?"
>
> "He was trespassing. He might get speared for it."
>
> "But as long as he stuck to the track, he'd always find people who shared his Dreaming? Who were, in fact, his brothers?"
>
> "Yes."
>
> "From whom he could expect hospitality?"
>
> "And vice versa."
>
> "So song is a kind of passport and meal-ticket?"
>
> "Again, it's more complicated." (p. 13)

Arkady offers another analogy to help Bruce understand the concept of a Songline. He explains that all of Australia can be read as a musical score: "There was hardly a rock or creek in the country that could not or had not been sung. One should perhaps visualize the Songlines as a spaghetti of *Iliads* and *Odysseys,* writhing this way and that, in which every 'episode' was readable in terms of geology."

"By episode," I asked, "you mean 'sacred site'?"

"I do."

"The kind of site you're surveying for the railway?"

"Put it this way," he said. "Anywhere in the bush you can point to some feature of the landscape and ask the Aboriginal with you, 'What's the story there?' or 'Who's that?' The chances are he'll answer 'Kangaroo' or 'Budgerigar' or 'Jew Lizard,' depending on which Ancestor walked that way."

"And the distance between two such sites can be measured as a stretch of song?"

"That", he said, "is the cause of all my troubles with the railway people." (pp. 12–13)

Arkady further explains that it is one thing to convince the railway people that some "heap of boulders were the eggs of the Rainbow Snake," but it is something else to convince them that "a featureless stretch of gravel was the musical equivalent of Beethoven's Opus 111" (p. 14).

Arkady then uses Chatwin's most convincing method of argument— an etymological one—to explain the heart of the aboriginal cosmology:

By singing the world into existence, he said, the Ancestors had been poets in the original sense of *poesis,* meaning "creation." No Aboriginal could conceive that the created world was in any way imperfect [a concept very close to the native Yaghans' belief, in *In Patagonia,* that their territory is always an Edenic paradise]. His religious life had a single aim: to keep the land the way it was and should be. The man who went "Walkabout" was making a ritual journey. He trod in the footprints of his Ancestor. He sang the Ancestor's stanza without changing a word or note—and so created the Creation. . . . Aboriginals could not believe the country existed until they could see and sing it—just as, in the Dreamtime, the country had not existed until the Ancestors sang it.

"So the land," I said, "must first exist as a concept in the mind? Then it must be sung? Only then can it be said to exist?"

"True."

"In other words, 'to exist' is 'to be perceived'?"

"Yes."

"Sounds suspiciously like Bishop Berkeley's Refutation of Matter."

"Or Pure Mind Buddhism," said Arkady, "which also sees the world as an illusion." (p. 14)

Arkady develops the concept of the Songlines even further by revealing the geographical genesis of the aboriginals' cosmology:

Aboriginals believed that all the "living things" had been made in secret beneath the earth's crust, as well as all the white man's gear—his aeroplanes, his guns, his Toyota Land Cruisers—and every invention that will ever be invented; slumbering below the surface, waiting their turn to be called.

"Perhaps," I suggested, "they could sing the railway back into the created world of God?"

"You bet," said Arkady. (pp. 14–15).

Chatwin was wise to employ the dialogic technique Diderot used in *Jacques Le Fataliste*—a variation on the Platonic dialogue—to clarify highly complicated religious and cosmological concepts so foreign to Europeans and Americans.

In the 1987 interview in *Granta,* Chatwin relates the concept of the Songlines to the "Walkabout," as examined in the seminal research of nineteenth-century English ethnologist W. E. Roth. Roth, he claims, defined the Walkabout as part of a "gigantic diplomatic and trading system which kept the most far-flung tribes in peaceful contact with each another. What has since emerged is that the trade-routes were also songs, and that the principal medium of exchange was song. A Songline changes languages from one people to the next, but the melody remains constant over colossal distances: so that, in theory at least, a man can sing his way across a landscape without ever having been there" ("Interview," 31).

Chatwin admits in the same interview that the concept of the Songlines is the single most fascinating idea he has ever come across but that he isn't sure exactly what conclusions to draw from them. He does find that their existence completely invalidates various theories that man "is a territorial predator whose impulse is to raid or destroy his neighbor" ("Interview," 31). Michael Ignatieff suggests, however, that Chatwin's journey into the complex cosmology of the aboriginals is also a personal one: "*Songlines* could be read as a pretty grandiose metaphysics of your own restlessness. It grounds your wanderlust in a big scheme that involves Darwinism, nomads, instincts—but a skeptic would say, 'Come off it, Bruce, the *real* story is that you're an Englishman who wanted to get out of Sotheby's, who wanted to get out of this bloody little country and see the world' " (p. 31). Chatwin does not deny that Ignatieff's conclusions are true.

In the beginning of chapter 4, the narrator, Bruce, explains to Arkady the etymological origins of his lifelong quest for the secret of the nomads. Chatwin's first long scholarly essay was entitled "The Nomadic Alternative" (1970), and he had come to Australia to test his all-consuming idea of "pastoral nomadism." Chatwin had found that the Greek word *nomos* meant "pasture": "A nomad moves from pasture to pasture. A pastoral nomad is a pleonasm" (*The Songlines,* 16). He then tells Arkady the story of his temporary blindness and his doctor's advice to travel to places with "long horizons," a traditional prescription for the alleviation of intense eye strain. Bruce went to the Sudan, where he became familiar with the Beja, a nomadic tribe with whom he traveled and studied. He tells Arkady that when "lying awake under the stars, the cities of the West seemed sad and alien—and the pretensions of the 'art world' idiotic" (p. 18). Bruce explains that his guide, Mahmoud, seemed utterly content, and that he and his tribe stood as a dramatic example of the victory of process over stasis: "The Pharaohs had vanished: Mahmoud and his people had lasted. I felt I had to know the secret of their timeless and irreverent vitality. . . . The more I read, the more convinced I became that nomads had been the crankhandle of history, if for no other reason than the great monotheisms had, all of them, surfaced from the pastoral milieu" (pp. 18–19). What Bruce found most alluring was the idea of a journey without an end, a kind of nonteleological journey whose only purpose was the continuation of its own circular, cyclic process. As an ancient Chinese dictum states, "The journey itself is Home."

Critic Jane Dorrell points out that the subject matter and theme of *The Songlines* were not new for Chatwin: "Chatwin had done for the Northern Territory what he did ten years ago for Patagonia. He had written an absorbing book on a disappearing world, a world in which it is said that 'by spending his whole life walking and singing his Ancestor's Songline a man eventually becomes the track, the ancestor and the song."[2] As in his three earlier books, Chatwin is meditating on ruins, in this case the ruins of a magnificently complete aboriginal world in which a person, by the sacramental agency of song, becomes one with his human and animal ancestor and thus part of the earth itself. When the aboriginals no longer have access to their Songlines, their Edenic paradise begins to fall into ruin. It is Arkady's major function to try to put off that inevitable fall as long as possible, but unfortunately, as in Chatwin's earlier works, the natives are hopelessly addicted to alcohol and drugs.

The narrative thrust is built also on Bruce and Arkady's confrontation with vivid characters throughout their journey, very much like the way that *In Patagonia's* plotless chronicle is structured around sometimes unforgettable characters, both native and immigrant, who enliven Chatwin's journey. Unlike *The Songlines,* however, the geographical movement of *In Patagonia* is from north to south, a pattern that encourages Dantean echoes; Chatwin does eventually descend into hades—the land of fire (Tierra del Fuego). The geographical movement of *The Songlines* is from south—actually, Alice Springs is in the center of Australia—to north and west. But Australia's north is south to peoples of the Northern Hemisphere, so a Dantean journey into a hellish desert can be expected. Indeed, toward the end of the novel, Bruce does make a dangerous journey into that desert and attempts to climb Mount Liebler.

The first of many vivid characters appear at Mrs. Lacey's Desert Bookstore in Alice Springs. Besides Mrs. Lacey, herself a pert, enterprising Australian in her sixties, Bruce encounters a painter and Pintupi elder named Stan. Stan has come to sell his aboriginal paintings to Enid Lacey, who in turn sells them to tourists at a hefty profit for both herself and Stan. Stan is obviously an alcoholic but has become well known for his ability to paint abstract renditions of aboriginal Dreamtime ancestors. But Stan is forbidden, Mrs. Lacey explains to the American tourists, to paint his own totemic Emu Dreaming—"No artist paints his own Dreaming. It's too powerful. It might kill him" (p. 26). Mrs. Lacey explains that Stan Tjakamarra

cannot paint an Emu Dreaming because an emu is his paternal totem and it would be a sacrilege to do so. He can paint honey-ant because that is the totem of his mother's brother's son. That's right, isn't Stan? Gideon's Dreaming is honey-ant?"

Stan blinked and said, "Right!"

"Gideon," she continued, "is Stan's ritual manager. They both tell each other what they can and cannot paint." (p. 27)

The delicate issue of totemic relationships is one of the book's most complex, as is the relationship of a tribal elder and his ritual manager. The ritual manager is the person who remembers the entire history of the ancestors' sacred geographical sites and who gives the tribe permission to disclose or not disclose certain secret, sacred information. In explicating the complex abstractions of Sam's painting, Mrs. Lacey explains to the anxious American tourists that Dreaming-tracks—or Songlines—may be anywhere, but only the Pintupi know where they are: "For all I know there's a Dreaming-track running right through the middle of my shop" (p. 28). But only the Pintupi can see and then sing it:

> "You can't have a track without a song."
> "And these tracks run every place?" the man asked. "All over Australia?"
> "Yes," said Mrs. Lacey, sighing with satisfaction at having found a catchy phrase. "The song and the land are one." (p. 28)

Chatwin's clever echo of the ancient Grail response "The King and the land are one!" helps give the concept of Songlines its proper importance in the aboriginal cosmology. The Pintupis' grail is not limited, though, to one symbolic object, as is the Christian Grail. Rather, the Pintupi grail's systems of Songlines expand its holiness to every part of the continent. The Songlines identify the sacredness of the aboriginal world and return the concept of "the holy" to its original meaning of "whole." There is no separation of sacred and profane, spirit and body, earth and soul: the halves of each pair are identical to each other and can be accessed through the agency of the Songlines at any given moment. There is also no such idea of "*in illo tempore*"—that is, an evocation of an earlier sacred time, or a referral to "*that* time"—in which the world existed in a prelapsarian, Edenic condition. The world is always in a paradisal state as it is being sung and as its rules are being followed by the members of the tribe.

After meeting such characters as Marian, a woman with whom Arkady has taught and who now works on women's land claims, Bruce encounters an overly aggressive and slightly hostile muscular man whom he calls "the Gym Bore." The Gym Bore warns Bruce that he should expect nothing from the aboriginals because he has just arrived in Australia. At a cookout Bruce is also introduced to a number of well-educated people who have been working with the aboriginals for years, "nurses, teachers, lawyers, linguists, architects. . . . They were young and had wonderful legs" (p. 42). Most of the people seem slightly hostile toward Bruce and suspect that his attitudes may be less radical than theirs. As Salman Rushdie remembers in *Imaginary Homelands,* "Later I discovered that many of the young white radicals I meet in Alice Springs, people working as lawyers for the Land Rights movement, or people working with the various tribes 'out bush,' distrust Bruce for his apparent political conservatism and his anthropological orientation. Bruce is untroubled, walking through the minefield of black Australian politics with unconcern" (*Imaginary Homelands,* 234).

Rushdie also comments on Chatwin's later claim that Rushdie was Arkady Volchok, and that the book's original title was *Arkady.* He and Chatwin had traveled together in Australia in early 1984: "Later, after the book is published, Bruce tells someone that 'of course' I am Arkady. This isn't true. I know one person in Alice Springs, like Arkady an Australian of Russian descent, also highly knowledgeable about aboriginal religion, who is a much more obvious model. Nor do I recognize a single line of our conversation in *The Songlines.* The truth is, 'of course,' that Bruce is Arkady as well as the character he calls Bruce. He is both sides of the dialogue" (*Imaginary Homelands, 233*). Although Rushdie admits that he and Chatwin traveled extensively throughout Australia and that he spent many hours listening to Chatwin talking—he was a monumental talker—he explains that the major significance of their time together was that they became fast friends:

> At the end of such a journey you either hate each other passionately or you discover you're in love.
> Speaking of myself, I fell in love. (p. 236)

In chapter 10, Bruce runs into the Gym Bore again, whose real name is Kidder and who continues to challenge him on his right to know anything about aboriginal culture and wisdom. Kidder asks Bruce if he wishes to be initiated into aboriginal religion, a process that involves a particularly painful form of circumcision

> which, as I doubtless knew, was to have your urethra peeled back like a banana skin and flayed with a stone knife.
> "Thank you," I said. "I'll pass." (*The Songlines, 42*)

Kidder, whose job is "community adviser" to the aboriginals, asserts that their sacred knowledge belongs exclusively to them and that outsiders like Bruce should move on. Undaunted, Bruce, when asked by Kidder what a *tjuringa* is, amazes him with his response: " 'A sacred board,' I said. 'An Aboriginal's "holy of holies." Or, if you like, his "soul." ' "

"A *tjuringa* is usually an oval-ended plaque, carved from stone or mulga wood and covered with patterns which represent the wanderings of its owner's Dreamtime Ancestor. In Aboriginal law, no uninitiated person was *ever* allowed to look on one" (p. 43). Later, at a party, a New Zealand barrister advises Bruce that he must meet a certain Father

Flynn, an ex-Benedictine priest and aboriginal, who is occupied with a small party of his own in a dark part of the garden. Father Flynn bears more than a little resemblance to Father Manuel Palacios in *In Patagonia,* a native but also a Salesian priest, "the Patagonian Polymath." It is important for Bruce to talk to Flynn because he is so well informed about aboriginal wisdom, but Flynn's greater advantage is his familiarity with a number of aboriginal languages. He informs Bruce that linguistic information means a lot in understanding the concept of a Songline: "All our words for country . . . are the same as the word for 'line' " (p. 56). He also explains to Bruce the necessity of nomadism for the aboriginals, who live in scrub desert where rain may not fall for years: "To move in such a landscape was survival: to stay in the same place was suicide. . . . [T]o feel 'at home' in that country depended on being able to leave it. Everyone had to have at least four 'ways out,' along which he could travel in a crisis. Every tribe—like it or not—had to cultivate relations with its neighbors" (p. 56). In particularly difficult times, one tribe will supply food for a neighboring tribe to save it from starvation.

Flynn further explains that the trade route is the Songline because "songs, not things, are the principal medium of exchange. Before the whites came . . . no one in Australia was landless, since everyone inherited, as his or her private property, a stretch of the Ancestor's song and the stretch of country over which the song passed. A man's verses were his title deeds to territory. He could lend them to others. He could borrow other verses in return. The one thing he couldn't do was sell or get rid of them" (p. 57).

Flynn goes on to detail a theoretical situation in which the elders of a particular snake clan decide it is time to sing their entire song cycle from beginning to end—something like reciting the New Testament by heart over several days:

> "Messages would be sent out, up and down the track, summoning song-owners to assemble at the Big Place. One after the other, each owner would then sing his stretch of the Ancestor's footprints. Always in the correct sequence!
>
> "To sing a verse out of order . . . was a crime. Usually meant the death penalty."
>
> "I can see that," I said. "It'd be the musical equivalent of an earthquake."
>
> "Worse," he scowled. "It would be to uncreate the Creation." (p. 58)

It is clear that aboriginal cosmology is constructed on a verbal and musical basis—it is a universe that, without words, does not exist. And if the verses are not sung in the proper order, reality is not simply destroyed it is uncreated. The verb "to uncreate" has virtually no equivalent in Western culture, with the possible exception of the French writer and mystic Simone Weil's concept of "decreation"; as described by Wallace Stevens, in decreation the creative imagination fictively approximates reality but is immediately forced to decreate that reality because it endlessly changes. Stevens's long poem "An Ordinary Evening in New Haven" embodies and enacts that process quite clearly.

Just as Bruce and Arkady think they have a firm grasp on these aboriginal cosmological complexities, Flynn brings in even more complications that deal with "dual paternity." In the mind of the native Australians, the concept of "father" includes both a human being and the earth. There is always

> a kind of parallel paternity which tied his soul to one particular point in the landscape.
>
> Each Ancestor, while singing his way across country, was believed to have left a trail of "life-cells" or "spirit-children" along the line of his footprints.
>
> "A kind of musical sperm," said Arkady, making everyone laugh again: even, this time, Flynn.
>
> The song was supposed to lie over the ground in an unbroken chain of couplets: a couplet for each pair of the Ancestor's footfalls, each formed from the names he "threw out" while walking. (p. 60)

Flynn then describes a scenario in which a pregnant woman walking along inadvertently steps on a couplet; a "spirit-child" then leaps up into her "through her toenail, up her vagina, or into an open callus on her foot—and works its way into her womb, and impregnates the foetus with song."

> "The baby's first kick", he said, "corresponds to the moment of 'spirit-conception'."
>
> The mother-to-be then marks the spot and rushes off to fetch the Elders. They then interpret the lie of the land and decide which Ancestor walked that way, and which stanzas will be the child's private property. They reserve him a "conception site"—coinciding with the nearest landmark on the Songline. They earmark his tjuringa in the tjuringa storehouse. (p. 60)

Chatwin further expands on this complex process in his *Granta* interview: "Each newborn baby inherits a section of the song as his birthright. His stanzas are his inalienable private property and define his territory" ("Interview," 31). By varying Bruce's sources of scholarly information, Chatwin keeps the complexity of the information fresh and compelling. Flynn's monologue delivers hard information and at the same time reveals his brilliant but quirky and conflicted personality.

Bruce finds that he must also seek out another priest, Father Terrence, an Irish priest who belongs to a Cistercian order—the Trappists—and who now lives on a beach on the Timor Sea. Terrence, in imitation of the great mendicant St. Francis, has found it necessary to rid himself of all material things and live in a hut. He spends his days praying, reading, and corresponding. He is also writing a manual of poverty. For him the enemy is things—possessions that eventually possess the owner. His spiritual models are the great desert fathers of the early church: "to be lost in the desert was to find one's way to God" (p. 64). Terrence, whose earlier counterpart is Theo the Tent in *On the Black Hill,* is another Franciscan model that Chatwin admires and envies.

Although Terrence admires Flynn for his genius, he believes that a most dangerous idea has corrupted him, the concept of syncretism—the same enemy that an African White Father, Father Zerringer, finds in Mama Wéwé's shrine in *The Viceroy of Ouidah.* Syncretism points up disturbing similarities between certain Christian beliefs and rituals and so-called pagan ones. Certainly the Christian concept of the Incarnation of Christ as both human and divine bares a dangerously close relationship to the aboriginal concept of Songlines insofar as both are grounded in a verbal universe. In Christianity the Bible opens with "In the beginning was the Word"; aboriginal cosmology begins with "In the beginning was the Song." Terrence finds Flynn's characterization of the aboriginals' condition very similar to that of Adam before the Fall and sees the Songlines as another version of Christ's "I am the Way." Terrence claims that Flynn lost his spiritual way because he never understood the simplicity of the story of the stable—that is, the manger in Bethlehem—and the nomadic plight of the holy family (p. 66).

Chapter 14 is the first in which other texts become crucial to understanding Chatwin's expanding awareness of the Songlines' tremendous range and application and of the extent to which they can explain the relationship between humanity and nature. Whenever the weather becomes unbearable, Bruce finds time to read and think about crucial books that have influenced him to pursue his sometimes dangerous journeys. Two of *The Songlines*'s seminal texts are Theodore Strehlow's *Songs of Central Australia* and an earlier work, *Aranda Traditions.* Chatwin cannot separate what he has read from the experience he is now having because his reading is what brought him to this strange land. In a sense Chatwin's readers are reading Chatwin reading Strehlow or any of the hundreds of texts he quotes after chapter 30.

Chatwin brilliantly demonstrates how his reading enters his intellectual and spiritual life, and also how reading incites him to action. His reading contributes to the construction of his reality and is as important as his actual presence in Australia. His first experience of Australia was in written texts, and his literal journey to and through Australia is another "text" that he adds to the initial ones. This book is, then, one of the clearest examples of the process of intertextuality *as it actually occurs.* Reading becomes so important, in fact, that by chapter 30 his text has literally become what he has read. The internal spiritual dialogue from this point on includes texts that have helped formulate his imagination of Australia, and *The Songlines* becomes Bruce Chatwin's imagination of his journey into Australia's remotest parts.

It is also clear that Bruce discovers Strehlow's findings to be a counterpart to his own activities, particularly Strehlow's serious attempts to come up with a "grand poetic theory" about the relationship of aboriginal song to the land and to draw analogous relationships with counterparts "in Hebrew, Ancient Greek, Old Norse or Old English: the literature we acknowledge as our own. Having grasped the connection of song and land, we wish to strike at the roots of song itself to find in song a key to unravelling the mystery of the human condition" (p. 69). In defining Strehlow's ambitious reach, Bruce reveals his own and fears that he may well suffer the same critical reproach that Strehlow did. When Strehlow's *Songs of Central Australia* was published in the early 1970s, it was bitterly criticized by Lands Rights activists (i.e., Gym Bores), who accused him of stealing sacred information from the elders and using it for his own purposes. Bruce feels the man's failure deeply: "Strehlow died at his desk in 1978, a broken man. . . . He was, I am convinced, a highly original thinker. His books are great and lonely books" (p. 69).

At the conclusion of chapter 14, Bruce, after hours of reading Strehlow's *Songs,* goes for a drink at the bar in the motel where he's staying. The reading experience has been so powerful that he decides to take a brandy back to his room: "Reading Strehlow had made me want to write something. I was not drunk—yet—but had not been nearly so drunk in ages. I got out a yellow pad and began to write" (p. 71).

It is clear that the act of reading has become for Bruce a transforming act in the process of scholarly discussion and at the same time con-

tributes to the creative text that follows chapter 14 in a section called
"In the Beginning . . ." This highly creative dream-vision is obviously
Chatwin's hypnogogic participation in a gradually expanding text that
insists the writer enter it in a creative mode simply because the dynamics of the mythopoeic process are what Chatwin has really been examining for the first 14 chapters of this book; Songlines are vivid examples of
mythopoesis. In short, Chatwin discovers his real subject only at this
point, and it is clear to him now that discovering and creating are not
separate activities.

"In the Beginning . . ." is Bruce's clear demonstration of his ability to
amalgamate and synthesize everything he has learned from his reading,
his conversations, his discussions, his dialogues with Arkady, and in his
fecund imagination in a kind of semi-intoxicated dream-vision state: he
is, in short, creating his own Dreamtime and Songline. Chatwin becomes
an Adamic namer within his Dreaming: "In the earth was an infinite
and murky plain, separated from the sky and from the grey salt sea and
smothered in a shadowy twilight" (p. 72). The last 7 paragraphs of this
12-paragraph chapter delineate the creation of the world, the ultimate
act of mythopoesis—literally, a making (*poeisis*) of myth and, therefore,
a world. In vividly surreal images Bruce dreams/writes his version of a
Genesis in which the ancient aboriginal ancestors arise from the primordial earth soup: "The mud fell from their thighs, like placenta from a
baby. Then, like the baby's first cry, each Ancestor opened his mouth
and called out, 'I AM!' 'I am—Snake . . . Cockatoo . . . Honey-Ant . . .
Honeysuckle. . . . And this first 'I am!,' this primordial act of naming,
was held, then and forever after, as the most sacred couplet of the
Ancestor's song" (p. 73).

Bruce's Dreaming then shows him the ancestors naming the objects
in the world with each footstep:

> The Ancients sang their way all over the world. They sang the rivers
> and ranges, salt-pans and sand dunes. They hunted, ate, made love,
> danced, killed: wherever their tracks led them they left a trail of music.
> They wrapped the whole world in a web of song: and at last, when
> the Earth was so sung, they felt tired. . . . Some sank into the ground
> where they stood. Some crawled into caves. . . .
> All of them went "back in." (p. 73)

It is at this point in the narrative, when Bruce surrenders himself to
the overwhelming visionary imperative to generate his own Dreamtime

and Songline, that an additional subject of the book surfaces. *The Songlines* now evolves into a text about the generation of narrative forms. Bruce becomes so profoundly engaged in his subject matter—which is nothing less than the dynamics of how words and music become a world—that he can no longer remain an objective collector of data or maintain a scholarly distance; he must enter the process. Once he becomes part of the mythopoeic process and surrenders himself to his own Dreamtime, he is required to generate forms that remain open. And since he has discovered that the world he is examining is a visionary one—the Dreamtime—he can enter it only by creating his own Songline. The book begins to open up and expand at this point because he finds he must accommodate its ever-expanding content—the genesis of his own Songline—a process that simply does not submit to traditional rational-intellectual analysis.

As Bruce and Arkady begin to prepare for their trip into the great Australian desert, Bruce collects his gear and is especially careful to bring along the notes he made over a 10-year period for the manuscript he wrote on pastoral nomadism. He mentions that he burned the manuscript but kept the notes and intends, when he finds a few days, to go over them and see what he can make of them: "They contained a mishmash of nearly indecipherable jottings, 'thoughts,' quotations, brief encounters, travel notes, notes for stories" (p. 75). These are the materials Bruce will eventually transform into art, since *The Songlines* has now become a self-referential text that demonstrates how it generates its own form. As *The Songlines* progresses, books and reading become increasingly important and begin to formulate into an additional and enlightening subtext that will, with "From the Notebooks," eventually take over the narrative. In an almost humorous gesture with obvious mythic resonances, Arkady presents Bruce with Ovid's *Metamorphoses*—the Ur-text of how to transform the commonplace into myth. In true Ovidian fashion, *The Songlines* metamorphoses back into its origins—the notes from which it came—and becomes a kind of multileveled hypertext akin to Charles Olson's *Maximus Poems*, William Carlos Williams's *Paterson*, and Ezra Pound's *Cantos* combined with Louis Zukofsky's literary musical score *A*. There need not be a question of direct or indirect influences regarding these modernist and postmodernist giants of American poetry, but they, like Chatwin, were forced to generate new, open forms due to the vastness of their subject and to the formal requirements of their aesthetic tasks.

On their journey, Arkady and Bruce immediately encounter some of the idiosyncratic but vivid characters who have chosen to live in such a remote place. They stop at the ramshackle house of Jim Hanlon, a 73-year-old Communist, who challenges Bruce at every opportunity and tries to berate him for wanting to write a book about the aboriginals and for appearing to be from the upper class. Hanlon, who has lived on his land for 30 years and sold most of it off, is living on welfare; he is obviously a dying man. But he apologizes to Bruce for flying at him, and after feeding Bruce and Arkady some bloody steaks he sends them on their way to visit Skull Creek Camp and Burnt Flat Hotel. Most of the aboriginal inhabitants of this next location seem to be sleeping off hangovers, and the whites spend much of their time abusing the natives. In chapter 19, Bruce and Arkady visit Middle Bore, where Arkady meets his old friend Alan, an aboriginal elder. They expected to meet Marian there, but she is behind schedule. Alan is *kirda*—the owner of the land that Arkady has come to survey. As the owner, or "boss," of the land, he is "responsible for its upkeep, for making sure its songs were sung and its rituals performed on time" (p. 98). However, it is Alan's *kutungurlu*—his manager or helper—who actually decides if the railroad will violate his and Alan's ancestral Songlines.

Alan and his ritual manager guide Arkady and Bruce to an actual Song-line; later that night, Alan acts out one of the totemic ancestral stories that took place on that Songline. Alan goes into a kind of trance and tells a very dark story about the Lizard, his wife, and the wife's unfaithfulness, and the Lizard's eventual death. Bruce calls it the story of an "antipodean Helen." Arkady tells Bruce that that story would be known thousands of miles away and that Alan would know the songs from many other parts of Australia. The melodic structure of the various songs would identify them immediately, for it is the songs' melodic contour rather than their words, that describes the nature of the land that the song passes over:

> So, if the Lizard Man were dragging his heels across the salt-pans of Lake Eyre, you could expect a succession of long flats, like Chopin's "Funeral March." . . .
>
> Certain phrases, certain combinations of musical notes, are thought to describe the action of the Ancestor's feet. One phrase would say "Salt-pan"; another "Creek-bed" . . . and so forth: An expert songman by listening to the order of succession, would count how many times his hero crossed a river, or scaled a ridge—and be able to calculate where, and how far along, a Songline was. . . .
>
> "So a musical phrase," I said, "is a map reference?"
>
> "Music," said Arkady, "is a memory bank for finding one's way about the world." (p. 108)

Bruce is so stimulated by the day's activities—the tracing of a Songline, the creation of his own Songline, and Arkady's brilliant explications of the ritual's applications—that he cannot sleep. Instead, his memory takes him back to an encounter with the great Austrian ethologist Konrad Lorenz, winner of the Nobel prize for his seminal books on aggression.

As in *In Patagonia,* Bruce's memory of an encounter with a famous person becomes part of his meditation on the relationship of man and nature and, specifically, on the origins of human aggression. But what reminds Bruce of Konrad Lorenz is the vociferous way in which Lorenz, like Alan's "man in blue" (an elder in Alan's tribe), acted out and mimed the actions of animals. Lorenz virtually invented the discipline of ethology—the comparative study of animal behavior in the animals' natural habitat; in a sense, Bruce and Arkady are conducting the same study, with humans. What remains with Bruce long after his visit to Lorenz, however, besides Lorenz's marvelous ability to mimic animals, is his explanation of his version of the Fall of Mankind: "Our fatal flaw, or Fall, he insisted, was to have developed 'artificial weapons' instead of natural ones. As a species, we thus lacked the instinctive inhibitions which prevented the professional carnivores from murdering their fellows" (p. 112). Bruce essentially agrees with Lorenz about animals' innate ability to ritualize aggression, a skill that Lorenz found many so-called savage tribes had adopted: "In the Orinco, there were Indians who would suppress tribal warfare with 'ritual' exchange of gifts" (p. 113). Once again, Bruce's experience in his journey evokes specific memories both of his reading and, in this instance, of an important exchange with an author whose books he read and greatly respects.

As Bruce is resting in the heat of the desert afternoon, he opens his copy of Ovid's *Metamorphoses*—having just watched Alan act out an aboriginal example of that process—and begins to find similarities among these ritualized Songlines, his reading, and the memory of his visit to Arkadia, in the Peloponnisos, years before. He is, appropriately, reading and remembering the story of Lykaeon's transformation into a wolf (remember that Arkady is named after Arkadia and that his Russian surname, Volchok, means "wolf"). Bruce begins to theorize that Ovid's constructions of the myths of Hyacinth and Adonis, of Deucalion and the Flood "and how all the 'living things' were created from the warm Nilotic ooze," were European versions of the same basic stories that appear among aboriginal myths. He then moves deeper into his imagination and finds profound mythic connections: "And it struck me, from what I now knew of the Songlines, that the whole of Classical mythology might represent the relics of a gigantic 'song map': that all the toing and fro-ing of gods and goddesses, the caves and sacred springs, the sphinxes and chimaeras, and all the men and women who became nightingales or ravens, echoes or narcissi, stones or stars—could all be interpreted in terms of totemic geography" (p. 117). It becomes more obvious as the book progresses that Bruce and Arkady are experiencing a variety of fascinating characters and religious rituals but are learning little they had not already researched and read about in depth. So what the text is recording primarily is the continuous development and expansion of Bruce's imagination as it becomes an interactive vortex of his present physical experience, his reading (and his memory of past reading), his note taking, and his memory of seminal intellectual and spiritual characters from his past. *The Songlines* is evolving into a multidimensional mapping of all of these activities, similar to the evolution in *In Patagonia* but under more compelling circumstances.

The other emerging process is that Arkady is becoming more than just a quirky intellectual who reads endlessly and plays his harpsichord. When he presents Bruce with a copy of Ovid's *Metamorphoses,* an act that alerts the reader not to miss the obvious transformations happening everywhere, he is identifying himself as Ovid. As Ovid, Arkady's gift to Bruce is to remind him that he—Arkady as Ovid—is leading Bruce into these fabulous areas. Formerly literal figures are now becoming archetypal—for example, Marian, who will eventually marry Arkady and whose name means both "sea" and "mother," is also beginning to become an important character, literally and mythically, in the book. Aboriginals, on the other hand, can function on both literal and mythical levels simultaneously and are not troubled by intellectual or spiritual dichotomies. Since they are attached to the land by primordial song and by totemic ancestors, they are unencumbered by dualities of, for example, mind and body, spirit and flesh. They are comfortable in the world because their minds have not separated them from the world. They *are* the world.

After a disturbing scene with local bigots in the bar at the Glen Armond—where Joe Hanlon collapsed the night before—Arkady, Bruce, and Marian decide to have a picnic in the desert on the road to Cullen. Their conversation turns toward hunting tribes, and Bruce recalls, with affection, some time he spent with the Nemadi in Mauritania in the western Sahara. The Nemadi, who were relegated to the Moorish caste system's eighth level—the lowest—were treated by the Moors as pariahs because they were genuine nomads and lived on what they hunted. The Nemadi, whose name means "master of dogs," always hunt with dogs and treat them with the utmost love and respect; the dogs are "said to eat even when their owners go hungry" (p. 131). The Nemadi's favorite food is antelope, which the dogs capture for them; the Nemadi then kill the antelope with a quick knife thrust, asking immediately for its forgiveness. Bruce then recalls meeting with an ancient Nemadi—more than 100 years old—and not being able to get her graceful kindness and humility out of his thoughts. His experience with her and with the gentle members of the Nemadi occasion Bruce's declaration on the moral nature of humanity:

> "But I live with that old woman's smile."
> The smile, I said, was like a message from the Golden Age, it had taught me to reject out of hand all the arguments for the nastiness of human nature. The idea of returning to an "original simplicity" was not naive or unscientific or out of touch with reality.
> "Renunciation," I said, "even at this late date, can work."
> "I'd agree with that," said Arkady. "The world, if it has a future, has an ascetic future." (p. 133)

Nowhere else in Chatwin's work does he so clearly identify himself as a philosophical romantic in the Rousseauist tradition as in the statement that human nature is basically good. He has observed the ascetic simplicity of the aboriginals and remembers the gentleness of the Nemadi and draws some hope for the future from their example. That hope resides in a return to a Franciscan simplicity. Chatwin is asserting a romantic redemption in a return to origins; as Andrew Harvey points out, "We will survive, he is telling us, if we return to the truths of the desert, and to our nomadic nature, with its essential unaggressiveness and reverence for the world: true freedom is the freedom of the soul from things, the nomad's irreverent and generous happiness of spirit; this freedom is not a fantasy of travelers or romantic poets or 'primitivist' anthropologists but a reality rooted in man's earliest experience of the earth still alight and shining in the lives of those nomadic peoples who have not been 'civilized' " ("Footprints," 27). What is becoming increasingly obvious is that Bruce could not have come to these dramatic philosophical conclusions unless and until he had traveled to landscapes that connected and resonated with each other; these travels, together with stimulating conversations with Arkady and his own reading, have culminated in decisive conclusions about the moral nature of mankind.

On their way to Cullen to meet the man Arkady must consult with, Titus Tjilkamata, they stop in Popaniji to visit a local teacher, an Australian woman named Lydia, who is barely holding her school together. Her assistant, Graham, an aboriginal educated in Canberra, has gotten involved in creating a rock band and has neglected his obligations to his tribe (in this case the Pintupi). He disappeared just when he was to be formally initiated into the tribe, and as a result the natives are angry with both him and Lydia.

Finally the group arrives at Cullen, a settlement that lies between two mountains, Mount Cullen and Mount Liebler. Cullen is a little town of about 400 members of the Pintupi tribe. The community store is supervised by Rolf Niehart, a classic Chatwinian Renaissance man of letters and important family background: "eight generations of Prussians, solid Lutheran with solid money, the most rooted community in Australia." Rolf, who is only about 4 feet 10, looks like he stepped off of a beach on the French Riviera. When he is not supervising the store, he reads books; his home is overflowing with them. He reads mostly English, American, French, German, Czech, Spanish, and Russian literature—he is currently reading Marcel Proust's *Remembrance of Things Past* in French—and also manages to keep up with the *New York Review of Books, Nouvelle Revue Francaise,* and other sophisticated literary journals. Rolf speaks English, German, and French and earned a degree at the Sorbonne, where his thesis was on "structural linguistics." The woman he lives with, Wendy, is also a linguistic scholar and is writing a Pintupi dictionary.

Arkady has heard rumors that Titus Tjilkamata, the important tribal elder he wants to consult, is in a foul mood. As a result, he enlists the help of Titus's ritual manager, Limpy, to accompany him some 25 miles southwest of Cullen to Titus's home. Arkady asks that Bruce remain in Cullen until he returns.

In the meantime, Rolf summons a Pintupi elder, Joshua, to give Bruce more information on the Dreamings: "Joshua was a famous Pintupi performer . . . who had performed in Europe and the United States" (p. 152). Joshua takes Bruce to his home between the two mountains and performs one of the Songlines connected with Mount Liebler, which happens to be covered with Songlines. Joshua then performs and tells the story of the Perenty Lizard, a Songline that follows a north-south axis. He then sings some Porcupine couplets and a Qantas Dreaming and tells Bruce about a meeting—hilarious to him—at which a Catholic monk sang Gregorian chant, a Tibetan lama sang his mantras, an African sang a chant, and Joshua sang his Dreaming. All had electrodes attached to their heads: "all four of them [were] singing their heads off, to test the effect of different songs styles on the rhythmic structure of the brain" (p. 155). The memory of the experiment strikes Joshua as so comic that he is bent over with laughter.

Later in the afternoon, Arkady returns from Titus's with stories of enormous complications involving the exchange of two sets of *tjuringas* from many years ago. Titus, who was been well educated at the Lutheran Mission on Horn River, is also a highly esteemed elder of the Pintupi tribe "who spoke six or seven Aboriginal languages and was famous, up and down the Western Desert, for his judgments on tribal law" (p. 156). Titus is happy with the Lands Rights Act and sees it as an opportunity for his people to return to their native country. He thinks that such a reengagement with their land would relieve the epidemic alcoholism that has blighted his land. But the white government insists on reserving the rights to underground minerals and requires licenses for any prospecting, an idea Titus does not like because he sees it as corrupting both the whites and his people. Unfortunately, his only weapon is noncooperation with the mining companies.

However, before the Lands Rights Act, Titus's grandfather exchanged two unmarked *tjuringas* with the Loritja clan, which gave each tribe access to the other's hunting grounds. But the *tjuringas* have never been returned, and therefore the agreement is still in effect. When the mining company got nowhere with Titus, they enlisted the help of members of the Loritja clan—now known as the Amadeus Mob—who claimed that they were the owners of the land and its songs and, as such, owned any royalty rights. The Mob committed the ultimate sacrilege by tampering with the *tjuringas* and engraving their own totemic designs on them, an act that constituted a grave forgery. The Amadeus Mob forged "the title deeds to Titus's birthright . . . [and] by altering the tjuringas, the Amadeus Mob had attempted to re-write the Creation. . . . Titus told Arkady how, at nights, he heard his Ancestors howling for vengeance— and how he felt forced to obey them" (pp. 158–59).

Arkady informs Bruce that the repercussions of this scandal will take weeks to untangle and that he will return to Cullen as soon as he can. Bruce, then, readies himself for a lengthy period of "settlement" and breaks out his reading and writing equipment—those now-famous *carnets moleskines* (moleskin notebooks) that he always bought at a Parisian *papeterie* in the Rue de l'Ancienne Comédie. Chatwin offers a rare glimpse into his personal writing habits and is also beginning to feel a disturbingly prophetic "presentiment that the 'travelling' phase of my life might be passing. I felt, before the malaise of settlement crept over me, that I should reopen these notebooks. I should set down on paper a resume of the ideas, quotations and encounters which had amused and obsessed me; and which I hoped would shed some light on what is, for me, the question of questions: the nature of human restlessness" (p. 161). It is at this point in the narrative that Bruce reveals the very heart of his and possibly mankind's, inability to sit still: "Pascal, in one of his gloomier *pensées,* gave it as his opinion that all our miseries stemmed from a single cause: our inability to remain quietly in a room" (p. 161).

It is also quite clear at this point that Bruce has been examining and analyzing the lives of both the aboriginal nomads and the nomad Bruce. But there are signs, too, that Bruce's quest to understand the nature of restlessness has become a part of what appears to be an enormous existential questioning of the purpose of life and the place of suffering in it. Bruce's philosophical mind finds that the answer to one question often leads to another whose answer may be unbearable: "Later, on further reflection, having discovered the cause of our misfortunes, he wished to understand the reason for them, he found one very good reason: namely, the natural unhappiness of our weak mortal condition; so unhappy that when we give it all our attention, nothing could console us" (p. 161). Bruce insists on knowing whether "our mania for the new was an instinctive migratory urge" (p. 161). Is Chatwin, having to face the devastating effects of AIDS and the resulting despair, admitting that the only alleviation is pursuing a program of distractions that might protect him from the horror of his condition? The almost purposeful abstractions of Bruce's language—in a writer who studiously avoids abstractions of any kind—suggests that these existential musings are both personal and universal, and that he is facing his own death.

Bruce begins to put together materials from his notebooks that evolve into some satisfactory answers to these pressing questions, which have occupied him for more than 20 years. He admits that his notes from South Africa and the information he has learned in Australia point to major epiphanies: "that Natural Selection has designed us—from the structure of our brain-cells to the structure of our big toe—for a career of seasonal journeys *on foot* through a blistering land of thornscrub or desert. . . . If this were so; if the desert were 'home'; if our instincts were forged in the desert—then it is easier to understand why greener pastures pall on us; why possessions exhaust us, and why Pascal's imaginary man found his comfortable lodgings a prison" (p. 162).

Ninety-eight of the remaining 131 pages of *The Songlines* consist of selections from Bruce's notebooks interspersed between—and sometimes attached to—the remaining nine chapters. This radical break in the chronological narrative disturbs some critics, whereas others see it as an indication of Chatwin's failing health and his inability to hold the narrative together. Chatwin himself confesses at the book's conclusion that he is so ill that he can't walk across a hotel room: "I wrote that last chapter about three old men dying under a gum tree, when I was just about to conk myself" ("Interview," 35).

Critic Roger Clarke characterizes the nearly 100 pages of quotations as the "shattered remains" of a book he once tried to write on nomads: "Chatwin just doesn't seem up to the magnificence of the questions he poses, and occasional chapters retreat into a shell-shocked and quivering palsy of learning—pages and pages of quotes, albeit very illuminating ones. . . . But he never makes a connection."[3] American travel writer Edward Hoagland considers the book "charming and impeccably stylish" but finds fault in Chatwin's narrative procedures: "[H]e has grafted one unfinished book onto a different one, hoping that the seams will fit. They don't entirely."[4] Andrew Harvey sees the quotations from the notebooks as Chatwin "counterpointing his Australian explorations with his earlier ones in Africa" ("Footprints," 27), and Jennifer Howard views the function of these quotations as providing "documentation for the Chatwinian theory that the nomad is the quintessential man . . . that we are born to wander."[5]

The scope of the book begins to expand considerably once Bruce begins synthesizing his past and present experiences with the immense range of reading, from which he has taken relevant quotations. One of the few ways that a writer can accommodate massive amounts of information from both life and reading is to permit those materials to form themselves into a kind of vast, open-form collage using such modernist techniques as juxtaposition and parataxis, methods that invite the reader to connect relevant motifs in imaginative ways. A creative writer and thinker like Chatwin cannot simply synthesize aboriginal art, religion, philosophy, and their geographical interconnections within the limits of a European linear discourse. The demands of his content insist that he employ forms that are more suitable to the aboriginals' imagination of both their cosmology and cosmogony (i.e., the origin and nature of their world). In his attempt to map the outlines of an aboriginal, atemporal, nonlinear, nondichotomous world, Chatwin may have felt that an open-form collage similar to ones Charles Olson used in mapping the spiritual and geographical levels of Gloucester, Massachusetts, in his 700-page *Maximus Poems* was more appropriate to his content. William Carlos Williams also employed open-form methods of collage and juxtaposition in constructing and mythologizing his hometown in his long poem *Paterson*. A description and analysis of aboriginal mythopoesis simply could not be satisfactorily encapsulated in standard European methods of analysis. As Olson once stated, "Form is never more than an extension of content."

An additional contribution that Chatwin made to contemporary literature was to restore the "commonplace book" to its earlier, exalted position in literature; that is, as a functioning book of spiritual precepts that guide human behavior and thought and not merely as a collection of favorite quotations and pet theories. The "Notebooks" section of *The Songlines* resembles Robert Burton's *Anatomy of Melancholy* insofar as it functions as a kind of anatomy of the human organism in its most basic activities: walking, moving, wandering. Chatwin's single most convincing etymological argument is the Tibetan term for "human being"—*a-Gro ba,* "a goer," or one who goes on migrations (*The Songlines,* 197). Another important function of the notebooks is that they guide the reading of the text and elevate a rather common and not particularly compelling journey (which by itself would constitute a *literal* commonplace book) to a higher level of revelation. In that sense, the notebooks transform an ordinary modern novel into a spiritual masterpiece by supplying a richness and depth that the narrative alone cannot generate or sustain. Chatwin uses the notebooks' precepts as a form of spiritual documentation, connecting them to the oldest and most common theme in literature and religion—the mythological journey of the hero. In short, the information in the notebooks vivifies and spiritually enriches a narrative that, in and of itself, is not particularly remarkable or deep.

A comprehensive summary of the 98 pages from Bruce's notebooks is clearly unnecessary, but a survey of their most important recurring motifs and interconnections will reveal some idea of the range of Chatwin's spectacular erudition. Paradoxically, Chatwin, the most private of humans, reveals himself by allowing us to observe the questions that torture him. The major motifs are familiar ones: settlement, pastoral nomadism, human origins, the origins of aggression, the Fall, Cain and Abel, language and etymology, progress and technology, the golden age, song, and most important, the sacred function of walking.

He begins his notebooks with the titans of modern literature and philosophy, quoting Baudelaire's definition of the great malady "horror of home" and Rimbaud's defining existential question "What am I doing here?" (Chatwin borrowed Rimbaud's question for the title of his 1989 collection of brilliant sketches and essays, *What Am I Doing Here.*) He then quotes Søren Kierkegaard, who says in a letter to a friend that as long as he walks every day "everything will be all right" (p. 171).

Bruce usually supplies the location of his observations and the source of his quotations. His notebooks contain entries written in China, Brazil, Cameroon, Benin, Mauritania, Timbuktu, Mali, Niger, Russia, Afghanistan, England, Paris, Austria, California, New York, South Africa, and India. The range of the works and authors he draws from is enormously comprehensive and erudite: Rimbaud, Baudelaire, William Blake, Arthur Koestler, Heidegger, John Donne, the Finnish epic the *Kalevala*, the *Chinese Book of Odes, Tristam Shandy,* Meister Eckhart, Turi's *Book of Lappland,* Christopher Marlowe, Sir Thomas Browne, Henri Focillon, Martin Buber, the Bible, Herman Melville, Josephus, Lancelot Andrewes, Herodotus, Ortega y Gasset, Konrad Lorenz, the *Odyssey,* the *Topeka Weekly Daily,* William James, and a number of other less well-known scholars, poets, scientists, and philosophers. His discussion of the mythological journey of the hero—and of the hero cycle—seems as if it were taken from Lord Raglan's *Hero* and Joseph Campbell's *Hero With a Thousand Faces,* though Chatwin does not mention Campbell by name.

The three most important clusters of quotations and meditations that occupy the notebooks document Chatwin's obsession with the persistent dichotomy of the wanderer versus the settler, the sacred dimension of walking, and the origins of aggression. Throughout *The Songlines* Bruce finds consistent evidence that the nomadic condition is a means of re-evoking an original innocence, a kind of prelapsarian regeneration of an Edenic condition in which such categories as time and place do not exist in opposition. The maintenance of nomadic pastoralism, in effect, is an atemporal proposition that subsumes the concept of time under place and shows that time is an abstraction that originates only in settlement. Bruce, in etymological studies of words that describe high finance and the stock market, finds linguistic subtexts that reveal that nomadism—particularly the movement of cattle from one pasture to another—is archaic proof that settlement constitutes a decisive fall from innocence into the corruption of possession and ownership. He finds that "Domesticated animals are 'currency'—'things that run'—from the French *courir.* In fact, almost all our monetary expressions—capital, stock, pecuniary, chattel, sterling—perhaps even the idea of 'growth' itself—have their origins in the pastoral world" (p. 185). The stock market was originally just that. As a result of these creative etymological meditations, Bruce sees the American cowboy as one of the last modern romantic nomadic figures.

Using the Old Testament as a text that portrays the Hebrews as nomadic wanderers, Chatwin "re-visions" the desert wanderings of the Jews "as a monumental dialogue between Him and His People in the rights and wrongs of living in the Land. . . . Was it a land for fields and houses?. . . Or was it a country of black tent and goat path? A nomad's country of milk and wild honey?. . . Or was it, as Heine surmised, 'a portable kingdom' which could only exist in men's hearts?" (p. 194). Chatwin develops his arguments by pointing out that "Jahweh, in origin, is a God of the Way. His sanctuary is the Mobile Ark, His House a tent. . . . He leads them out of Egypt, away from the fleshpots and the overseer's lash, a journey of three days into the harsh clean air of Sinai" (p. 194). The notebooks demonstrate better than anything Chatwin ever wrote the depth and freshness of his imagination, particularly when he deals with language issues, such as etymology, semantics, and comparative linguistics. His ability to view things from different perspectives also enables him to support his sometimes tenuous philosophical speculations. For example, he sees the great Old Testament prophets, like Isaiah, Jeremiah, Amos, and Hosea, as "nomadic revivalists who howled abuse at the decadence of civilization. By sinking roots in the land, by 'laying house to house and field to field,' by turning Temple into a sculpture gallery, the people had turned from their God" (p. 195). Bruce sees these prophets as looking to "a day of Restoration when the Jews would return to the frugal asceticism of nomadic life. In the Vision of Isaiah they are promised a Saviour, whose name would be Emmanuel, and who would be a herdsman" (p. 195). In this context, one of the Bible's best-known quotations—"The Lord is my shepherd"—takes on new dimensions and relevance.

Bruce then piles on more support from the writings of the Greek Hesiod that the Men of the Golden Race wandered freely, ate their meals in common, and had no possessions (p. 204). So too did the early Christians, as embodied in the Desert Fathers' return to ascetic wandering; St. Francis of Assisi founded the Roman Catholic church's first mendicant order, the Franciscans, who took a vow of absolute poverty and lived on the road as beggars—that is, homeless mendicants.

Bruce offers his most compelling proof of the corrupting potential of settlement in the findings of a Hungarian epidemiologist whom he met at the Simonaspetras monastery on Mount Athos. The man, who had abandoned his research as an epidemiologist and taken to climbing the sacred mountains of the world, became convinced that man "was not meant to settle down."

> This was something he had learnt from his study of epidemics. The story of infectious disease was a story of men brewing in their own filth. . . . "Make no mistake," he said. "Epidemics are going to make nuclear weapons seem like useless toys." (p. 197)

In between his discussions on wandering and the sacred function of walking, Chatwin plunges into a complex analysis and rejection of the findings of South African professor of anatomy Raymond Dart and of the man who popularized his theories, anthropologist Robert Ardrey. Chatwin finds repellent Dart's notion that mankind evolved from lower animals *"because* we were killers and cannibals; that the weapon fathered the Man; that all subsequent history revolved around the possession and development of superior weapons" (p. 237). Ardrey, particularly in his best-selling *Territorial Imperative,* subscribed to Dart's bleak ideas, but his theory that animals map out their own specific geographical terri-tory, claim a kind of ownership of it, and thereby defend it to the death was for Chatwin just another antiromantic philosophy used to support the concept of settlement.

Another means of supporting his theories about the spiritual efficacy of nomadism Bruce uses is the consistent and recurring pattern of the mythological journey of the hero found throughout Western and East-ern mythology and religion. Joseph Campbell calls this pattern of sepa-ration, initiation, and return the "monomyth,"[6] the basis of all narrative. Bruce calls it the

> "Hero and his Road of Trials," in which a young man . . . receives a "call." He travels to a distant country where some giant or monster threatens to destroy the population. In a superhuman battle, he over-comes the Power of Darkness, proves his manhood, and receives his reward: a wife, treasure, land, fame.
>
> These he enjoys into late middle age when, once again, the clouds darken. Again, restlessness stirs him. Again he leaves . . . to set off for some mysterious destination and vanishes. (p. 217)

The hero is driven, then, despite his worldly success and happiness, to renew his wandering—that is, to revert back to a purer state of Edenic innocence. "The Hero Cycle represents an unchangeable paradigm of

'ideal' behaviour for the human male. . . . Each section of the myth—
like a link in a behavioural chain—will correspond to one of the classic
Ages of Man. Each Age opens with some fresh barrier to be scaled or
ordeal to be endured" (pp. 217–18). Chatwin also seems fascinated with
how the role of the hero is transformed into the role of the stranger once
the hero leaves the safety and security of his territory. There is a com-
monly held theory that there is only one narrative (Campbell's monomyth), which has two perspectives to it: 1) a young man leaves his home
and embarks on a long journey; 2) a stranger comes into town. The
monomyth is, then, the story of a wandering stranger.

An interesting though minor revelation is Chatwin's quotation from
P. J. Hamilton Grierson's *Silent Trade* that concerns the linguistic relationship between the Middle Latin *wargus* (which became the Late Latin
expulsus), which means both "stranger" and "wolf." It is obvious that
Arkady Volchok's surname comes from *wargus,* and he is both a "wolf"
and a "stranger" in Australia (p. 220).

Next to the recurring motif of the nomads versus the settlers, the
motif of walking takes center stage throughout the notebooks. Ironically, the one long walk Bruce himself attempts ends prematurely, as
heat and wild animals force him off Mount Liebler and back to the comfort and coolness of his trailer. But he includes in the notebooks his note
that in the East, wandering—especially walking—"re-establishes the
original harmony which once existed between man and the universe" (p.
178). He records on the next page a Sufi religious concept, *siyahat,*
which means that the

> action or rhythm of walking—was used as a technique for dissolving the
> attachments of the world and allowing men to lose themselves in God.
>   The aim of the dervish was to become a "dead man walking": one
> whose body stays alive on the earth yet whose soul is already in heaven.
> (p. 179)

How different that phrase is from its American use in prisons, where
"dead man walking" refers to the prisoner's last walk, to his execution.
Bruce also extracts from a Sufi manual, the *Kashf-al-Mahjub,* that a
dervish, toward the end of his journey, "becomes the Way not the way-
farer" (p. 179). Arkady reminds Bruce that the aboriginals hold the same
belief: " 'Many men afterwards become country, in that place, Ancestors.'
. . . By spending his whole life walking and singing his Ancestor's Songline,
a man eventually becomes the track, the Ancestor and the song" (p. 179).

Bruce further notes that in early Christianity there were two distinct kinds of walking pilgrimages. The first was a wandering in search of God in imitation of Jesus and Abraham, who were examples of nomadic prophets. The other pilgrimage was a penitential one, in which the sinner walked and assumed the role of a beggar, forever lamenting his sins. Sacred walking was a way of trying to attain his salvation on earth and atoning for his sins, usually sins of violence: "The idea that walking dissolved crimes of violence goes back to the wanderings forced on Cain to atone for the murder of his brother" (p. 180). Bruce encountered a similar figure in his travels in Mauritania. There he was called the *bhagi,* or "holy wanderer." He traveled from oasis to oasis and recited the Koran by heart for the edification of the faithful. His recitation so accelerated that he finally attained a trancelike state and appeared to the crowd to be speaking directly from God (p. 181).

Bruce then searches for evidence of the efficacy of walking and its relationship with infants and their care. He once discovered in Dr. John Bowlby's book *Attachment and Loss* evidence that walking directly influences the infant's mental and emotional health. Bowlby found that infants inevitably cried when they were left alone and that the quickest way to silence them was for the mother to rock her baby as she walked around (p. 229). Outside of the relentless search for sustenance, a baby not even old enough to walk puts all energies into attempting to do so. Bruce finds further evidence of the importance of walking in his notes from Osip Mandelstam's *Conversations about Dante.* Mandelstam found Dante greatly concerned with "the human gait, the measure and rhythm of walking, the foot and its shape. The step, linked to the breathing and saturated with thought: this Dante understands as the beginning of prosody" (p. 230). Further, Proust asserted that the " 'walks' of childhood form the raw material of our intelligence" (p. 272). Chatwin said in his *Granta* interview that Mandelstam's comments on Dante's connection of the importance of the foot with writing is "a key text" ("Interview," 37). Ignatieff concludes that the connection is also

> "talismanic for a book like yours about the relationship between walking and writing."

CHATWIN: "Absolutely. Mandelstam himself could only compose on the hoof. He had to be walking, when actually writing a poem. He had an idea that the production of words in the larynx was dependent on the action of the feet."

IGNATIEFF: "You believe this . . . ?"

CHATWIN: "Oh, yes. Like dogma!" (p. 37)

Bruce reverts intermittently to the narrative, which is coming to its conclusion, but only to reveal that Arkady has not yet returned from his difficult negotiations with Titus and the Amadeus Mob. The information in the notebooks has undoubtedly expanded the depth and spiritual significance of an ordinary trip into the dry heart of aboriginal Australia. Events that would have appeared trivial before the "Notebooks" section now take on mythic dimensions.

Finally, after three weeks, Arkady returns to Cullen and brings mostly good news. Titus and the railway seem to have worked out their difficulties; his Songlines will not be violated if the company extends the railroad, although there is some question about whether it will be able to afford to do so. Arkady announces, almost triumphantly, that due to budgetary problems he is out of a job. The other good news is that Arkady and Marian are deeply in love and will marry. The beginning of the penultimate chapter finds Bruce, Arkady, Marian, Limpy, and the man from Amadeus driving out for a final conference with Titus about the missing *tjuringas*. After several hours, Titus declares that the *tjuringas* have been returned to their proper owners and that the creation will no longer be uncreated.

In the final chapter Bruce bids farewell to Rolf and Wendy. Limpy insists on taking Bruce, Arkady, and Marian to visit Cycad Valley, a location very important on his Songline but a place he has never before visited: "Limpy's Dreaming, the Native Cat, ran straight down the middle of the stream-bed" (*The Songlines,* 291). The major reason Limpy wants to visit this ancestral area is that three of his distant relatives are dying right next to their *tjuringa* storehouse. After a difficult seven-hour journey, they arrive at the site, then continue deeper into the desert on foot. Bruce enters into his notebooks essential information about the connection between dying, one's *tjuringa,* and Songlines: "In Aboriginal Australia, there are specific rules for 'going back' (or, rather, for singing your way to where you belong: to your 'conception site,' to the place where your tjuringa is stored. Only then can you become—or re-become—the Ancestor" (p. 293).

The last scene is a fitting closing to this, Chatwin's longest and most complex book, because it brings together in a brilliantly comprehensive image the way the Songlines sacramentalize every human event and transfigure the individual, the song, the land, and the ancestors into one profound event—that of "going back in":

> In a clearing there were . . . three dying men. They were almost skeletons. Their beards and hair had gone. . . . When they heard who Limpy was, all three smiled, spontaneously, the same toothless grin. . . .
> They were all right. They knew where they were going, smiling at death in the shade of a ghost-gum. (p. 294)

Chatwin could not have concluded his sprawling book with a more appropriate image; *The Songlines* is a profound examination and analysis of the sacred, or holy, as it is lived and practiced by a disappearing race of doomed people. As such, the book is his final meditation and judgment on the incalculable damage done by a European technological culture on the instinctual lives of the vulnerable aboriginals of Australia.

Though the message of *The Songlines* is essentially a dark, pessimistic one, the good-natured humor and serene acceptance of the aboriginals are the images the readers of the book carry away with them and keep. There is a scene early in the book in which Arkady is attempting to bring Bruce to a deeper understanding and appreciation of the profound but practical application and meaning of the Songlines in the natives' daily lives: " 'Sometimes,' said Arkady, 'I'll be driving my "Old Men" through the desert, and we'll come to a ridge of sandhills, and suddenly they'll all start singing. "What are you mob singing?" I'll ask, and they'll say, "Singing up the country, boss. Makes the country come up quicker" ' " (p. 14).

Chapter Six
Utz: "Museum or Mausoleum?"

To the casual reader it might be difficult to find many similarities between the macrocosm of *The Songlines* and the microcosm of *Utz*. How could the same author move so casually from cosmic mappings of aboriginal mythopoesis to the incredibly attenuated world of one lone collector of precious Meissen figurines? Although critic Michael Dirda asserts that Chatwin "never published the same kind of book twice," similar thematic and structural patterns do, however, reappear throughout the major works, including *Utz*. Dirda also adds, correctly, that "each is an off-beat masterpiece."[1]

What unifies all five of these wildly diverse books is that they all share, in various degrees, the common theme of the fall of a once-glorious Eden into a devastated wasteland. *The Songlines* carefully delineates the dynamics of that fall in the relentless, arrogant, and devious methods by which the colonials seized the aboriginals' lands and dispatched them into reservations, where they were, and are, plagued by alcoholism, drugs, despair, and early death. The aboriginals' Eden collapsed into a spiritual wasteland. *Utz* outlines, in a much subtler way, that Western civilization—as seen in one of its most cultivated centers, Prague—fell from its glorious eighteenth-century heyday into a shabby, desperate, and ultimately empty place. That, at least, is the view of one Kaspar Joachim Utz, the central character in, according to some, Chatwin's most accomplished book.

On closer examination, other resonating parallels between Chatwin's earlier works and *Utz* begin to surface. John Lanchester, speaking of the eighteenth-century flavor of *The Songlines,* claims that *Utz*, Chatwin's next novel, may very well be the opposite of what readers expect: "Extrapolating negatively, then, one can guess that Chatwin's new novel [*Utz*] is unsprawling and unmetaphysical, un-18th century in tone and in technique, set in the Old World and with a central theme which has something to do with not being a nomad. And so it proves" ("A Pom," 10). But who could have guessed that *On the Black Hill*'s anchoritic world would follow the cultural exoticisms of *In Patagonia* and *The Viceroy of Ouidah*? Just as the macrocosmic content and themes of

Chatwin's first two novels were succeeded by the modest world of *On the Black Hill,* so too does *Utz's* miniaturized world supplant *The Songlines's* massive one. Nicholas Murray asserts that, even though this was Chatwin's shortest book, "a case could be made for its being his most perfect work" (*Bruce Chatwin,* 109).

As is the case for three of Chatwin's other books, *Utz* came out of an assignment for Sotheby's for which he had to travel to Prague to consult with a collector of rare Meissen porcelain figurines. Chatwin characterized the collector as a monk who had "shrunk his horizons down to those of his best friends, who were all porcelain figures seven inches high" (*Bruce Chatwin,* 108). But Chatwin saw in that man a figure like himself; Chatwin's fantasy too was to "sit in a cell and never move again" (p. 108). One prototype, however, was never enough for Bruce Chatwin's fecund imagination. Indeed, Murray found evidence in two of Chatwin's essays of two other real-life characters whom Chatwin visited and interviewed; both essays appear in Chatwin's collection *What Am I Doing Here.* The first character was the legendary Russian architect Konstantin Melnikov, who lived for 40 years in isolation, thanks to the Communist authorities, in an ultramodern house in Moscow, where he reigned as one of the last of the leftist artists from the 1920s. The other prototype was the Soviet Union's leading private art collector, George Costakis, who "had rescued the products of the Futurist school and turned his house into a museum" (p. 107). The authorities allowed Costakis to keep the collection in his home provided he left it to one of the state museums after his death. The parallels between these three figures and Kaspar Utz are impossible to ignore.

Michael Dirda also finds literary prototypes for Kaspar Utz in such well-known Russian and east European writers as Turgenev, Gogol, and Chekhov, and in Elias Canetti's *Auto-da-fé:* "Even closer to home, there are echoes of Kafka and allusions to the Jewish monster of Prague, The Golem, immortalized in the novels of Gustave Meyrink" ("Collector," 1).

Thematically, *Utz* is richer than both *In Patagonia* and *Viceroy* and combines the lessons of both *The Songlines* and *On the Black Hill.* Besides the fall and the Eden/wasteland dichotomies, *Utz* explores the additional themes of artistic obsession, mutability, exile, and mortality—all of which are consonant with Chatwin's own obsessions at the time of his impending death. During the writing of *Utz* he must have known that AIDS was going to kill him soon, a possibility that makes his meditations on art and its relationship with death almost unbearably poignant and courageous. There is little question that *Utz* can and should be read as his final musings on his own all-too-short life.

Though *Utz,* like Chatwin's previous novels, is a meditation on the ruins of culture and society, it is additionally a meditation on Chatwin's own sad ruins, as AIDS is causing his formerly attractive body to waste away. One of the book's most profoundly moving moments takes place when the narrator muses about the permanence of mirrors and the impermanence of life, a classic ode on mutability. He describes Utz's face as " 'waxy in texture,' but now in the candlelight its texture seemed like melted wax. I looked at the ageless complexion of the Dresden ladies. Things, I reflected, are tougher than people. Things are the changeless mirror in which we watch ourselves disintegrate. Nothing is more age-ing than a collection of works of art."[2] Ironically, though, *Utz* is also Chatwin's most comic novel and shows his ability to laugh at himself, the feckless American collector, and at the general silliness of art's entire commercialized enterprise. Partly for these reasons, Salman Rushdie viewed *Utz* as a fresh development in Chatwin's literary career: "The thing I find saddest about *Utz* is that it suggests to me that Bruce was indeed beginning that new, light-spirited phase of flight. *Utz* is all we have of what had become possible for him once his Australian odyssey helped him express the ideas which he carried about for so many years" (*Imaginary Homelands,* 235).

Though much of the novel's energy comes from the vividness of a few idiosyncratic characters, the city of Prague is also a major character; Kaspar Utz describes his love-hate relationship with its beauty and shoddiness. He cannot stay away from it but finds he must holiday at the French resort of Vichy once a year, in spite of finding its decadence stifling after a few days.

Besides being a meditation on the fall of Western culture, there is little question that *Utz* is a detective novel. The book's central mystery is the disappearance of a priceless collection of rare Meissen figurines. What happened to it? Did Utz destroy it, or did Marta the maid? Solving that mystery is what occupies the narrator, a sleuth in the tradition of Graham Greene, Eric Ambler, or John le Carré, though with considerably more humor, during the last third of the novel. Gabriele Annan suggests that *Utz's* mystery is not " 'whodunit,' but why did he do it."[3]

Critic John Krizanc characterizes the work as "the first epic novella" that manages to cover a variety of subjects, such as "the psychopathology of the compulsive collector . . . the legend of the Golem . . . a history of Czechoslovakia . . . [and] the technique of bringing an operatic diva to orgasm."[4] Critic Peter Conrad sees the novel's sprawling canvas as evidence that it could be considered a postmodern work. He calls it "that punctiliously postmodern thing, a novel about its own problems in getting itself written."[5] Fred Shafer suggests that *Utz*'s form and function are one insofar as the novel is "a finely polished miniature."[6] It is remarkable that Chatwin manages to cover a larger range of topics and themes in this novella than he did in either *Viceroy* or *On the Black Hill,* and in a lapidary prose style that combines both wit and wisdom.

There is little question, though, that *Utz* is very much a dialogic novel in which Chatwin uses dialogue throughout (as does Diderot in *Jacques Le Fataliste*), as he did in *The Songlines.* Utz, the master, conveys the bulk of his esoteric information to the narrator through dialogue: the narrator asks questions and Utz answers them, though at times in indirect and oblique ways. Much of the character of both men can be read in the way they regard each other. Utz is understandably paranoid about anyone asking questions about his priceless figurines, whereas the narrator finds himself learning about such esoteric topics as alchemy, hermeticism, the history of the Austro-Hungarian empire, the cabala, and other related occult, historical, and political traditions. The narrator undergoes a fall from his relative innocence to the complexity and depth of central European greed and corruption and, most important, realizes that things are never as they first appear. As Gabriele Annan puts it, "*Utz* is a minefield of clues, false, ambiguous, some possibly real. Nothing is what it seems: even the stuffed bear in a Prague restaurant is not a brown bear from the Carpathians, but a grizzly shot in the Yukon" ("Rules of the Game," 6).

Much of the novel's humor comes out of similar ironic reversals of expectations. For example, *Utz* reverses the traditional quest for the grail that is fundamental in Western literature. In a sense, *Utz* is about the curse of possessing the grail, because in this work the problem is that Utz *possesses* his treasure—more than 1,000 Meissen figurines worth millions. His quest has been wildly successful, and his task is now to discover how to keep his collection out of the hands of those who don't appreciate its aesthetic value—the philistine bureaucrats who merely count and label and put away. Like the mindless museumgoers in T. S. Eliot's "Love Song of J. Alfred Prufrock," who "come and go talking of Michelangelo" and miss the profound message of his passionate artistic expression, the bureaucratic proles are incapable of comprehending the spiritual significance of such precious objects.

Chatwin—again reversing expectations—shows, however, that the curse of possession may well have inadvertently helped Utz to find true love. The Meissen figurines function somewhat like the alchemical philosopher's stone or the grail in that they have the power to transform lead into gold, sickness into health, despair into redemptive hope. Though it appears that the treasure is irrevocably gone and that Utz is responsible for its disappearance, its potential to transform is still in operation. Its restorative power works paradoxically insofar as Utz's rejection of his obsession enables him to be transformed by his powerful love for Marta. Not only are things not what they seem, they are frequently the exact opposite of what they seem and function as alchemical exemplars of the transmuting power of selflessness that comes from rejecting material objects; that is, an emptying of self. Chatwin's unspoken model is again St. Francis of Assisi, the nomadic mendicant who understood that possessing material objects never liberates and often becomes a curse.

The opening of *Utz* is a delightful illustration of comic reanimation. The story begins at the moment of Kaspar Joachim Utz's death, on 7 March 1974. Utz died in his apartment at no. 5 Siroka Street, which overlooks the Jewish Cemetery. The funeral, which Utz himself planned meticulously, is attended by only two people: Dr. Orlik and Utz's longtime companion and housekeeper, Marta. The funeral is held at the church of St. Sigismund, a German name for a Burgundian saint and king that means "victory"—not for the Czechs but for their German invaders. Seemingly irrelevant allusions and geographical locations take on added significance as the narrative moves forward, and many of these details are used ironically. For example, the organist is too lazy to get out of bed, so he hires one of the janitors to play the two chords he learned the day before. The hired pallbearers make little attempt to hide their boredom. The priest barely gets through the funeral and refuses to go to the cemetery. Utz even arranged and paid for the valedictory breakfast at the fancy Hotel Bristol, but only Dr. Orlik and Marta attend. After a few glasses of tokay, they toast not Utz but the Yukon Bear—their country's fraternal protector from invaders.

The second chapter—none of the chapters or sections are labeled—reverts back to the summer of 1967, a year before the Soviet invasion of Czechoslovakia. The unnamed narrator, who recalls the reason for his visit to the country, is certainly Bruce Chatwin, who visited Czechoslovakia in 1966 for his employer, Sotheby's, to consult with a collector of rare Meissen figurines just before leaving the firm. The purpose of the narrator's visit, however, is to do some "historical research. The editor of a magazine, knowing of my interest in the Northern Renaissance, had commissioned me to write an article on the Emperor Rudolf's passion for collecting erotica: a passion which, in his later years, was his only cure for depression. I intended the article to be part of a larger work on the psychology—or psychopathology—of the compulsive collector" (*Utz*, 12). Although he claims that this project comes to nothing, the psychopathology of the compulsive collector is exactly what *Utz* is about.

Again moving back, to just before his visit to Prague, the narrator tells of stopping at the Schloss Ambras to see the "cabinet of curiosities" assembled by the emperor Rudolf's uncle, the notoriously famous Archduke Ferdinand of Austria, whose assassination occasioned World War I. Listing both Ferdinand's and Rudolf's treasures, the narrator alludes, comically, to some priceless, legendary treasures: "the Hapsburg family narwhal horn, and a Late Roman agate tazza that might or might not be the Holy Grail . . . Rudolf's treasures—his mandragoras . . . his bezoar stone, his unicorn cup . . . his nails from Noah's Ark and the phial of dust from which God created Adam—had long ago vanished from Prague" (p. 13).

A few sentences later the narrator speaks of wanting to look for clues to Rudolf's exotic interests in astrology and astronomy: "(Tycho Brahé and Kepler were his protégés). Or search with his alchemists for the philosopher's Stone. Or debate with learned rabbis the mysteries of the Cabbala" (p. 14). Though such descriptions attest to Chatwin's marvelous handling of the most precious and sophisticated details and reveal his comprehensive knowledge of the ancient and modern art worlds, they also begin to add up to a number of meaningful motifs, which he develops throughout the rest of the novel. For example, images of the Holy Grail consistently surround the priceless Meissen figurines, which become, in effect, a version of the Grail. And certainly the fact that an eighteenth-century alchemist, Johannes Böttger, created porcelain from the clay found in Dresden and Meissen foreshadows the narrator's growing interest in alchemical processes as an analogue of creativity. Chatwin cleverly constructs several subtexts beneath the obvious narrative out of alchemical, gnostic, cabalistic, hermetic, and astrological lore, subtexts that deepen and enrich—sometimes quite comically—a thin plot line. All of this seemingly unimportant information, or "fluff," is a cleverly constructed overture that presents important motifs that will develop into themes as the novel moves forward *and* backward.

In the next section the narrator meets a historian who, once hearing of his interests in the history of porcelain and its connections to some of eastern Europe's most exotic figures, sends him to Utz, whom he calls "a Rudolf of our time" (p. 16).

Chatwin then gives a detailed biography of Kaspar Utz's family, but not before announcing that he is the owner of "a spectacular collection of Meissen porcelain which, through his adroit manoeuvers, had survived the Second World War and the years of Stalinism in Czechoslovakia. By 1967 it numbered over a thousand pieces—all crammed into the tiny two-roomed flat on Siroka Street" (p. 16). The Utz family were originally Saxon landowners in the Sudetenland but maintained a house in Dresden. Chatwin then—almost as a foil in this mystery novel—plays with the etymology of the name Utz. (Once he begins to delve into etymologies, the reader knows he is getting serious.) Using Grimm's *Etymological Wordbook,* he claims the word " 'utz' carries any number of negative connotations: 'drunk,' 'dimwit,' 'card-sharp' . . . in the dialect of Lower Swabia, ['utz'] is the equivalent of 'Any old Tom, Dick or Harry' " (pp. 16–17). When he looks up the name in the *Oxford Dictionary of Surnames,* a curious reader finds that Utz is the diminutive Czech equivalent of the German name Ulrich, whose Old High German source is Odalric, meaning "prosperous and powerful": odal equals prosperity and riches equals power. St. Ulrich of Augsburg, a tenth-century bishop, was invoked during mouse and rat plagues—certainly comically apt metaphors for the country's Russian and German invaders. St. Ulrich is also symbolized in Christian iconography as a fish; Utz makes his first appearance and first acquaintance with the narrator in the Restaurant Pstruh (the Trout Restaurant) in Prague. St. Ulrich was also the first German bishop given the right to mint coins, a vaguely alchemical activity.

It was at the family's summer chateau, Ceske Krízove, that the child Kaspar fell in love with porcelain figurines. He found himself "[b]ewitched by a figurine of Harlequin that had been modelled by the greatest of Meissen modellers, J. J. Kaendler. The Harlequin sat on a tree trunk. His taut frame was sheathed in a costume of multi-coloured chevrons. In one hand he waved an oxidized silver tankard; in the other a floppy yellow hat. Over his face there was a leering orange mask; 'I want him,' said Kaspar" (p. 18).

Four years later, Utz owned that Harlequin figure and began to collect others one by one. The young Kaspar "had found his vocation: he would devote his life to collecting—'rescuing' as he came to call it—the porcelains of the Meissen factory" (p. 19). He also began to publish articles on the figurines in respectable journals.

As the years rolled by Utz came to identify museums and their curators as the enemy of art because they prevented human contact with these precious figurines. He became an advocate for the private ownership of such treasures, and believed that museums should be looted every 50 years and their collections returned to circulation. The young Kaspar insisted that these objects must be touched and that their owners needed to touch them: "As a young child will reach out to handle the thing it names, so the passionate collector . . . restores to the object the life-giving touch of its maker" (p. 20). Here, Chatwin entertains notions about the artist and his creation as agents of the transforming power of art, notions that resemble claims made of such objects as the Holy Grail or the philosopher's stone.

Utz's pathological need to collect—to rescue—these figures brought with it an insensitivity to whatever political turmoil happened to be taking place. Indeed, he looked upon national chaos as an opportunity for a serious collector and, in fact, "welcomed the cataclysms that flung fresh work onto the market. 'Wars, pogroms and revolutions,' he used to say, 'offer excellent opportunities for the collector.' The stock market crash was one such opportunity. Kristallnacht was another. That same week he hastened to Berlin to buy porcelains, in U.S. dollars, from Jewish connoisseurs who wished to emigrate. At the end of the war he would offer a similar service to aristocrats fleeing from the Soviet Army" (p. 21).

Though Utz was disinterested in politics generally—and part Jewish—he was not above using his father's World War I decoration to save himself from Reinhard Heydrich, the butcher of Prague's thugs who came to arrest him one day. Though Utz somehow remained unharmed in Prague during the war, he was treated by some patriotic Czechs as a collaborator because he had passed on some important information to members of Goering's art squad. However, he claimed that such information could have been easily obtained by anyone who knew how to use an art library and that his act had actually saved a number of his Jewish friends from the gas chamber. Utz asserted, "What, after all, was the value of a Titian or a Tiepolo if one human life could be saved?" (p. 24). Several critics doubt that this kind of humanistic sentiment is consistent with Utz's all-consuming greed for Dresden porcelain at almost *any* price.

Even when the Soviets invaded Prague and nationalized all the art museums, Utz somehow worked out a deal whereby they permitted him to keep his collection but only on the condition that it become the property of the state upon his death, a condition similar to the one George Kostakis made with the Soviet government.

Chapter 6 begins with a description of Utz's appearance by the narrator as he meets with him and Dr. Orlik at the Restaurant Pstruh, where

Dr. Orlik and Utz have dined every Thursday since 1946. Dr. Orlik is an old friend of Utz's and a well-known scholar in two very different areas: he is a trained paleontologist who specializes in the study of the woolly mammoth and is also a specialist in the study of flies. If one has any doubt that Chatwin is using the etymological histories of proper names other than Utz ironically to depict character, one need only consider the comic possibilities of both of Dr. Vaclav Orlik's names. Dr. Orlik's surname—a Czech version of the Russian Orlov—means "eagle" or "king of the birds," but Dr. Orlik's primary interest is in the eagle's exact opposite, the fly. Chatwin adds to the reader's growing suspicions that he is using names ironically when he describes Dr. Orlik's hand: "His hand—rather a crustacean claw than a hand—gave mine a painful nip and moved on to attack the pretzels. His forehead was scoured with deep furrows. I stared with amazement at the see-saw motion of his jaw" (p. 29). There can be little doubt that Chatwin's attribution of animal-like characteristics to Dr. Orlik's anatomy is intended for minor but nonetheless comic effect.

Dr. Orlik's first name, Vaclav, is the Russian name for the patron saint of Bohemia, St. Wenceslas, for whom Wenceslas Square, where he, Utz, and the narrator are having lunch at Restaurant Pstruh, was named. As mentioned previously, the Czech word *pstruh* means "trout," this particular restaurant's specialty. However, the few remaining trout are being devoured by the "four fat Party Members." That a Czech citizen who virulently hates the Russian-Communist usurpers has a Russianized name of the patron saint of Bohemia is an ironic twist. Again, the characters' proper names are not only not what they seem but are, at times, the exact opposite. Once the reader becomes conscious of the naturalistic pattern of names that seems to be emerging, an already comic scene becomes even funnier, particularly the one in which Dr. Orlik questions the narrator about a famous English scientist, Professor Horsefield, who wrote favorably about one of Dr. Orlik's articles 40 years earlier in the *Journal of Animal Psychology*. Chatwin may be humorously suggesting that Czechoslovakia has become, under the deterministic Marxists, a case study of animal psychology rather than any kind of human environment where art can grow and develop in an atmosphere of free expression.

Dr. Orlik and the narrator choose to eat carp instead of the specialty of the house, but the word "carp" has been misspelled on the menu to read "crap," which fosters a lengthy and often hilarious dialogue. Indeed, the word "crap" would undoubtedly apply to the depths to which the grand Czech cultural world has fallen under the mean-spirited Communists. Appropriately, Dr. Orlik's interests changed from the regal eagle (of his name) to the *Musca domestica*—the common housefly, whose favorite nesting place and eatery is crap.

Kaspar Utz's first name is another example of Chatwin's gnomic sense of humor. The name Kaspar comes from a Persian word meaning "treasurer," and certainly Utz's function throughout the book is keeper of the great treasure. Kaspar is also the name of one of the Three Kings, or Wise Men—the Magi—who brought gifts to the infant Jesus from the East. ("The Infant of Prague" is the only officially sanctioned simulacrum of Christ as an infant.) Kaspar is the king who brought gold; the other two, Melchior and Balthazar, brought frankincense and myrrh, respectively. These figures are sometimes thought of as sorcerers, astrologers, or alchemists—bearers of the riches of the East, where both porcelain and alchemy originated. Certainly Utz can be viewed as a modern-day alchemist who transforms clay into gold, that is, rare Dresden figurines into huge money-making opportunities. One wonders if Chatwin is also alluding, waggishly, to the cartoon character Casper the ghost; officially, Kaspar Utz is a ghost throughout the book since he is dead from the first page. Like the dead throughout James Joyce's *The Dead*, the memory of whom takes center stage throughout, Kaspar's Utz's ghostly presence makes it seem as though he were alive throughout the novel.

After their tasty carp at the Restaurant Pstruh, Utz takes the narrator on a guided tour of some of Prague's most famous landmarks: several baroque, or rococo, palaces—the Vrtba, the Pálffy, and the Lobkovic. That evening they end up at the Old Jewish Cemetery, where Utz begins to tell the narrator some stories about the famous rabbi Loew, who is buried there. This rabbi was the undisputed leader of the Jews in Prague in the sixteenth century and was also the creator of the famous Yossel the Golem from the mud of the River Vltava. Rabbi Loew was also a devout cabalist. But what fascinates Utz most is the connection between stories of the golem—an artificial, or mechanical, man made from clay—and the creation story from the Torah. God fashioned Adam out of clay; Adam (whose name means "clay" in Hebrew) became, then, besides the first person, the first ceramic sculpture. Utz then relates a number of stories about golems that became more powerful than their creators and then destroyed them. They could become a kind of Frankenstein monster if they were not kept under control. It is also clear that golem makers were alchemists of a sort who possessed arcane secrets that were considered sinful and idolatrous. The Jews of the six-teenth century believed that a man-made figure was a blasphemy and by its very nature sought out its own destruction. The narrator also begins to see that Utz's gnostic utterances suggest that he believes porcelains—like golems—may be living creatures of a sort, and that art collecting may be a form of idolatry.

Chapter 11 opens at the threshold to Utz's apartment, and in the entranceway sits the threshold guardian and housekeeper, Marta, who is preparing some snacks for Utz and the narrator. In chapters 11 to 14, Chatwin describes the interior of Utz's home, a Meissen sanctuary filled with precious pieces of porcelain, many of which were modeled by either Kaendler, Eberlein, or Böttger himself. It is the most extensive collec-tion the narrator has ever seen. But what strikes him most is the dra-matic manner in which Utz has arranged his treasure: "It was a narrow room, made narrower by the double bank of plate-glass shelves, all of them crammed with porcelain, that reached from floor to ceiling. The shelves were backed with mirror, so that you had the illusion of entering an enfilade of glittering chambers, a 'dream palace' multiplied to infin-ity, through which human forms flitted like insubstantial shadows" (p. 49). No other image in the novel so profoundly or so accurately illus-trates the temporality of human existence.

An opulent collection in such depressed surroundings makes it seem even more magnificent, and the narrator remembers researching artists such as Kaendler and a strange pathological condition called *Porzel-lankrankheit*—"porcelain sickness"—which debilitated Augustus the Strong so thoroughly that his government fell into a crisis of power. The narrator notices that Utz has arranged—or staged, as it were—the col-lection "to reflect the moods and facets of the 'Porcelain Century': the wit, the charm, the gallantry, the love of the exotic, the heartlessness and light-hearted gaiety—before they were swept away by revolution and the tramp of armies" (p. 51).

The banks of shelves are sometimes arranged in rows of five or six fig-ures, and the most impressive display is that of eighteenth-century fig-urines of characters from "the Commedia dell' Arte: Harlequin and Columbine, Brighella and Pantaloon, Scaramouche and Truffaldino" (p. 52). Next come the ladies of the court: "Madame Pompadour, in a lilac dress scattered with roses, sang the aria from Lully's 'Acis and Galatea' which she had sung in real life" (p. 53). Next come characters from "the lower orders": miners, rope-makers, and a drunken fisherman. And then a mélange of shepherds, Tartars, Malabars, "a party of freemasons," and

"an endlessly grieving Mater Dolorosa" (p. 53). On lower levels are figures from the animal kingdom: monkeys, partridges, parrots, a camel, a
Lipizzaner, and the required pug dog. Utz then shows him the seven figures of Harlequin, pointing out the one his grandmother gave him when
he was a boy, the one that ignited his desire for others of its kind.

Chatwin inevitably arrives at the creation of a mythopoeic world in
all of his books: Mama Wéwé's syncretic menagerie in *Viceroy,* the native
museums of the Salesian fathers in *In Patagonia,* the aboriginals' portable
mythopoeic *tjuringas* in *The Songlines,* and *The Broad and Narrow Path* in
On the Black Hill. All of the novels' main characters require a private
enshrinement of their sense of the sacred to sustain them in their wasteland world and give that world a spiritual dimension and meaning it
would not otherwise have. In short, their private shrines transform the
fallen world around them and restore it to its previous Edenic innocence.
Utz's "cabinet of curiosities" is his private shrine.

Utz's narration then moves back to 1952, when three Communist
bureaucrats invaded his apartment to photograph all of his treasures so
that on his death the state would know what might be missing. Utz
confessed that he felt so violated that he entertained thoughts of suicide.
Instead, he decided that he needed a vacation away from Prague. On his
way to a spa at Vichy in France, he would stop in Switzerland to begin
to make plans to escape—with his treasures—the confines of east European Communism.

Utz then gives the narrator a history of his domestic servant, Marta,
whose name alludes to the biblical housekeeper and servant Martha
from the story about Christ's visit to the home of Lazarus and his sisters
Mary and Martha. As Christ is holding forth, Lazarus and Mary listen
intently while Martha performs all the household duties, like cooking
and keeping the guests happy. Christ calls attention to Martha's
unselfishness and states that her devotion to menial domestic chores is
every bit as important as listening to him speak. Utz wants the narrator
to know that Marta is much more than a domestic but leaves him ignorant as to why. Chatwin saves the explanation of Utz's secrecy for the
end of the book.

Utz first observed Martha as he was passing through her village of Kostelec and saw her being hounded down a street by a mob of brutal villagers
who could have come out of Jerzy Kosinski's *Painted Bird.* He took her
back to his family's summer estate at Ceske Krízove, where she became a
domestic servant and attended his every need. Though there were rumors
that she was his lover, her real value lay in her utter loyalty: "Only she

knew the hay-loft where the Hebrew scholar Dr. Kraus—and his Tal-
muds—was in hiding: she would risk her life to fetch him food. Only she
had the key to the cellar where, throughout the War, the porcelains were
stored" (p. 63). She has been with Utz from the early days of the Communist takeover in the late 1940s and would stay till the end of his life in
1973. She now sleeps in an attic room a few doors down Siroka Street.

The novel's next seven chapters detail Utz's ultimately unsatisfactory
trip to Vichy, the overly rich food, and the cold women. His journey
echoes similar journeys taken by some of Thomas Mann's lonely and for-
lorn bachelors—Gustave von Aschenbach from *Death in Venice,* Tonio
Kröger, who travels north in the novella of the same name, and the
character from Anton Chekhov's great story "The Lady with the Dog";
Utz, however, unlike that ultimately unfortunate male, failed to meet
any women who were even slightly interested in him; he is a short, ugly
man. If readers of *Utz* don't make these connections to characters and
situations out of Mann and Chekhov, Chatwin mentions that Utz read
Mann's *Magic Mountain* (p. 65) on the train (he didn't want to be too
obvious) and that a woman with a dog who interested him reminded
him of the woman in the Chekhov story (p. 76). Utz found France decadent and began to yearn for the clarity and wholesomeness of Prague.
But in spite of these feelings he continued to make the journey annually.
Utz then reveals that he keeps an additional collection of Meissen figurines in a bank in Geneva, a collection he intends to use as a bargaining
agent when he eventually decides to escape the confines of Communism.

Utz is, though, a divided man: he oscillates between his hatred of the
bureaucratic proles who run the government and his disgust over the
excesses of capitalism he sees in France. Though the barbed wire at
the Czech frontier depresses him, he is relieved "that there were no more
advertizing billboards" (p. 88). As long as he is able to escape his homeland for a vacation, he will remain there: "He was not going to join the
flow of exiles. He would not sit complaining in rented rooms. He knew
that anti-Communist rhetoric was as deadly as its Communist counterpart. He would not give up his country. Not for them!" (p. 87). Knowing how disgusted Chatwin himself became with the capitalistic greed
and competition that he witnessed at Sotheby's, it seems appropriate
that Utz expresses similar bitter feelings.

The pathetic but loyal Marta appears more frequently as Utz's narration continues. It's almost as if in telling his story to the narrator he is
uncovering his true feelings about Marta's importance to his happiness
and well-being. Could he actually be in love with her?

As he is talking to the narrator, Utz begins to realize how enslaving his treasure has become. He knows that he, too, is suffering from a severe case of *Porzellankranheit*—"porcelain sickness." But he finds himself caught between the sacramental sustenance that comes from touching his Grail-like objects and the lure of selling his treasure to the capitalists of the West. He is also haunted by the fate of the alchemist who invented porcelain: "In 1719 Böttger dies, of drink, depression, delusion, and chemical poisoning" (p. 108). In Utz's oscillations between his sedentary life at Siroka Street and his journeys to Vichy, Geneva, and sometimes Paris, another recurring Chatwinian pattern surfaces—that pull between Cain the city founder, and thus the ironic effects of civilization, and the pastoral Abel.

After Utz relates a hilarious story about his acquisition of a famous Neapolitan porcelain, "The Spaghetti Eater," from a Dr. Marius Frankfurter of New York, he and the narrator have a modest dinner prepared by the faithful Marta. During dinner Utz goes into a lengthy dissertation on the etymological origins of the word *porcelain* and claims that it was coined by Marco Polo. Cowrie shells were once used as currency in Africa and Asia—Chatwin's readers will recall their use as money by the kings of Dahomey in *Viceroy*. Because the shells resemble pigs, Marco Polo called them "porcelain shells"—*porcella* means "little sow" in Italian. Utz inquires whether the narrator has read the letters of the Italian Jesuit Father Mateo Ricci on his visits to China, or Father d'Entrecolles's description of the manufacture of porcelain. And does he understand the immense importance and influence of Chinese porcelain on the European imagination during the seventeenth century? The Chinese built pagodas of porcelain and considered them their "gold." When Utz begins to detail the life of the inventor of European porcelain, Johannes Böttger, the narrator scurries for his notebook.

Chatwin uses these seeming diversions the same way he uses large sections of biographical and historical facts in *The Songlines* and *In Patagonia*. The information is itself compelling, but it also serves to document Utz's intellectual life and thereby expand a very thin plot. Once again, the depth and exactitude of the enormous range of information Chatwin provides, in this case about the history of porcelain and its alchemical background, is stunning. But it is also evident that such information was more than dry fact for Chatwin's creative imagination: it was high drama that clarified the roots of pathological collectors of every kind from the beginning of history, particularly those living in Europe in the seventeenth and eighteenth centuries.

Such information also serves as a reminder that studies in alchemy are not to be relegated to the realm of the occult but are vitally important to a proper understanding of the history of science, religion, psychology, and the development of the imagination. Carl Jung wrote two volumes on alchemy, and the works of such major mythopoeic American poets as Charles Olson, Robert Duncan, Jerome Rothenberg, Robert Kelly, and Clayton Eshleman were more than casually influenced not only by Jung but also by the same scholars Böttger read: Raymond Lull, Paracelsus, and Van Helmont. Modern writers' interest in alchemy comes out of their conviction that creativity is a kind of alchemical process in which the imagination transmutes the leaden quotidian into the gold of artistic creation.

The next lengthy section is devoted to Utz's detailed narration of the life and times of Johannes Böttger, who invented porcelain in Europe only after a number of life-threatening experiments. We also learn of the pursuits of a pederastic monk and of the ladies of the court of King Frederick William. The young Böttger obtained a vial of red tincture, "or Ruby Lion, a grain of which will transmute lead into gold . . . and performs his first 'successful' transmutation" (p. 106). From then on he was treated like royalty but was kept in prison working on the "arcanum universale," or the philosopher's stone. When he failed, he was put in another prison but was released when he helped another chemist to create both red and white porcelain, to the delight of King Augustus the Strong, who had virtually bankrupted his treasury importing Chinese porcelain. Since Böttger mined the clay from areas around Dresden and Meissen, the Royal Saxon Porcelain Manufactory was started at Meissen and began to produce porcelain for commercial sale. Thus began the production of what would become the world's most valuable and expensive figurines. Utz updates the story by telling the narrator that during inflation problems in Germany in 1923 "the Dresden banks issued emergency money, in red and white 'Böttger' porcelain" (p. 108).

In chapter 33 Utz continues his role as the master teaching his student, in the tradition of Diderot's *Jacques Le Fataliste,* by insisting that the early alchemists were not interested only in transmuting lead into gold and becoming rich: "He felt it was foolish to attribute to former ages the materialist concerns of this one. . . . It was a mystical exercise. The search for gold and the search for porcelain had been facets of an identical quest: to find the substance of immortality" (p. 109). Utz admits that he took up his own alchemical studies to elevate his obsession for porcelain "onto a metaphysical plane: so that if the Communists took the collection, he would nonetheless continue to possess it" (pp. 109–10). His readings of Jung, Goethe, Dr. Dee, and other scholars of hermeticism and alchemy helped him arrive at such a mystical level. He explains the differences between the Chinese alchemists' belief that god was the "body of the gods" and the Roman Catholic dogma that the body of Christ is "the perfect, untarnishable substance, an elixir which could snatch one from the Jaws of Death" (p. 110). He uses another analogy, of the way precious stones and metals were believed "to mature in the womb of the earth" just as a fetus grows into a baby in the mother's womb. The job of the alchemist, then, is to "speed up the process with the help of two 'tinctures': The White Stone, with which base metals were converted into silver; the Red Stone which was 'the last work of alchemy'—gold itself!" (p. 110). Utz then theorizes that porcelain may be both dead and alive and that the biblical parable of Shadrach, Meshach, and Abednego is really about the creation of ceramic figures because they obviously survived the fire.

It becomes increasingly clear, however, that Utz is trying to show the naive narrator deeper truths about alchemy and that Böttger's red and white ware corresponded to alchemical red and white tinctures. It is also becoming obvious that to the eighteenth-century imagination, porcelain possessed magical and mystical powers that prolonged life, increased potency, and made the possessor virtually invulnerable: "Porcelain . . . was the antidote to decay" (p. 112). So it would follow that the larger one's collection of figurines, the longer one will live, and the inevitable fall into time and mortality can be put off. Possessing a collection serves the function of transforming a wasteland into a temporary Eden as long as one *possesses* it.

After their modest dinner, Utz puts on a recording of the recitative of Zerbinetta and Harlequin from Richard Strauss's opera *Ariadne auf Naxos,* and the mixture of wine, candlelight, and music helps the narrator enter a quasivisionary realm that takes him out of himself and beyond time and place. He observes Utz's face as though it were preserved in wax—like a living corpse—and begins to see how the porcelain figures might possess timeless dimensions: "Things, I reflected, are tougher than people. Things are the changeless mirror in which we watch ourselves disintegrate" (p. 113). This scene, and this particular statement, can be viewed as the novel's emotional and spiritual climax because it encapsulates the core message—the theme of the book—that Utz is trying to teach the narrator. But that message is simultaneously so complex and so simple that it has taken him nine hours to explicate it and any number of examples to document his proofs. The novel is, then, about a classic literary theme that became increasingly important from the eighteenth century to the present: *Vita brevis ars longus*. A loose translation of that epigram is "Life is short and art is long." Utz then begins to lift figurines of the characters from the *Commedia dell'arte* and put them in the spotlight, "where they appear to skate over the glass of the table, pivoting on their bases of gilded foam, as if they would forever go on laughing, whirling, improvising. Scaramouche would strum his guitar. Brighella would forever liberate people's purses. . . . The coils of spaghetti would be eternally poised above Pulchinella's nostrils. . . . Columbine would be endlessly in love with Harlequin—'absolutely mad to trust him' " (p. 113).

It is at this climactic moment that the narrator connects everything that Utz has told him to the possibility that Utz himself has "become" one of his own figurines; that his collection has come to possess him, not in a tragic way but in a redemptive way in which he feels himself part of an immortally pure and ecstatically shining world where he is invulnerable, happy, and satisfied:

> "And Harlequin. . . . *The* Harlequin . . . the arch-improviser, the zany, trickster, master of the volte face . . . would forever strut in his variegated plumage, tiptoe into bedrooms . . . dance in the teeth of catastrophe. . . . Mr. Chameleon himself!"
>
> And I realized, as Utz pivoted the figure in the candlelight, that I had misjudged him; that he, too, was dancing; that, for him, this world of little figures was the real world. And that, compared to them, the Gestapo, the Secret Police . . . were creatures of tinsel. And the events of this sombre century—the bombardments, blitzkriegs, putsches, purges—were, so far as he was concerned, so many "noises off." (p. 114)

The one mythic figure that the narrator overlooks, Hermes the Trickster, is alive and well in the ugly little body but rich soul of Kaspar Utz. Gnosticism and alchemy always belonged to the hermetic world, the realm of Hermes-Mercury, the perpetual nomad, the god of travelers, the thief, and most important, the messenger of the gods. Undoubtedly, Utz *is* Harlequin, both trickster and divine messenger. With that in mind, Utz invites his young initiate to take a walk around Prague.

After a brisk trip around the Old Town Square, Utz declares his hatred for Prague, to the narrator's shock. Then, as is appropriate for a Hermes figure, Utz shakes the young man's hand and announces, "I will leave you now. I will go to the brothel" (p. 115). Since James Joyce's

Ulysses, brothels have symbolized a descent into hades, hell, the underworld. It is clear that Utz has taken the narrator on an extensive trip
into the underworld of not only the history of European art but of the
gnostic-hermetic alchemists, an underworld that gave birth to modern
science, modern literature, and art. Chatwin's return to origins is a pattern he follows from *In Patagonia* to *Utz,* his brilliantly comic but intellectually challenging last novel. One cannot begin to understand the
wasteland of the present day unless one goes back to the Edenic innocence and purity of the beginning. The lesson that Utz silently teaches is
the same lesson that John Keats shows his readers in one of English literature's greatest poems, "Ode on a Grecian Urn." Keats calls the urn a
"Cold Pastoral! / When old age shall this generation waste, / Thou shalt
remain, in midst of other woe / Than ours."

The narrator never sees Utz again, although he receives a postcard
from him of the tomb of the great Danish astronomer Tycho Brahé. Six
years later he receives a note from Dr. Orlik telling of Utz's death. The
young man realizes that he spent only a little more than nine hours with
him in 1967 and in a Dantean sense entered the Ninth Circle with him.
The remainder of the novel deals with the Soviet occupation of Czechoslovakia in 1968 and the effects it had on its citizens.

In chapter 37, it is 1974, and the narrator revisits Prague after a visit
to the Soviet Union, which is in much better shape than he ever
expected. He finds Prague, by contrast, a veritable wasteland—"mourn-
ful and gloomy." Many of the great churches are closed, as are most of
the museums. He visits Utz's old apartment and gets little information
from the retired opera singer who lives on the floor below and who was,
he discovers, one of Utz's many mistresses. He meets with a suspicious
female curator who tells him, as did Dr. Frankfurter of New York, that
the priceless Meissen figurines have mysteriously disappeared. Utz had
been given permission to import his second collection of 267 objects
from Switzerland to his apartment. Two days after his funeral, however,
the stunned officials found the apartment empty.

The narrator has lunch with Dr. Orlik at the Restaurant Pstruh the
next day and, though learning nothing about the collection's disappearance, discovers all kinds of new information about Utz's hidden life. He
and Marta were actually married in a civil ceremony in 1952 so that he
would not lose his two-room apartment on Siroka Street. Dr. Orlik also
tells about Utz's very rich sexual life and that he had had a succession of
lovers—beautiful operetta singers—over many years, much to the sorrow of Marta, who would disappear when they came to the apartment.

Sometimes she would stay with friends, but often she would spend the night at the Central Railway Station, "her heart in shreds, crossing herself at the thought of thrashing limbs and pink satin" (p. 137). They later married in a religious ceremony at the Church of St. Nikolaus in the spring of 1968, and, it seems, lived quite happily till Utz's death in 1974. Marta's daily prayers were answered.

The last three chapters of Utz, 46 to 48, are accounts of the narrator's attempts to discover exactly what happened to the priceless Meissen figurines. Utz's former mistress who lives in his old apartment building claims to have heard Utz and Marta hammering away at what she presumed was the collection. But the narrator insists on pursuing the mystery further and ferrets out the garbagemen who would have hauled the shards to the dump. He follows one of them, who picks up the garbage at no. 5 Siroka Street, and asks to be put in contact with other drivers who may know something about the broken porcelain. He then meets with several men—some of whom are highly educated writers and philosophers—at their favorite beer-drinking place, the city dump outside Prague, the ultimate wasteland. Finally he finds a man named Kosik, who "had done the garbage round in the Old Jewish Quarter. He would thus have emptied Utz's dustbins" (p. 149). Though Kosik can remember nothing to indicate that Utz or Marta destroyed the collection, he does recall a couple who resembled the pair periodically coming out to the dump in a cab and walking along a lane.

In frustration, the narrator proposes several crucial questions about the fate of the collection: had the couple smuggled it out of Prague? No. There was no evidence of that. Had the officials of the state museum smuggled it abroad? If they had, Dr. Frankfurter would have known about it immediately. Did Utz himself destroy his precious treasure? Searching for an answer, the narrator then delves, in typical Chatwinian fashion, into the etymology of the word *iconoclasm:* "Is there, alongside the tendency to worship images—which Baudelaire called 'my unique, my private passion'—a counter-tendency to smash them to bits? Do images, in fact, demand their own destruction?" (p. 151). Or was it the highly religious Marta, the domestic servant of ultimate common sense, who regarded Utz's real-life mistresses and his fictive mistresses as belonging to the same category of "trash"? He concludes that none of these theories can adequately account for the figurines' disappearance.

But in forging a synthesis of all of these theories, Chatwin arrives at a strikingly lucid articulation of one of the novel's principal themes: "I believe that, in reviewing his life during those final months, he regretted having always played the trickster. He regretted having wheedled himself and the collection out of every tight corner. He had tried to preserve in microcosm the elegance of European court life. But the price was too high. He hated the grovelling and the compromise—and in the end the porcelains disgusted him" (p. 152). Certainly Chatwin expands the novel's macrocosmic theme of the attempt to preserve the Edenic condition of eighteenth-century court life and microcosmically save it from the wasteland decadence of the nineteenth century and the fall of the Austro-Hungarian empire, an era that had its pristine birth when Charlemagne was crowned Holy Roman Emperor in A.D. 800. Quite simply, the monumental effort required to keep his idealized mythopoeic world functioning in such an ambience of shoddy dissimulation became overwhelming. He discovered this only after he had found the ideal of true love, one he never knew he was looking for.

Several commentators find such a solution too easy and even a bit sentimental. The narrator theorizes that it was Utz's falling in love with the maid, faithful Marta, that saved his soul but destroyed the collection. One act depended on the other. Adam Mars-Jones, a sympathetic critic, states, *"Utz,* though for all its slightness, contains much that Chatwin's admirers will enjoy, even if Utz's final renunciation of precious things in favor of a precious person—as fondly imagined by the narrator—seems sentimental."[7] As Murray succinctly puts it, "Life, in short, triumphed over art" (*Bruce Chatwin,* 117).

The narrator summarizes his theory in a final revision of all of his previously unsatisfactory conclusions. Utz changes when Marta emerges from the bathroom in her pink dressing-gown after their wedding and, "unloosening the girdle, let it slide to the floor and embraced him as a true wife. And from that hour, they passed their days in passionate adoration of each other, resenting anything that might come between them. And the porcelains were bits of old crockery that simply had to go" (p. 152). Although such an ending might strain a reader's credulity, there is nothing inconsistent with its fairy-tale formula if one keeps in mind that the richest part of Utz's spiritual and emotional life was his adoration of the inert but glorious figures—that, in short, his life found its most authentic response in the aesthetically fictive, mythic worlds of alchemical transformation. But what he obviously learned—if the narrator's story is true—was that one's private world can be ultimately redemptive: that the promise of idealized love is possible in the real world. And in that sense, the collection possessed the transformative power of the Grail or the philosopher's stone in bringing Utz into the realm of the love, passion, and paradise that these cold figures had always intimated. Art accomplished its end by moving the viewer from memory and desire into the heart of what it permanently promises: love. The ending might resemble a fairy tale, but what had Utz's life been up to then but a grim fairy tale?

In the last chapter, the narrator, unable to stop his search for the solution to this mystery, goes to Marta's home village, Kostelec, which "lies close to the Austrian border, near the watershed between the Danube and the Elbe. The wheatfields have been invaded by biblical 'tares': but the cornflowers, the poppies, knapweed, scabious, and larkspur make one rejoice in the beauty of a European countryside as yet unpoisoned by selective weedkillers. On the edge of the village there are water-meadows and, beyond, there is a lake where carp are raised, half-encircled with a stand of pines" (p. 153). What could be a more obvious representation of a pastoral Eden than pristine, untouched (by weed-killers), paradisal Kostelec? The area also closely resembles the marvelous settings depicted in the brothers Grimm's fairy tales, and Chatwin moves, etymologically, from "grim" to "Grimm." As he enters a wicket gate, "a snow-white gander flapped towards me, craning his neck and hissing" (p. 154). In case we haven't yet picked up on the obvious allusions to myth and fairy tales, Chatwin blatantly uses the term "snow-white" to nudge us into that mind-set. An old woman comes to the door: "I murmured a word or two and her face lit up in an astounded smile. And she raised her eyes to the rainbow and said, '*Ja! Ich bin die Baronin von Utz*' " ("Yes, I am the Baroness von Utz"; p. 154). Yet another fairy tale, "Cinderella," comes true as Marta, the domestic servant, enters the realm of royalty.

Appropriately enough, there is a rainbow at the end of the novel and, by extension, that mythic pot of gold. True love—and maybe a hidden treasure somewhere—concludes Bruce Chatwin's most accomplished novel. Utz's "museum" has moved from "mausoleum" to paradise.

Chapter Seven

What Am I Doing Here
and *Anatomy of Restlessness:*
"The Search for the Miraculous"

Critic Diane Ackerman asserts that "Many of the essays in *What Am I Doing Here* are examples of Chatwin at his best—part observer, part interviewer, part scholar. What brings them alive is his special talent for noticing life's strange, riveting details."[1] Few would question her comprehensive summary of Chatwin's talent as an observer, an interviewer, and consummate scholar, but it is his genius in choosing the most telling details that vivify these pieces into literature. Chatwin himself defines his genres as "fragments, stories, profiles and travelogues" and claims that all of them—with the exception of his profile on Mrs. Gandhi—were "my ideas" (*WH,* vii). Almost all of the book's "stories" had been previously published, in *Granta,* the (London) *Sunday Times Magazine, House & Garden,* the *New York Review of Books, Esquire,* the *New York Times Magazine,* and several other journals, but the first three appeared in the collection for the first time. Chatwin cautions the reader, though, to pay attention to the unconventional way he uses the word *story:* "The word 'story' is intended to alert the reader to the fact that, however closely the narrative may fit the facts, the fictional process has been at work (p. vii). Few statements could more accurately describe the characteristic ways Chatwin interwove fact and fiction throughout his career.

Bruce Chatwin organized this collection as he was dying of AIDS and wrote the first three stories literally on his deathbed. Instead of arranging them chronologically, he gathered them under subject and theme. For accurate critical evaluation, he said, "They can be judged by their dates" (p. vii).

Chatwin's organization is like a kind of symphonic sonata form; the book starts out in a gentle, impressionistic, even comic mood, and the remaining 10 sections are filled with gradually increasing drama that reaches an emotional culmination in sections four through seven and calms a bit in section eight. Section nine comes to a disturbing climax, with pieces on Mrs. Gandhi and Ernst Jünger, and sections 10 and 11 (he entitles section 10 "Coda") conclude the collection on a light note. Not only is Chatwin's prose style highly melodic, the movement of his imagination in structuring the collection is impeccably musical also. Further, both the opening "stories" and the concluding "tales" are intensely personal, a mode rarely found in Chatwin's consistently private disposition.

The musical subtext, or sonata form, works beautifully within each section, which has its own exposition, climax, and conclusion. Section 2, "Strange Encounters," for instance, begins with the previously published "A Coup," which became the factual basis of *The Viceroy of Ouidah*, and after two shorter but nonetheless compelling stories reaches a marvelous climax in one of the most impressive pieces Chatwin ever wrote, "The Chinese Geomancer." Section 3, "Friends," contains a dramatic and detailed piece on one of Chatwin's heroes, Howard Hodgkin, and concludes with the shortest vignette in the book, "At Dinner with Diana Vreeland." Section 4, "Encounters," is just that—intense and sometimes disturbing encounters with such cultural giants as André Malraux and Werner Herzog. In the middle of the collection rests the central essay, not only in the book but in Chatwin's own lifelong struggle to define and understand human restlessness. "Nomad Invasions" is a radical revision and clarification of his scholarly 1970 essay "The Nomadic Alternative." It is fitting that this essay should occupy the central position in *What Am I Doing Here*. Chatwin's fascination with structure obviously was a permanent part of his prevailing architectonic imagination.

Second only to human restlessness, Chatwin was obsessed with obsession; his most revealing pieces are on the obsessiveness of certain artists, politicians, writers, and cultures. Salman Rushdie, undoubtedly Chatwin's most dependable psychoanalyst and admirer, treats this collection as if it were "an autobiography of the mind," although he laments that Chatwin did not reveal more of himself in these essays: "In this book, as in life, Bruce Chatwin is secretive about the workings of his heart. I wish it were not so, for he was a man of great heart and deep feeling, but he rarely let it into his prose" (*Imaginary Homelands*, 239). However, just as Chatwin used the notebooks in *The Songlines* as a kind of anatomy of the human organism in its most basic activities of wandering and walking, so too can these pieces be viewed as an anatomy of Bruce Chatwin's imagination involved in its most basic activity of reconstructing his experiences into meaningful literary expression. His principal means of anatomizing experience and transforming it into literature is to mythologize it, a method that expands the significance of the experience from a personal to a mythical realm that transcends time and place. Indeed, it would seem no accident that his second collection of essays should be entitled *Anatomy of Restlessness* (1996).

The opening stories "Assunta" and "Assunta 2" are personal anecdotes that illustrate a clash of cultural beliefs. Assunta is the Sicilian cleaning lady and tea maker in the National Health Service hospital where Bruce is deathly ill. She relieves Bruce's claustrophobia by telling him stories about her English neighbor, whose enormous pregnant snake crawls into Assunta's garden and terrifies her. Assunta cannot believe that such a monster could ever be domesticated and actually live in her neighbor's house and sends for the police. "Assunta 2" is an allegory about how doctors don't always know either the cause or the cure of disease; Assunta tells Bruce her woeful tale of her last pregnancy. The doctors tell her that the baby in her womb has neither arms nor legs, and they recommend an abortion. Assunta does not believe either their diagnosis or prognosis and insists on having the baby. After Assunta spends three months in the hospital, the baby is born perfectly normal. The story so moves Bruce that he weeps unashamedly. Assunta becomes for him more than just a Sicilian cleaning lady and tea maker. Mythically, she is the nourishing mother—the *Alma Redemptoris Mater,* bringing life from her Mediterranean spiritual resources. Chatwin seems incapable of not finding the mythic in the individual or the individual in the mythic.

The deeply moving "Your Father's Eyes Are Blue Again" is a rare insight into Chatwin's family and, even rarer, into his feelings of affection toward both parents. The title is taken from his mother's comment after successful cataract surgery and from Chatwin's admission that his father had the most beautiful blue eyes he had ever seen in a man. He mentions that his mother, Margharita, had lively brown eyes "with suggestions of Southern ancestry" (*WH,* 9). Certainly this observation brings to mind one of Chatwin's favorite writers, Thomas Mann, whose Tonio Kröger—like several of Mann's young male characters—is torn between his father's cerebral northern origins (the blue-eyed Krögers) and his mother's southern passion (represented in Tonio himself). Chatwin's story then follows the fate of his grandfather's yacht, the *Aireymouse,* and Bruce's father's yearning for its lost glory. The family had to sell it during hard financial times, but it became his father's persistent dream that he would one day see that mythic treasure again. The story ends when his father receives a phone call from the new owner of the *Aireymouse,* who needs help from Mr. Chatwin in restoring her. Though this story was written months before Chatwin's death, it is clearly an optimistic tale about his father's recaptured dream—a Proustian redemption of lost time. Chatwin remained a devoted romantic right up to his death, in January of 1989.

Critical opinions on the merits of these "stories" are sharply divided. Diane Ackerman views them as "the weakest part of this collection, and they read more like outtakes from his other books than self-contained works of fiction" ("Home," 11). Critic James Chatto, on the other hand, finds the Assunta stories "as powerful and moving as anything he ever wrote" ("Abroad Canvas," 44). Chatto also claims that "Chatwin was fascinated by collectors and perpetually sought to understand them through their collections. *What Am I Doing Here* is his own collection of the people, places, and ideas that he found interesting and as such is revealingly autobiographical" (p. 44). Even more enlightening is that Chatto takes Chatwin's suggestion literally that these pieces can be best judged by their dates. Analyzing them chronologically "immediately uncovers the development of his style, the movement from documentary to fiction, from an occasionally pedantic learning to genuine insight, and the fine-tuning of his beautiful, ascetic prose" (p. 44). Chatto also finds a unifying theme that runs throughout the collection and that clarifies Chatwin's reasons for writing about the people he did: "Their interest for Chatwin . . . lies in their stubborn individualism and courage" (p. 44). The humble but vivid Assunta shares these virtues with such luminaries as André Malraux, Werner Herzog, and Mrs. Gandhi. Most important, Chatto points out that Chatwin himself clearly articulates his major purpose in life in "On Yeti Tracks," one of the key texts in the collection: "My whole life has been a search for the miraculous" (*WH,* 283).

After the uncharacteristic intimacy of the first three stories, the remaining 31 pieces cover subjects and themes similar to those found throughout his five books: mythopoesis, human restlessness, nomadism and settlement, colonialism, artistic obsessiveness, and the nature of genius. Although most of the pieces were journalistic assignments that were "his ideas," he managed, according to Hans Magnus Enzensberger, to "steer clear of the pitfalls of the commission. Not for him the know-all attitude, the jaded taste and the flashiness of instant reportage. Here is the uncommon spectacle of a writer using the press on his own terms, using the tools and opportunities of journalism to the advantage of literature. This gives a rare freshness even to his most ephemeral pages" ("Much Left Unsaid," 657). Enzensberger, himself a well-known novelist, poet, and nonfiction writer, appreciates the novelistic genius behind Chatwin's professional journalism better than most; he also points out that Chatwin's greatest gift, that of a storyteller, is what he will be most remembered for. But Chatwin was a storyteller who moved far beyond the boundaries of storytelling by "assimilating in his tales elements of reportage, autobiography, ethnology, the Continental tradition of the essay, and even gossip. Yet underneath the brilliance of the text, there is a haunting presence, something sparse and solitary and moving, as in Turgenev's prose" (p. 657).

Chatwin's organization of the book's 11 sections moves from the personal present out into the world and then back to the personal present. The titles he gives to each section are as follows: 1) "Written for Friends and Family," 2) "Strange Encounters," 3) "Friends," 4) "Encounters," 5) "Russia," 6) "China," 7) "People," 8) "Travel," 9) "Two More People," 10) "Coda", 11) "Tales of the Art World." Geographically the pieces move west from England to the United States for a short visit to an American demagogue, Mel Lyman, and then explore, at their extremes, the southern part of South America ("Chiloe"), the eastern origins of the Huns ("Nomad Invasions"), and one of the remotest parts of the world, Tibet ("On Yeti Tracks"). The inner geography he explores moves from the public side of Mrs. Gandhi to the private mythic worlds of composer Kevin Volans and artist Donald Evans and the oracular world of André Malraux, who, Chatwin suggests, inhabits the "mythical present."

It becomes increasingly evident that a number of these pieces are connected to Chatwin's books in either remote or direct ways. The figures of the architect Konstantine Melnikov and of the collector George Costakis are clearly prototypes of Kaspar Utz. And the profile of German filmmaker, Werner Herzog, is relevant to the composition of *The Viceroy of Ouidah*. Chatwin's explication of the South African composer Kevin Volans's project to connect music with the local geography resonates with Chatwin's similar project with the aboriginals in *The Songlines*. German mathematician and geographer Maria Reiche's lifelong quest to understand the purpose and function of the enigmatic "Nazca lines" on the Peruvian pampa parallels Chatwin's own attempts to plumb the depths of other kinds of lines in central Australia. And the early "story" of a Chinese salesman's bout with venereal disease, "Until My Blood Is Pure," eerily foreshadows Chatwin's own battle with the blood infection caused by AIDS, which eventually killed him—and the

1977 story was written long before the term *AIDS* existed. Both "The Albatross" and "Chiloe" could be outtakes from *In Patagonia*.

Section 2 of Chatwin's evolving symphonic suite, "Strange Encounters," depicts one of his mythic descents into the underworld, in this case of a Boston-based Manson-like cult group lead by Mel Lyman. Chatwin calls the piece a story, but the characters are unmistakably familiar. The story, which tells of a thriving drug culture in the middle of Roxbury, Massachusetts, run by a modern-day fascist, is a brilliant study of the nature of demagoguery in which the demagogue is on LSD and speed. "The Chinese Geomancer" is one of Chatwin's most compelling pieces because of its easy integration of complex Asian religious beliefs with such practical problems as constructing a building. A geomancer is a professional who surveys the spiritual appropriateness of a building's location. In the story, the Hong Kong and Shanghai Bank call in Mr. Lung, the geomancer, before their building is erected to "survey the site for malign or demonic presences, and to ensure that the design itself was propitious" (*WH*, 50). The contrast with Westerners' crass materialistic concerns in locating their skyscrapers is staggering. Chatwin uses his interview-essay as a springboard to explore the spiritual richness of Chinese cosmology, in which the earth is a mirror of the heavens—a theory similar to the beliefs of European hermetic alchemists in the sixteenth and seventeenth centuries. In both cases, planets are "living sentient beings shot through and through with currents of energy—some positive, some negative—like the messages that course through our own nervous systems. The positive currents—those carrying good 'chih,' or life force—are known as 'dragon lines.' They are thought to follow the flow of underground water, and the direction of magnetic fields beneath the earth's surface. The business of a geomancer is to make certain, with the help of a magnetic compass, that a building, a room, a grave or a marriage bed is aligned to one or other of the 'dragon-lines' and shielded from dangerous cross-currents" (*WH*, 51). It is quite obvious that dragon-lines are very close to the Songlines of the so-called primitive aboriginals, though they are used for different reasons and are not dependent on ancestral patterns.

Extrapolating from the numinous information he receives from Mr. Lung, Chatwin moves on to a serious meditation on the solid grounding of Chinese spiritual beliefs. In the tradition of such classical English essayists as Oliver Goldsmith, John Ruskin, and William Hazlitt, he finds connections he had not considered before. He now sees that geomancy, or *feng-shui*, is more than a frivolous anachronism; rather, it is a "vital connection to the making of the Chinese landscape in which houses, temples and cities were always cited in harmony with trees and hills and water" (*WH,* 52). Chatwin then makes the imaginative leap to a new understanding of the place of geography in Chinese belief systems: "Perhaps the *rootedness* of Chinese civilization; the Chinese sense of belonging to the Earth; their capacity to live without friction in colossal numbers—have all, in the long run, resulted from their adherence to the principles of feng-shui?" (*WH,* 52). The geomancer's need to find and follow the flow of the dragon-lines gives new meaning to the trite phrase "go with the flow."

Following Chatwin's piece on the world's greatest collector of Greek vases, George Ortiz—Ortiz's connection to Kaspar Utz is hard to ignore—Chatwin explores the musical world of South African composer Kevin Volans, who can be viewed as a kind of European-trained musical geomancer. Volans, after studying with Karlheinz Stockhausen in Germany, finds that serialism is, in effect, dead and has vanished into the lifeless abstractions of an exhausted idiom. Back in his homeland, Volans begins to notice the incredible richness of the native culture around him, which he had earlier dismissed as primitive. Earlier in the century Stravinsky had found similar tremendous vitality in the so-called primitivism of mother Russia, just as Picasso derived similar sustenance from African art. Volans begins to study the relationship of native South African music to its geography and discovers the universal and the mythic in the local geography of his homeland. Much like poets Robert Kelly and Jerome Rothenberg, the formulators of a unique American school of poetry known as deep imagism, Volans seeks wisdom in the archetypal unconscious that the blacks of his land preserved in their rituals and songs. Volans and Chatwin become fast friends, and Volans calls his *String Quartet No. 3* "The Songlines." Its three movements are 1) "Striding Dance," 2) "Songline," and 3) "Standing Dance." The piece vividly represents and evokes both the simplicity and the complexity of Chatwin's *Songlines*. Volans accomplishes this seemingly impossible task with great success; a 1994 recording of the piece, made in Amsterdam in Volans's presence by the renowned British chamber group, the Balanescu Quartet, is available on Argo CD. On the recording's back cover, Volans's dedication appears in parenthesis just below the quartet's title: "Dedicated to Bruce Chatwin."

In the booklet accompanying the CD, Volans recalls writing *"The Songlines* quartet in the summer of 1988 whilst staying with Bruce and Elizabeth in Oxfordshire. Bruce and I were planning the opera *The Man with Footsoles of Wind,* which was intended as an extension in another medium of some ideas in Bruce's novel *The Songlines.* The quartet was written as a prelude to the opera, and indeed the same material appears in both pieces. Chatwin described his novel as 'an imaginary conversation on an imaginary journey.' For me, the conversation in this quartet is between abstract and concrete imagery in music. The journey is an exploration of the nature of material."[2] Chatwin announces at the conclusion of his essay that *The Songlines* quartet—no. 3—will be given its premiere by the American Kronos Quartet in November of 1988.

Murray states that Volans was so captivated by Chatwin that he dedicated another album to Chatwin after his death called *Cover Him With Grass: In Memoriam Bruce Chatwin* (Landor Barcelona CD, CTLCD 111). Murray also reports that a performance of Chatwin and Volans's collaborative work based on the poetry of Rimbaud and a libretto by Chatwin called *L'homme aux Semelles de Vent* (*The Man with Footsoles of Wind*) was premiered by the Kronos Quartet at Lincoln Center in New York City on 26 November 1988 (*Bruce Chatwin,* 129).

Chatwin's profile of the British painter Howard Hodgkin is the longest and most complex in section 2 of the collection. Hodgkin came from a well-to-do family of the upper middle class, a "family of well-ordered minds and well-furnished houses. The Hodgkins are one of those puritanical public-spirited dynasties that constitute . . . 'the intellectual aristocracy of England.' . . . A nineteenth-century Hodgkin discovered Hodgkin's disease (of the spleen and lymphatic glands); a twentieth-century cousin shared the Nobel Prize for Medicine" (*WH,* 70–71). During the war Hodgkin was sent to America and from then on viewed America as a paradise and England as a wasteland, even though he pursued his art studies at various English schools. As Hodgkin's artistic talent matured, he also became a collector of Japanese, Indian, and Middle Eastern artwork. Chatwin cleverly traces the serpentine world of art collectors in describing their initial contact: "I knew a man in France, who knew a woman in Switzerland, who was the widow of a famous German scholar of Islamic art, who owned a great masterpiece of Indian painting" (p. 75). But what interests Chatwin is the way Eastern art influenced Hodgkin's work and enabled him to include an erotic element in his later paintings. His work is never pornographic, but one can sense hidden erotic subtexts. Chatwin's Flaubertian analogy of Hodgkin's newfound eroticism is brilliant: "Descriptions of the sexual act are as boring as descriptions of landscape seen from the air—and as flat: Whereas Flaubert's description of Emma Bovary's room in a *hotel de passe* in Rouen, before and after, but not *during* the sexual act, is surely the most erotic passage in modern literature" (p. 78).

"At Dinner With Diana Vreeland," by far the shortest vignette in the book, nonetheless contains volumes of insights into one of the fashion world's most enduring icons. The piece is barely half a page, but it shows what a phenomenally gifted miniaturist Chatwin is; he also possesses a comic sense that rivals Noel Coward's in creating an imagistic scene of the most telling details. Chatwin reveals, for instance, the heart of Vreeland's artistic genius: "Her glass of neat vodka sat on the white damask tablecloth. Beyond the smear of lipstick, a twist of lemon floated among the ice-cubes. We were sitting side by side, on a banquette" (p. 79). Diana Vreeland inquires as to what the young Chatwin is writing about. He mentions Wales and she mistakes the word for whales: "Blue whales! . . . Sperrrm whales! . . . THE WHITE WHALE!" Chatwin corrects her and tells her that he means Welsh Wales. Vreeland's response is a perfect prose haiku: " 'Oh! Wales. I do know Wales. Little grey houses . . . covered in roses . . . in the rain . . .' " (p. 79).

This vignette presents the first of what Salman Rushdie calls a gallery of strong, older women of a special genre: "Bruce was much attracted (and attractive) to formidable ladies of a certain age, and this volume offers us quite a gallery of them: the aforesaid Nadezhda Mandelstam and Diana Vreeland, but also Madeleine Vionnet, 'the Architect of Couture,' who designed her clothes on a doll because she didn't dare tell her father the extent of her business . . . ; and Maria Reiche, spending her life trying to decode the mystery of the lines and patterns on the Peruvian pampa. And the piece on Mrs. Gandhi is as wonderful in writing as when he told it aloud" (*Imaginary Homelands,* 239). Diane Ackerman detects a similar penchant: "Chatwin seemed especially to prefer vibrant, earthy, outspoken, slightly farouche older women" (p. 11).

The details of Chatwin's writing again tell all in his presentation of the ruined beauty of Osip Mandelstam's bedridden widow, Nadezhda:

> Her hair was coarse, like lichen, and the light from the bedside lamp shone through it. White metal fastenings glittered among the brown stumps of her teeth. A cigarette stuck to her lower lip. Her nose was a weapon. You knew for certain she was one of the most powerful women in the world, and knew she knew it. . . .
> "Tell me, my dear . . ." She waved me to a chair and, as she waved, one of her breasts tumbled out of her nightie. "Tell me," she shoved it back, "are there any grand poets left in your country?" (*WH,* 84)

The collection's longest and most comprehensive profile is the one on André Malraux, and it's quite obvious that Chatwin spent a great deal of time researching the background of this multifaceted character. This piece provides the additional benefit of an in-depth character analysis of Charles De Gaulle, for whom Malraux worked in a number of governmental capacities. Some might even suggest that the essay reveals as much about De Gaulle as it does about Malraux.

Malraux was a genuine Renaissance man of the twentieth century, as Chatwin's opening sentence proclaims: "The career of André Malraux has startled, entertained and sometimes alarmed the French. As archaeologist, writer of revolutionary novels, compulsive traveller and talker, war hero, philosopher of art and Gaullist minister, he is their only living first-class adventurer. At 73 he is a national institution but an institution of a most unpredictable kind. They consult him as an oracle; and if his replies bewilder, none will deny him one of the most original minds of our time" (*WH,* 114). Malraux's intimate connection—almost symbiotic —with the intellectual and artistic fate of postwar France as envisioned by De Gaulle is one of the profile's subthemes. As Chatwin suggests, "Malraux's rediscovery of France prepared the intellectual groundwork for his friendship with General de Gaulle" (p. 117). First as De Gaulle's minister of information and then, after 1958, as his minister for cultural affairs, Malraux expanded France's global involvements and contacts with world leaders when he initiated visits with Nasser, Kennedy, Nehru, and Mao Tse-tung. He also began the immense task of scrubbing the 600-year-old grime off of all of Paris's prominent buildings, metamorphosing the old myth of Paris as "the city of light" into a stunning reality.

Chatwin finds crucial similarities between De Gaulle and Malraux, the most important of which is that they were both intellectuals and adventurers and "were fascinated with the exercise of power and the archetypal hero who saves his country" (p. 117). They also shared a disdain for politicians and industrialists and an adoration for the subtle musicalities of the French language. They detested the "machine" and were contemptible of the promises of technology. But behind these romantic convictions lay Malraux's romantic belief in the essential nobility of man that conditioned De Gaulle's growing sympathy to the idea of decolonization. However, behind these Voltairean assumptions, Chatwin finds Malraux continuously mistaking "the event with the archetypal situation. Alexander the Great, Saint-Just, Dostoyevsky, Michelangelo or Nietzsche are his intellectual companions and he moves among them on familiar terms. Legendary figures take substance; works of art come alive; modern people dissolve into myth" (p. 118). Malraux's profound intellectual gifts, then, can occasionally be undercut by his peculiar sense of reality: "Malraux inhabits the Mythical Present" (p. 118). All events—historical, religious, artistic—exist in a kind of atemporal, synchronous present, and only the man who is in daily contact with this present by way of art, music, literature, and history is capable of understanding and controlling human destiny. It is instructive that Malraux's best known novel is called *La Condition Humaine* (which Chatwin translates as *Man's Fate*). One of the first questions that Malraux asked Chatwin upon first meeting him was a perfect illustration of Malraux's inhabiting the mythical present: "And Genghis Khan? How would you have stopped him?" (p. 120).

After fascinating accounts of Malraux and Hemingway's mutual hatred for one another and lengthy examinations of De Gaulle's troubled feelings for both the British and the Americans, Malraux reveals his views on the nature of heroism, past and present. He points out that the French, since the eighteenth century, have revered the intellectual hero, or the *homme de bibliothèque* (the writer in his library), a tradition that began with Voltaire and Diderot. Malraux points out, though, that his personal model is an authentically modern hero, Anatole France, who "was a gigantic talent. He had a state funeral. But Anatole France was not only an *homme de bibliothèque;* his heroes were *hommes de bibliothèque"* (p. 133). Clearly Malraux's career fuses the hero of action with the "scholar in his library."

Chatwin concludes his interview with Malraux as Malraux laments the loss of new horizons for the hero-adventurer to explore, though his last words are "And Tibet . . . there is always Tibet . . ." (p. 135).

None of the collection's other 34 pieces approaches the depth and range of the Malraux essay, though Chatwin's troubled review of Ernest Jünger's *Diaries* approaches its intensity.

In the essay entitled "Russia," on Russia's last private art collector, George Costakis, Chatwin reveals obvious parallels between Costakis and the genius for intrigue of Kaspar Utz. More important, though, are Chatwin's penetrating views about the Russian imagination's belief in the power of art to transform the world. Chatwin has little doubt that two Russian artists, Kasimir Malevich and Vassily Kandinsky, are the fathers of what became abstract expressionism in America in the 1940s and 1950s and that to understand that movement properly, critics must see it in its original "Slavic context" (p. 154). Chatwin has ingenious insights into the

way Slavic spirituality—and its torturous dichotomies—laid the groundwork for modern art. Kandinsky had for years "been painting the private
landscapes of the mind," a sacrilegious act in an Orthodox Christian culture. But he also believed in the power of the imagination to heal itself
and to turn humanity away from the seductiveness of materialism. The
image-icon must go because it represents the religious and political establishment. Malevich's monochromatic canvases themselves became non-
morphological images of his iconoclastic impulses to smash all human
images to bits. Chatwin makes giant imaginative leaps to incorporate
his old theory about pastoral nomadism and theorizes that "Anarchic
peoples, like desert nomads, hate and destroy images, and a similar
image-breaking streak runs through Russian history" (p. 163). The
essay, actually only peripherally about Costakis, is a comprehensive theoretical discussion of what Chatwin believes to be the richest and most
compelling topic in the history of modern art and literature. Famous
names appear, such as those of poets Mayakovsky and Esenin; architect-
artist-engineers Vladimir Tatlin and Konstantin Tsiolkovsky; and artist
Alexander Rodchenko. Chatwin ties them all together. But he does not
leave out the kind of esoteric cults he calls "leveling movements—with
mystics of all kinds, the Brodiagi or perpetual pilgrims, flagellants,
Adventists, people in search of the Seventh Dimension and the famous
Molokany, or Milk Drinkers, who influenced Tolstoy" (p. 163). Few of
Chatwin's essays demonstrate so vividly the enormous range of his imagination as this one.

Chatwin's next, more recondite piece, "The Volga," traces Russia's
geography in the heart of the country. What makes this journey doubly
provocative is that most of the tourists on the boat trip down the Volga
are German military veterans (or their widows) of the bloodiest cam-
paign of World War II: the Siege of Stalingrad. In a novelistic narrative
that echoes such writers as Graham Greene and Eric Ambler, Chatwin
periodically focuses on characters like a "Prussian Junker, Von F—a
proud ex-aviator with the planed-off skull of Bismarck and a stump of
an arm on which he balanced his Leica" (p. 170). He and Chatwin occasionally take walks on shore, where the Prussian airs his imperious views
on Soviet technological achievements: "East minus West equals Zero"
(p. 170). Their boat, the *Maxim Gorky,* begins its ten-day southern journey at Kazan and proceeds to its destination of Rostov-on-Don, Gorky's
birthplace. Once again, an actual southern journey becomes a mythic
descent into hell, in this case the most devastating battleground of
World War II, Stalingrad—now renamed Volgograd.

But that southern descent also brings Chatwin into an even more powerful resonating mythic boundary: where West meets East at Rostov. Chatwin presents that dramatic line in an almost casual scene of Western ignorance, in which one of the German tourists-pilgrims asks, "What are all these North Vietnamese doing here?" Chatwin corrects the questioner, pointing out that the people are not Vietnamese but Kalmucks. The Kalmucks "live across the river in their own republic. They were the last Mongolian people to ride over into Europe" (p. 191). Chatwin is, once again, fascinated with origins and migratory boundary lines. He beholds the actual geographical location where the Huns concluded their massive Western nomadic migrations 1,000 years earlier.

The Volga also runs through the hometowns of Lenin, Tolstoy, and Gorky, and Chatwin ponders the Eastern influences on the imaginations of the three revolutionary writers and thinkers: "The Volga is the nomadic frontier of Modern Europe, just as the Rhine-and-Danube was the barbarian frontier of the Roman empire. Once Ivan crossed the Volga, he set Russia on her course of eastward expansion, which would roll on and on until the Czar's colonists met the Americans at the Russian river in Northern California" (p. 173). But Chatwin's most strangely moving experience is his visit to Volgograd, particularly the hill of Mamayev Kurgan, the location of Stalingrad's deadliest battle and now the site of a monumental complex dedicated to "the Fallen Dead." Chatwin lets the facts speak for themselves: "During the battle, whoever held the hill held Stalingrad; and though the Germans took the water-tower on the summit, Marshal Zhukov's men hung on to the eastern flank. When they cleared the site, an average of 825 bullets and bits of shrapnel were found on each square metre" (p. 188).

Once again Chatwin's extensive knowledge of the etymology of place names enriches his account: " 'Kurgan' is a Turko-Tartar word meaning 'hill,' 'mound' or 'grave'—and Mamayev Kurgan, with its grave, its temples and the 'sacred way,' reminded me of the great temple complexes of ancient Asia" (pp. 188–89). Chatwin reads into all these modern monuments mythic admonitions: "I could hardly help feeling that *The Motherland* [a giant statue of a woman dominating the entire complex] represented Asia, warning the West never to try and cross the Volga, never to set foot in the heartland" (p. 189). One of the lessons that the West may have learned in the twentieth century is that crossing that line brings with it the assurance of defeat. The essay's concluding image of the stature of Maxim Gorky "staring from his pedestal, across the gently flowing Don, towards the plains of Asia" quietly but cogently

serves as a warning to ponder deeply before entering upon such an ominous eastern journey (p. 191). At the conclusion of Steven Spielberg's
epic movie on the Holocaust, *Schindler's List,* a large group of survivors
of the death camp encounter a Russian soldier on horseback and ask him
in which direction they should move. All he says is, "Don't go East.
Whatever you do, *never* go East!"

Of course, the next major section of this collection is called "China,"
as Chatwin continues east and, thus, his movement back to origins.
Chatwin commented earlier on the strange coincidence that sometimes
"fiction and real life all came together: the year before [his trip to Aus-
tralia] I had been to China and picked up a completely unknown disease
of the bone marrow" ("Interview," 35). It was the result of that disease—really AIDS—that caused his death two years later.

Though "Heavenly Horses" is a delightful tale about the Chinese
emperor Wu-ti's (145–87 B.C.) spectacular horse-rustling practices, its
subtext rehearses one of Chatwin's favorite topics: the central place of
horses in the Western migration of the Mongolian hordes—the Huns—
and their devastating invasions of Europe. It's that "ocean of grass" that
extends eastward from Manchuria to the Hungarian plain that consistently interested Chatwin over the years and fed his enduring obsession
with nomadic migration. Once again, though, it's Chatwin's vivid imaginative leaps—here, into the mythical function of horses—that gives
this essay its compelling edge. He theorizes about the connection of
hobbyhorses and merry-go-rounds: they are "the last vestiges of the
'vehicles' in European folklore which helped one get out of one's self"
and are also mythical vehicles that transport the soul, after death, to
heaven. He reminds his readers that in Chinese mythology it is the horse
that carries off the emperor to "the Land of Perpetual Peace. The Royal
Mother of the West would be standing on her jade ramparts to greet
him" (p. 205).

After an affectionate portrait of one of China's most famous non-
Chinese botanists, Dr. Joseph F. Rock, whose detailed descriptions of the
customs, legends, and landscape of southwest China gave Ezra Pound his
idea of paradise, the central essay in the collection appears. "Nomad
Invasions" is a "re-visioning" and reduction of Chatwin's essay "The
Nomadic Alternative," a highly scholarly work (abounding with footnotes) that appeared in a volume entitled *"Animal Style" Art from East to
West,* published by the Asia Society in 1970. Accompanying this earlier
essay are page after page of photographs of ornaments, weapons, animal
statuary, and other ancient items from fifth-century central Siberia, Ire-

land, Alaska, Romania, Scythia, Crimea, and other countries and cultures. Chatwin catalogs and annotates each object in great detail and attaches a detailed bibliography. His scholarship is of the highest level. But what makes the main essay of "The Nomadic Alternative" so readable in spite of its almost overwhelming scholarship is Chatwin's ability to take heavily archaeological and anthropological information and relate it to the literature of many cultures, thereby illustrating and making available to the general reader very esoteric material. "The Nomadic Alternative" is studded with references to ancient Greek poets, like Alcman, dramatists, like Aristophanes, the philosopher Diogenes the Cynic, and historian Herodotus. Chatwin also quotes sources few would be familiar with, such as Bishop Ivo of Narbonne, *The Annals of the Bamboo Books,* and Aristeas of Proconnessus's epic poem (now lost) the *Arismaspeia* ("The Nomadic Alternative," 180–81). "Nomad Invasions," however, was published in 1972, two years after "The Nomadic Alternative" and leaves out all of the heavy scholarly footnotes and commentary.

Much of the information in "Nomad Invasions" should be familiar to readers of Chatwin's books and essays since it is an in-depth rehashing of his favorite subject: the struggle of the nomads versus the settlers, as embodied in the Cain and Abel myth. Chatwin also later used much of the material in the "Notebooks" section in *The Songlines.* However, none of his other essays document the significance of mythic geography as thoroughly or as convincingly as "Nomad Invasions," and the essay is especially enlightening to modern readers who are trying to understand the fearful apprehension Americans and Western Europeans had for anything coming from the East, for example the "Red Menace" of Soviet Communism or the "Yellow Peril" of China. This primitive, mythic mind-set continues to dictate international politics to an astonishing degree.

Chatwin shows how the settlers "won" because "civilization"—always identified with settlers—determines who the "savages" are by "recording" in literature its victories over the nomadic invaders. Genghis Khan was the European and Christian culture's first Antichrist. Chatwin then asserts that one of the causes of aggression was not the "territorial imperative" propounded by Robert Ardrey but rather "the monotony of prolonged settlement or regular work" (*WH,* 221–22). He redefines aggression: "Much of what the ethologists have designated 'aggression' is simply an angered response to the frustrations of confinement" (p. 222). Certainly the growing incidence of "prison riots" would attest to Chatwin's informed insights.

Chatwin even brings in the support of medieval Christianity (in an ironic way) when he points out that the church "instituted pilgrimage *on foot* as a cure for homicidal spleen" (*WH, 222*). He also connects the cultural idea of trespassing not, as one would expect, with settlers but with the cooperation of nomadic herdsmen with their fellow nomads' grazing rights. Abraham was, after all, a herdsman and instituted early laws regarding relationships between nomadic herdsmen: "But once a split-away group trespasses on the pastures of others because of overstocking, old boundaries and agreements are destroyed" (*WH, 225*). Such informative theories shed new light on the issue of trespassing so central to the Lord's Prayer's "forgive us our trespasses as we forgive those who trespass against us." Such a prayer, then, can be read anew as a document about "steppe pastoralism" and grazing rights. Chatwin concludes his essay in discussing the "great transformation from food-gathering to food-producing, known as the Neolithic Revolution in the Old World," and brilliantly ties together all of the many strands of nomad-and-settler conflicts over thousands of years.

The seventh section of *What Am I Doing Here,* "People," contains a long and important journalistic piece Chatwin wrote for the *Sunday Times Magazine* called "The Very Sad Story of Salah Bougrine." An Algerian, Bougrine was a victim of a 1969 attack in Nice by two Europeans and a French Muslim. The attack was so severe that it had left him severely brain damaged. In August of 1973, Bougrine inexplicably attacked and killed a bus driver in Marseilles. The crowd on the bus beat him nearly to death, and Bougrine spent several months in a hospital. As a result of the bus driver's death, the number of vicious attacks on Algerians and Arabs of every kind increased. Chatwin went to Marseilles to interview Salah Bougrine's family and several French politicians to try to clarify the growing mutual hatred of the French and the Algerians and trace its source back to De Gaulle's decolonization of Algeria in the early 1960s. Though most Algerians were forced to live in the squalor of the slums of many French cities, that life was preferable to the utter poverty of the little villages they were forced to abandon. Chatwin's analysis of the complicated conflicts between the French and their ex-colonials' attempts to be fair to both sides, though he clearly sympathizes with the Muslim Algerians.

What makes Chatwin's review of a book on artist Donald Evans so compelling is that he could very well be talking about himself. Evans was an American artist who immigrated to Amsterdam and died in a fire there in April 1977. He had become famous for painting several thousand miniature watercolors in the form of postage stamps: "These stamps were 'issued' in sets by forty-two countries, each corresponding to a phase, a friendship, a mood, or a preoccupation in the artist's life. In style, they more or less resemble 'colonial' stamps of the late nineteenth century" (*WH, 263*). Chatwin describes Donald Evans's childhood as a process of creating his own mythopoeic world: "he built sandcastles, and cardboard villages and palaces. He pored over maps and encyclopedias and dreamed the geography of a world that would be better than the one in which he lived. He also collected stamps—and, at the time of the coronation of Elizabeth II, drew his own commemorative issue for the coronation of his own imaginary queen" (*WH, 264–65*). Though Chatwin studiously avoids the slightest hint of sentimentality by delving into the child's pathetic loneliness, he could be describing his own isolation from his fellow classmates as a young public-school student in the 1950s. Chatwin clarifies possible reasons for Evans's move to Holland in 1972 by pointing to that country's geographical advantages: "He felt reborn there; and, one day, after stamping an antique envelope with the postmark 'Achterdijk,' he addressed it to an imaginary correspondent, 'De Heer Naaktgeboren' (Mr. Naked-Born)—which was a surrogate name for himself. He loved the flat wind-blown landscapes of Holland and the high varied skies. He liked the open-mindedness of the Dutch, and paid them the compliment of learning their language" (*WH, 266*).

Though some would treat Donald Evans as a member of the dropout generation of the 1960s who moved to other countries for some peace, Chatwin sees him as the antithesis of those years: "I can't think of any other artist who expressed more succinctly and beautifully the best aspirations of those years: the flight from war and the machine; the asceticism; the nomadic restlessness; the yearning for sensual cloud-cuckoo-lands; the retreat from public into private obsessions, from the big and noisy to the small and still" (*WH, 268*). There are few passages in any of Bruce Chatwin's works that could more accurately describe everything precious to him than his moving testament to the unique imagination and life of Donald Evans.

Section 8, "Travel," contains two classic Chatwin pieces. One, "On Yeti Tracks," is on his trip to Tibet with his wife, Elizabeth, and the other is "A Lament for Afghanistan." "On Yeti Tracks" records, among other things, a meeting with a genuine holy wanderer who had finally settled down, after 28 years, into a hermitage: "Mountains and solitude were essential to a life of prayer" (*WH, 278*). "A Lament for Afghanistan" is not so much about that particular country but really a homage

to one of Chatwin's childhood idols, the travel writer and historian Robert
Byron. In fact, it is an "in-the-footsteps-of" homage to Byron's most
famous book—and Chatwin's bible—*The Road to Oxiana:* "Long ago, I
raised it to the status of 'sacred text,' and thus beyond criticism. My
own copy—now spineless and floodstained after four journeys to Central Asia—has been with me since the age of fifteen. . . . By the time I
was twenty-two, I had read everything I could—by and about him—
and that summer set out on my own journey to Oxiana" (*WH,* 287).
Byron's scholarly works on the origins of Islamic architecture and his
book *The Byzantine Achievement* became key texts in the formulation of
Chatwin's own critical and artistic imagination and contributed sub-
stantially to his keen insights into what constitutes the value of art. The
ostensible occasion for Chatwin's lament in the essay is the Soviet
takeover of Afghanistan, but his deeper lament is a warning to any
invaders of Afghanistan that doing so might "awaken the sleeping
giants of Central Asia," a prophecy that eventually came true and cost
the Soviet Union worldwide embarrassment and the lives of thousands
of their soldiers.

    Section 9, "Two More People," contains two lengthy essays, one a
profile of Mrs. Gandhi and the other a book review of *The Diaries of
Ernst Jünger.* What stands out in "On the Road with Mrs. G." is the
woman's incredible perseverance, fueled by her equally incorrigible ego.
This is the only piece in the collection that was not Chatwin's idea; it
was a specific assignment for the *Sunday Times.* The profile appears frus-
tratingly chaotic until one realizes that life in India, particularly political
life, is permanently chaotic and sometimes dangerously so. Salman
Rushdie recalls that Chatwin retold anecdotes about the trip with Mrs.
Gandhi over and over, and what strikes Rushdie as so humorous is the
marvelous irony of Mrs. Gandhi's criticism of Mrs. Thatcher's arrogant
ambition in wanting to be prime minister of England in light of Mrs.
Gandhi's own ambitions to run for the presidency of India. He quotes
Chatwin quoting Mrs. Gandhi: " 'How that woman wants to be PM!
When she came here to Delhi she was so nervous. I felt like telling her,
"If you want to be PM that badly, you'll never make it" ' " (*WH,* 339).
The most telling and funny observation that Chatwin makes about Mrs.
Gandhi's relentless political aspirations is found in an offhand comment
she makes as she asks him to get her more cashew nuts: "You've no idea
how tiring it is to be a goddess" (*WH,* 326).

    Though ostensibly a book review for *History Today* and not an assign-
ment requiring interviews and travel, "Ernst Jünger: An Aesthete at

War" contains some of Chatwin's most profound insights on what constitutes modern heroism; it can be read as a comparison of the French
hero (à la André Malraux) to the Teutonic man of action and letters,
Ernst Jünger. Chatwin was reviewing Jünger's three-volume *Diaries,*
but Jünger was a highly respected novelist of two best-selling works:
"Storm of Steel (1920), a relentless glorification of modern warfare, and
On the Marble Cliffs (1939), his allegorical, anti-Nazi capriccio that
describes an assassination attempt on a tyrant" (*WH,* 299). Chatwin sees
the latter novelistic attempt as prophetic of Colonel von Stauffenberg's
failed coup in 1944. But what seems to attract Chatwin most is Jünger's
Renaissance many-sidedness. Not only was he a novelist, but he was also
an aesthete, a perceptive essayist, a political theorist, a brave soldier, and
a taxonomic botanist. Besides botany, his other scientific specialty was
entomology, with a subspecialty in the beetle. Chatwin has mixed feelings about his writing and describes his style as hard and lucid. In it he
finds a kind of self-regarding dandyism and cold-blooded banality
relieved, at times, by "flashes of aphoristic brilliance" but indicative of
"an anaesthetized sensibility" (*WH,* 300). But what Chatwin finds
both compelling and revolting is Jünger's behavior in occupied Paris
during the 1940s. He tells stories of visiting sympathizers, like the
renowned actor and playwright Sacha Guitry, and of Marie-Louise Bous-
quet's salon full of " 'collaborationist' colleagues—Montherlant, Jou-
handreau, Leautaud, and Drieu la Rochelle, the editor of *Nouvelle Revue
Francais"* (*WH,* 309). He also called upon Picasso, Braque, and one of
the highest-ranking German officers and plotters to assassinate Hitler,
the very erudite General von Stülpnagel. But when Chatwin himself visits the spry 80-year-old Jünger at his comfortable home in Germany
after the war, he receives only memorized excerpts from the diaries. A
line from Tolstoy strikes a chord in Chatwin: "There is no point in visiting a great writer because he is incarnate in his works' " (*WH,* 315).
What seems to disturb Chatwin most is the ease and serenity with
which Jünger looks upon the accomplishments of his long life and,
seemingly, a complete lack of remorse over anything he ever did.
    The last four pieces in section 11, entitled "Tales from the Art
World," are light and charming miniprofiles of several idiosyncratic collectors he encountered while working at Sotheby's. The last piece, "My
Modi," is a brief and poignant portrait of Beatrice Lillie and a Modigliani
she bought in 1944 from Sotheby's as an investment. Years later she was
forced to sell the painting to pay her nursing bills. Chatwin remembers
her, however, as having been utterly charming and witty when they

sang songs together in 1963. At the conclusion of "My Modi," Chatwin becomes uncharacteristically personal in recalling a long-awaited meeting with playwright master Noel Coward at a small London luncheon party at the home of Ian Fleming's widow. Present were Merle Oberon, Lady Diana Cooper, Coward, and Chatwin. As Coward left "his last lunch party in London before he crept off to die in Jamaica," he came over to Chatwin and stated bluntly, "I have very much enjoyed meeting you, but unfortunately, we will never meet again because very shortly I will be dead. *But* if you'll take one parting word of advice, 'Never let anything artistic stand in your way' " (*WH,* 366). Chatwin admits that he has always taken that advice very seriously.

One cannot view Coward's straightforward admission that he was a dying man as anything other than Chatwin's own courageous admission of his own impending death. Rather than an elegiac or morbid farewell, he chose to create the witty aura of a Noel Coward play, an act that shows clearly that Chatwin optimistically and gratefully regarded his life as one of privilege, fulfillment, and luck.

Anatomy of Restlessness: Selected Writings, 1969–1989

An additional collection of prose writings, *Anatomy of Restlessness: Selected Writings,* edited by Jan Borm and Matthew Graves, was published by Viking in 1996. The subject matter is the very same as that of *What Am I Doing Here:* nomadism versus settlement, journeys to exotic locations, and art. "Restlessness" is a word that the editors use to characterize the range of the book's content. Though the topics are not new, Chatwin's prose style is as vividly literate as anything he wrote, including a proposal in letter form to an editor for a book on nomads. Chatwin wrote well all the time, regardless of the occasion.

The book is divided into five major sections: "Horreur Du Domicile," "Stories," "The Nomadic Alternative," "Reviews," and "Art and the Image-Breaker." "Horreur Du Domicile" contains a reprint of Chatwin's essay in the *New York Times Book Review* called "I Always Wanted to Go to Patagonia—The Making of a Writer," a topic covered in greater depth in *In Patagonia.*[3] "A Place to Hang Your Hat," first published in *House and Garden* in 1984, describes Chatwin's small flat in London and his conflicted views on domesticity. "A Tower in Tuscany" is a lively description of an exotic tower in Italy that Chatwin used as a refuge in which to write. "Gone to Timbuctoo," a piece published in *Vogue* in

1970, echoes the legendary telegram he sent to the *Sunday Times* announcing his trip to Patagonia.

The stories in the section called "Stories" are reminiscent of those published in *What Am I Doing Here* and were all, except for "The Attractions of France," published in magazines or in altered forms in other books by Chatwin. "Bedouins" is quite obviously another version of the same story published in the "Notebooks" section of *The Songlines* (pp. 211–12). The delightful story "Milk," a witty initiation tale taken from Chatwin's African notebooks, was published in the *London Magazine*. "The Estate of Maximillian Tod," which first appeared in the *Saturday Night Reader* in 1970, spotlights one of Chatwin's favorite themes: the psychopathology of the obsessive collector. The main character certainly adumbrates Kaspar Utz.

In section 3, "The Nomadic Alternative," Chatwin explores his favorite topic in three very entertaining and scholarly essays. The title article is a reprint of his 1970 essay of the same name, and its publication here will do much to educate readers of the highly erudite scholarship upon which the public's enduring obsession with Chatwin depends. In "Letter to Tom Maschler," an unpublished letter to an editor at Jonathan Cape, Chatwin proposes a book on nomads. The letter, which earned him a book contract and became part of the manuscript of *In Patagonia,* is in effect a simplified version of "The Nomadic Alternative." The fourth essay in the section, "It's a nomad NOMAD world," is a further refinement of information from "The Nomadic Alternative" and *What Am I Doing Here*'s "Nomad Invasions."

The four reviews from section 4, called "Reviews," contain cogent and sometimes witty critical comments on biographies, anthropological treatises, and historical books. Chatwin's review of Wilfred Thesiger's *Desert, Marsh and Mountain,* entitled "Abel the Nomad," reveals Chatwin's sympathies with the book's topic of pastoral nomadism. In his 1976 review in the *Times Literary Supplement* of Osvaldo Bayer's three-volume treatment of the anarchists of Patagonia in an essay of the same title Chatwin uses fictional techniques to characterize the brutal battle between the Patagonian government and the infuriated peons. Although he generally praises John Pope-Hennessy's biography of Robert Louis Stevenson, he criticizes the biographer for neglecting Stevenson's Scottish background—especially his Edinburgh background—in "The Road to the Isles." The review was published in 1974 in the *Times Literary Supplement*. "Variations on an Idée Fixe" is Chatwin's review of Konrad Lorenz's *The Year of the Greylag Goose* (1979); though he finds it satisfactory, it is not in the same august category as Lorenz's earlier masterpiece, *On Aggression*.

Section 5 contains two lengthy essays on art and culture. "Among the Ruins" concerns the lives of decadent narcissists who lived on the Isle of Capri, and "The Morality of Things" explores the problems that may accompany possession. Possession as a component of settlement was a constant preoccupation of Chatwin's throughout his life. The essay was originally a typescript of a talk Chatwin gave in 1973, which was privately published in a limited edition in 1993.

Chapter Eight
Far Journeys: Photographs and Notebooks, "Numinous Visionary"

According to Francis Wyndham, one of the editors of this rich and unique collection of photographs, very few of Chatwin's friends knew of his interest in photography. Wyndham claims never to have seen him with a camera. Rebecca West, though, was so impressed by his photographs in *In Patagonia* that she told him that "not one word of the text was necessary" (*FJ,* 10). This handsome coffee-table volume is large, and the 30 pages of text are divided into two columns that would make up two pages in a normal-size book. The rest of the 160 pages contain photographs of the most diverse kind.

The book opens with a three-page introduction by Wyndham, followed by black-and-white photographs of pages of Chatwin's famous *moleskinne* notebooks, on which he drew various animals and art pieces he wanted to preserve. These are followed by several photographs of Chatwin's own art work—Joseph Cornell-like boxed assemblages of materials he had collected during his travels: West African jujus juxtaposed with a dried gecko, a guinea fowl feather, and two toes from a bird's claw. The assemblage resembles Mama Wéwé's syncretic shrine that so upset the White Fathers of Africa in *The Viceroy of Ouidah.*

The following six pages contain selected stark black-and-white photographs that appear in *In Patagonia.* The photographs are not of people but of an empty railway station, an isolated caboose, and a house fallen into ruin and evoke an atmosphere of poignant stasis. On pages 24 and 25, a vibrant color photograph of a nomad tent in vivid blues and whites relieves the Patagonian stasis. By including this photo, the editors, who knew of Chatwin's celebration of nomad virtues, show sensitivity to his long-held views on the robustness of nomadic lifestyles and values.

The next 18 pages contain Chatwin's most well-known color photographs—several of which appeared in the *New Yorker* in July of 1993. One, of a shopfront in Nouakchott, Mauritania, was also used as the cover for *What Am I Doing Here.* Though most of the pictures were taken in Mauritania (one was taken in Tunisia and one in Maghreb), they could have been taken anywhere because they demonstrate Chatwin's incredibly sensitive eye and his ability to recognize and create significance in the most quotidian scene. His concentrated attention transforms a simple scene or object into a mythic event. For example, his photograph of a brilliantly painted pirogue on a beach in Mauritania could easily be mistaken for a Kenneth Noland or a David Hockney painting.

The book contains many more examples of Chatwin's ability to make the most commonplace object seem numinous; he imbues the banal with a kind of sacramental aura by the sheer power of his visionary camera's eye. A collage of red, black, and blue boards, for instance, could be mistaken—with squinted eyes—for a classic Robert Motherwell study of the juxtaposition of lines and circles. The Mauritanian shopfront in Nouakchutt looks, from afar, like a Mark Rothko or a Hans Hofmann abstract expressionist painting. The photograph of a series of vertical parallel lines of various colors (which adorn the inside covers of the book) looks *exactly* like some of Barnett Newman's linear abstractions, the works for which he is known as one of America's most prominent abstract expressionists. And a shanty-town shack in Mauritania, as Wyndham suggests, could be a Rauschenberg assemblage.

But Wyndham warns, correctly, that Chatwin wasn't consciously thinking, " 'Now I'm going to do a Rauschenberg.' What excited him was that he had happened upon the basic elements of artistic inspiration in their original utilitarian form" (p. 10). Wyndham makes some other important comments, noting Chatwin's literary influences on his painterly imagination and finding that they intersect at Gustave Flaubert. Like Flaubert, Chatwin was not interested in "subjective self-expression. . . . The details over which he paused would in many cases have been passed over by anybody else. Their value is that they provide a luminous glimpse of how he saw the world—that is, of a rigorously organized, highly developed and unusually compelling inner visual landscape. They are deeply personal, but not introspective" (p. 10).

Wyndham explains clearly his method of editing the selections of Chatwin's text from his 50 pocket-size notebooks: "The extracts I have chosen only rarely have a direct connection with the photographs they accompany but I think they convey the general nature of his visual appetite, the kind of colours, forms and images which arrested the attention of his ever-curious gaze. . . . The contrast between these unconsidered entries and his finished work is extreme. He laboured to perfect his prose with a Flaubertian integrity and I would guess that artless spontaneity was among the qualities that he least desired the result to express" (*FJ,* 13). It is difficult at times, however, to distinguish the vivid insights of these notebook entries from many of the passages from his books. Wyndham also omitted many passages from the notebooks in which Chatwin intermingles quotations from other sources with his own observations. Instead, he concentrates on "visual rather than intellectual impressions" (p. 13).

Wyndham includes in his introduction a key passage that gives readers an additional insight into what drove Chatwin to begin his first book on nomadism: "This book is written in answer to a need to explain my own restlessness—coupled with a morbid preoccupation with roots. No fixed home till I was five and thereafter *battling,* desperate attempts on my part to *escape*—if not physically, then by the invention of mystical paradises" (*FJ,* 13). Certainly Chatwin's viewing just about everything as either a wasteland ruin or an Edenic paradise or, more likely, as the movement from one condition to the other, can be detected in these notebooks, a text written long before he ever published a word.

Few have analyzed so intelligently and persuasively as Wyndham the mythic way in which Chatwin's imagination—and life—operated: "he conceived of travelling as an end in itself (a realization of the *idea* of flight and escape, but an escape from nothing in particular and a flight to almost anything, a circular tour of the earth which must end where it began and then start again)" (p. 13). In short, Chatwin saw himself involved in what Nietzsche called the "myth of eternal recurrence," the hope and despair of all of the great European romantic poets, philosophers, and historians down to the present time. In a sense, Wyndham suggests that Chatwin's faithfulness to his inner drive continually to be on the move was a means of assuaging his restlessness and that he really believed "that true rest could only be found in motion: he spent years accumulating data (anthropological, archaeological, philosophical, geographical, historical, scientific, metaphysical, mythical) in order to construct a framework to support this feeling and establish it as a theory" (p. 13). Chatwin's belief in the absolute validity of his feelings makes him a contemporary romantic of the first order.

The remainder of the book is divided into three main chapters: 1) "In Mauritania," 2) "The Road to Ouidah," and 3) "From Hell to Heaven: Four Weeks in Afghanistan." "In Mauritania" is made up of 28 sections of various length, "The Road to Ouidah" of 18 entries, and "From Hell to Heaven: Four Weeks in Afghanistan," 21 sections. Most of the entries were written between 1969 and 1971, but many of the photographs are not dated. Probably he took photographs of the countries he visited as he entered his observations into the notebooks, but since he visited

Afghanistan at least three different times, it is difficult to attribute exact dates to many of the pictures taken there.

Sometimes Chatwin does include the place, the date, and the time he took a photo. At other times he gives only a date or only a place. Occasionally he mentions the town and the country, sometimes only the country, and sometimes only a date. There is no consistency in his attribution. The few people he photographed are left nameless, and the only women he photographed are pictured from the rear (Muslim women at a shrine in Pakistan, p. 141). In his rare pictures of men the men are usually stunningly handsome and project more than a little sexual attraction. A beautiful young man in white garments in the photograph called "Inhabitant of Mali," for example, possesses an angelic aura with quietly sensuous overtones. A photograph of five very handsome and eager young men standing at the window of the Palace Hotel in Pakistan suggests that the institution may be more than just a hotel.

As expected, three persistent subjects run throughout the collection of photographs: ruins, gardens, and doorways. Chatwin's doorways are never simply doorways: they are quasimythic thresholds to an area of some transforming possibility. But few photographers can capture a sense of emptiness as effectively as Chatwin does in his picture of the famous straw-hatted houses in an empty Dogon village in Mali or of an abandoned Buddhist temple in Bali. Chatwin also loved the ascetic barrenness of Sherpa houses in Nepal—without their inhabitants—and the desert barrenness of the Peruvian pampa intersected by elaborate Nazca lines, which Maria Reiche has been studying for 40 years. Two photographs of Professor Reiche show only her back and thus what she sees from her eyes.

The ruins Chatwin photographed include the great pyramids at Merowe, Sudan, which are black, bleak, and threatening; a disused mine in Wyoming; and Butch Cassidy's log cabin in Cholila in Patagonia. Most striking, though, are pictures of the ruins of a derelict Russian Orthodox church in which a huge icon of St. John the Evangelist rests sacrilegiously on a filthy floor. He also found a Dadaist storefront display in Katmandu, Nepal, of false teeth and dusty Christmas lights juxtaposed with a photograph of an Asian beauty. Another storefront in Lisbon, Portugal, shows a television set recycled as a birdcage full of green parakeets. And although he describes Nouakchott, Mauritania, as a "place of indescribable desolation," some of his most striking photographs are of the beauteous forms found amid utter poverty.

The most handsome photographs are of "found" art—the marvelous blues on the dome of the Mausoleum of Gohar Shad in Afghanistan, the various blues on a billowing nomad tent in Mauritania, and the always-piercing blue of the skies of the Sudan and Mali. Roger Clarke suggests that Chatwin's affinity for blue comes from "Chatwin's blue eye, drawn to the color of itself" ("Wandering Star," 36). A gathering of colorful *Chadors* (silk cloths) in Afghanistan resembles a Frank Stella assemblage. The massive blues of every shade and reflection that dominate the magnificent Bodnath Stupa in Katmandu and the windblown prayer flags at Hhumbu, Nepal, are the most stunningly numinous photographs of the entire collection and appear, appropriately, near the book's conclusion.

Chatwin's prose, though unrevised, is as vividly rendered as his visionary photographs and can imbue mythic dimensions to anything. Who else could transform a camel's anus into an object of serious attention: "The camel has the most elegant arsehole of any beast I know, none of the flushing flesh pink of the rectum which shows in a horse. And it produces the most exquisite turd—a neat elliptical shape which rapidly hardens in the sun. The shape and texture of a pecan nut" (*FJ*, 73). In Tamaské, Niger, he notices a woman clearly at the end of her tether: "Next to the milk sellers was a broken woman, legs spindles and scabbed, her hair matted not tied with plaits like her companions, when she crouched on the ground not covering her sex. Breasts withered into leathery pouches that never nursed a child. A woman broken in pieces. On her head arranged in a pile broken calabashes, all fragmented like her life yet neatly piled in a pyramid on her head" (p. 69). Though Wyndham characterizes Chatwin as "an aesthetic puritan," his description of the woman clearly reveals a sense of deep sympathy.

Chapter 4, "From Hell to Heaven: Four Weeks in Afghanistan," contains the book's greatest range of Chatwin's emotional and physical reactions. It's no wonder that Chatwin's first words, upon arriving in mid-July in southern Afghanistan in 1969, are "Here's a real hell hole! The heat is unbearable, all-enveloping and hazy" (*FJ*, 122). He and his wife, Elizabeth, were accompanying the poet Peter Levi on Chatwin's third trip to that obscure but gorgeous country. Levi later published a very successful book on that visit—with many references to Chatwin and his wife—entitled *The Light Garden of the Angel King* (1972). After Levi's book came out, Chatwin changed his mind about writing a book about that exotic land. As they progressed out of the enervating heat and encountered the gardens in some of Afghanistan's villages and towns, Chatwin began to see the place as distinctly Edenic because of the way gardens served as refuges from the outside world, as protected and peaceful centers for the family; that is, the gardens were a personal paradise. Chatwin's lifelong search for and creation of mystical paradises found their counterparts in Afghanistan: "Behind the walls enclosed

gardens, tangled and luxuriant. The closed world of the family. Sometimes the door is open and a woman, her face half-covered by a veil,
shoots an oblique glance in your direction" (p. 131).

But all is not paradisal in this vast country. Having enjoyed the abun-
dant beauties of Kunduz, he finds Herat (near the Iranian border) fallen
into narcotic chaos: "The indescribable filth of the Bahzad hotel. Painted
mint green with sickly pink columns and silver plastic table-tops. Torn
menus. Incredible sluttishness of the waiters, tousle-haired with wan
smiles. Hashish takes its effect. The boredom of the *hashishim*—incom-
municable internal visions" (*FJ,* 132). Has anyone articulated so profoundly the damage done by drugs as Chatwin does in that aphoristic
final phrase?

However, at the mausoleum of Gohar Shad, in Herat, he finds
renewed spiritual sustenance. His prose combines the specificity of Louis
Agassiz with the poetic vision of Allen Ginsberg: "White flowers with
green centres—yellow with turquoise. Petals within hexagons. Three
successive domes like tiered beehives. . . . Gleams of gold. Tombs of
saints. . . . Marble and basalt pebbles laid on the tombs from which
grow ancient trees spreading branches, pines and white figs, grey green
leaves dappling the glaucous shade. Children chanting their lessons in
unison. Kites magic in the sky. Symbolism of prayer flags attached to
the hang of the trees, orange, blue and green. Saint's body directly giv-
ing life-giving shade" (*FJ,* 133). Few passages so lucidly embody the
Edenic ideal that Chatwin pursued all of his life.

Not surprisingly, the last photographs are of the heaven he speaks of
in the title of chapter 3. There are three photographs of Kardamili,
Mani, Greece, on the southern tip of the Peloponnesian peninsula—
ancient Arkadia itself. Their subjects are a donkey grazing in an orchard
of some sort—a soothing Arkadian scene, a natural garden of daisies
and poppies wide-eyed and celebrating the persistence of life among the
ruins of an ancient temple, and Chatwin (from the rear) walking into
this sublimely beautiful garden. The ancient inscription on the tomb of
a shepherd in a painting of Poussin, "Et in Arcadia ego," resonates with
Chatwin's own descent into mortality because the inscription, whose
translation is "Also in Arcadia [am] I," traditionally signifies that death
is ever present even in the midst of an ideal Edenic life. The editors of
Far Journeys could not have more effectively brought together Chatwin's
most important concerns, both artistically and actually, in the conclusion of this stunningly handsome volume.

Notes and References

Chapter One

1. Salman Rushdie, *Imaginary Homelands* (New York: Granta Books, 1991), 237; hereafter cited in the text.
2. Roger Clarke, "Wandering Star," *New Statesman and Society* (22 October 1993): 36; hereafter cited in the text.
3. Nicholas Murray, *Bruce Chatwin* (Mid Glamorgan: Seren Books, 1993), 21; hereafter cited in the text.
4. Bruce Chatwin and Paul Theroux, *Nowhere Is a Place: Travels in Patagonia* (San Francisco: Sierra Club Books, 1985), 15; hereafter cited in the text as *NP*.
5. C. Bruce Chatwin, "The Nomadic Alternative," in *"Animal Style" Art from East to West*, ed. Emma Bunker, C. Bruce Chatwin, and Ann Farkas (New York: The Asia Society, 1970), 7; hereafter cited in the text.
6. Colin Thubron, "Bruce Chatwin: In Love with Fantastical Tales," *The Sunday Times* (London) (22 January 1989): G9; hereafter cited in the text as "Fantastical Tales."
7. Michael Ignatieff, "An Interview with Bruce Chatwin," *Granta* 21 (Spring 1987): 27; hereafter cited in the text as "Interview."
8. Rushdie, "Before the Voice We Lost Fell Silent," *The Observer* (14 May 1989): 48.
9. Ignatieff, "On Bruce Chatwin," *The New York Review of Books* (2 March 1989): 4; hereafter cited in the text.

Chapter Two

1. Bruce Chatwin, *In Patagonia* (New York: Penguin Books, 1977), 1; hereafter cited in the text.
2. Alastair Reid, "The Giant Ground Sloth and Other Wonders," *The New Yorker* (9 October 1978): 186.
3. Hilton Kramer, "Patagonia Revisited," *The New York Times Book Review* (30 July 1978): 3, 16.
4. David Rieff, "Bruce Chatwin," in *Contemporary Literary Criticism* vol. 57 (Detroit: Gale Research, 1989), 138.
5. Hans Magnus Enzensberger, "Much Left Unsaid," *The Times Literary Supplement* (16 June 1989): 657; hereafter cited in the text.
6. James Chatto, "Abroad Canvas," *Punch* (26 May 1989): 44; hereafter cited in the text.

7.   James Lanchester, "A Pom by the Name of Bruce," *The London Review of Books* (28 September 1988): 10; hereafter cited in the text as "A Pom."

8.   Guy Davenport, *The Geography of the Imagination* (New York: Pantheon Books, 1992), 18–19.

9.   Genesis 3.19, New English Bible.

10.   John Pilkington, *An Englishman in Patagonia* (London: Century Press, 1991), 123.

Chapter Three

1.   Bruce Chatwin, *Far Journeys: Photographs and Notebooks,* ed. David King and Francis Wyndham (New York: Viking, 1993), 75; hereafter cited in the text as *FJ.*

2.   Chatwin, *The Viceroy of Ouidah* (New York: Penguin Books, 1981), 1; hereafter cited in the text as *VO.*

3.   Samuel Decaldo, *Historical Dictionary of Dahomey (Peoples' Republic of Benin)* (Metuchen, N.J.: Scarecrow Press, 1976), 52; hereafter cited in the text as *HDD.*

4.   Andrew Harvey, "Footprints of the Ancestors," *The New York Times Book Review* (2 August 1987): 1; hereafter cited in the text as "Footprints."

5.   Mary Hope, "The Viceroy of Ouidah," *The Spectator* (15 November 1980): 21.

6.   Richard Hall, "Nightmare in the Darkness of Dahomey," *Book World* in *The Washington Post* (4 January 1981): 4; hereafter cited in the text as "Nightmare."

7.   Chatwin, *What Am I Doing Here* (New York: Viking, 1989), 137–38; hereafter cited in the text as *WH.*

8.   Victoria Glendenning, "Death in Dahomey," *The Listener* (27 November 1980): 733.

9.   Melville Herskovits, *Dahomey: An Ancient West African Nation,* vol. 2 (Evanston, Ill.: Northwestern University Press, 1967), 245; hereafter cited in the text as *Dahomey.*

Chapter Four

1.   Karl Miller, *Doubles: Studies in Literary History* (London: Oxford University Press, 1985), 404; hereafter cited in the text as *Doubles.*

2.   John Updike, "The Jones Boys," *The New Yorker* (21 May 1983): 128; hereafter cited in the text.

3.   V. S. Pritchett, "Make It Strange," *The New York Review of Books* (20 January 1983): 6.

4.   Pritchett, *Lasting Impressions: Essays 1961–1987* (New York: Random House, 1990), 42; hereafter cited in the text as *Lasting Impressions.*

5.   Francis King, "Ties of Blood," *The Spectator* (2 October 1982): 24.

6. Lorna Sage, "Bachelor Sanctuary," *The Observer* (3 October 1982): 33.
7. Bruce Chatwin, *On the Black Hill* (New York: Penguin Books, 1984), 13; hereafter cited in the text as *OBH*.

Chapter Five

1. Bruce Chatwin, *The Songlines* (New York: Penguin Books, 1987), 1; hereafter cited in the text as *The Songlines*.
2. Jane Dorrell, "The Ancestor and the Song," *Books* (July 1987): 22.
3. Roger Clarke, "Walkabout," *The Listener* (9 July 1987): 29.
4. Edward Hoagland, "Walkabout on the Wild Side," *Book World* in *The Washington Post* (2 August 1987): 2.
5. Jennifer Howard, "*The Songlines*," *The American Spectator* (November 1987): 45.
6. Joseph Campbell, *The Hero with a Thousand Faces* (Princeton: Princeton University Press, 1973), 30.

Chapter Six

1. Michael Dirda, "Bruce Chatwin and the Collector of Prague," *Book Week* in *The Washington Post* (22 January 1989): 1; hereafter cited in the text as "Collector."
2. Bruce Chatwin, *Utz* (New York: Penguin Books, 1988), 113; hereafter cited in the text.
3. Gabriele Annan, "Rules of the Game," *The New York Review of Books* (2 February 1989): 6; hereafter cited in the text.
4. John Krizanc, "The Pathology of the Compulsive Collector," *The Toronto Globe and Mail* (24 December 1988): 1.
5. Peter Conrad, "9 Hours—a Review of Utz," *The Observer* (22 September 1988): 43.
6. Fred Shafer, "A Finely Polished Miniature from Novelist Bruce Chatwin," *Chicago Tribune: Books* (8 January 1989): 6.
7. Adam Mars-Jones, "Taking the Cure," *The Times Literary Supplement* (22–29 September 1988): 1041.

Chapter Seven

1. Diane Ackerman, "Home Was Where the Road Was," *The New York Times Book Review* (10 September 1989): 11; hereafter cited in the text as "Home."
2. Kevin Volans, liner notes for *String Quartet No. Three: The Songlines (In Memoriam: Bruce Chatwin)*, Argo 440 687–2, 3.
3. Bruce Chatwin, *Anatomy of Restlessness: Selected Writings 1969–1989*, ed. Jan Borm and Matthew Graves (New York: Viking, 1996).

Selected Bibliography

PRIMARY SOURCES

Books

Anatomy of Restlessness: Selected Writings, 1969–1989. Ed. Jan Borm and Matthew Graves. New York: Viking, 1996.
In Patagonia. New York: Penguin Books, 1977.
Nowhere Is a Place: Travels in Patagonia (with Paul Theroux). San Francisco: Sierra Club Books, 1986.
On the Black Hill. New York: Penguin Books, 1984.
The Songlines. New York: Penguin Books, 1987.
Utz. New York: Penguin Books, 1988.
The Viceroy of Ouidah. New York: Penguin Books, 1981.
What Am I Doing Here. New York: Viking Penguin Books, 1989.

Journals

Far Journeys: Photographs and Notebooks. Edited by David King and Francis Wyndham. New York: Viking Penguin, 1993.

Articles and Introductions

Bedford, Sybille. *A Visit to Don Otavia.* New York: E. P. Dutton, 1990. Chatwin wrote a short introduction: see pages 11–12.
Mandelstam, Osip. *Journey to Armenia.* Translated by Clarence Brown. London: Redstone Press, 1989. Chatwin wrote a short introduction: see pages 6–9.
Chatwin, Bruce. "The Nomadic Alternative." In *"Animal Style" Art from East to West.* Edited by Emma Bunker, C. Bruce Chatwin, and Anne Farkas. New York: Asia Society, 1970: 176–84. Chatwin's first major publication.

SECONDARY SOURCES

Books

Murray, Nicholas. *Bruce Chatwin.* Mid Glamorgan, Wales: Seren Books, 1993. The only book-length biographical and critical study of Chatwin's work.

It is a very scholarly—though short—work, with intelligent critical opinions about Chatwin's complex life. It is stylishly written, highly informative, and full of insight and wit.

Articles and Parts of Books

Ackerman, Diane. "Home Was Where the Road Was." *The New York Times Book Review* (10 September 1989): 9, 11. Considers *What Am I Doing Here* to be the best representation of Chatwin as an observer, interviewer, and scholar.

Annan, Gabriele. "Rules of the Game." *The New York Review of Books*. Vol. 36, no. 1 (2 February 1989): 6. Finds inventive use of arcane, esoteric materials throughout *Utz*.

Auchincloss, Eve. "*In Patagonia*." *Book World* in *The Washington Post* (3 December 1978): E4. Finds *In Patagonia* highly original, poised, and a classic.

Brown, Ruth. "*The Songlines* and the Empire That Never Was." *Kunapipi* 3, no. 3 (1991): 5–13. A scholarly analysis of Australian aboriginals and their depiction in *The Songlines*.

Clapp, Susannah. "The Life and Early Death of Bruce Chatwin." *The New Yorker* (23 and 30 December 1996): 90–101. A comprehensive memoir of Chatwin's life.

Clarke, Roger. "Walkabout." *The Listener* 118, no. 3019 (9 July 1987): 29. Sees *The Songlines* as the brilliant "shattered remains" of Chatwin's proposed book on nomadism, which he never wrote.

———. "Wandering Star." *New Statesman and Society* 6 (22 October 1993): 36. A witty review of Nicholas Murray's book on Chatwin and of *Far Journeys*. Finds Chatwin's works "rare and wonderful."

Dirda, Michael. "Bruce Chatwin and the Collector of Prague." *Book World* in *The Washington Post* (22 January 1989): 1, 5. Calls all of Chatwin's five books "off-beat masterpieces" and finds *Utz*'s main character "cunningly achieved."

Dorrell, Jane. "The Ancestor and the Song." *Books*, no. 4 (4 July 1987): 21–22. Finds in *The Songlines* Chatwin's disconcerting concerns about the disappearing world of native cultures.

Eisenberg, Evan. "The Voyage Out: Bruce Chatwin's Long and Winding Road." *The Village Voice Literary Supplement* 72 (March 1989): 25–27. A comprehensive biographical and literary analysis of Chatwin's books.

Enzensberger, Hans Magnus. "Much Left Unsaid." *The Times Literary Supplement*, no. 4498 (16 June 1989): 657. One of Chatwin's keenest critics, who, though critical of the author's structural sense, finds his style evocative of Turgenev.

Estes, David. "Bruce Chatwin's *In Patagonia:* Travelling in Textualized Terrain." *New Orleans Review* 18, no. 2 (Summer 1991): 67–77. A revealing analysis of *In Patagonia* as classic travel literature.

Forster, Margaret. "Out of the Ordinary." *Manchester Guardian Weekly* (28 May 1989): 29. High praise for essays in *What Am I Doing Here,* a book that demonstrates Chatwin's disdain for the humdrum and predictable.

French, Howard. "At African Heart of Voodoo: Pride over Heritage." *The New Times* (10 March 1996): A3. Discusses relevant historical background of Ouidah, Benin, which sheds contemporary light on *The Viceroy of Ouidah.*

Glendinning, Victoria. "Death in Dahomey." *The Listener* 104, no. 2689 (27 November 1980): 733. Finds death at the center of the clashing myths of Europe and Africa in *The Viceroy of Ouidah.*

Goodman, Walter. "*The Songlines.*" *The New York Times* (29 July 1987): C20. Finds *The Songlines* a rich source of information in the areas of anthropology, religion, and philosophy.

Hall, Richard. "Nightmare in the Darkness of Dahomey." *Book World* in *The Washington Post* (4 January 1981): 4. Finds the structure of *Viceroy* imaginatively adroit because it moves backward in time.

Harvey, Andrew. "Footprints of the Ancestor." *The New York Times Book Review* (2 August 1987): 1, 27, 29. One of the most original and creative analyses of *The Songlines* and of the effects of Chatwin's influence on young British writers of the 1980s.

Hemming, John. "A Trader from the Badlands." *The Times Literary Supplement,* no. 4053 (5 December 1980): 1380. Finds *The Viceroy of Ouidah* compact but a powerful book nonetheless.

Hoagland, Edward. "Walkabout on the Wild Side." *Book World* in *The Washington Post* (2 August 1987): 1–2. Admires *The Songlines* but is disturbed by the novel's confusing structure.

Howard, Jennifer. "*The Songlines.*" *The American Spectator* 20, no. 11 (November 1987): 44–46. Finds Chatwin's romantic faith in humanity's goodness refreshing but laments his shallow depiction of the aboriginals.

Huggan, Graham. "Maps, Dreams, and the Presentation of Ethnographic Narrative: Hugh Brody's 'Maps and Dreams' and Bruce Chatwin's 'The Songlines.' " *Ariel* 22, no. 1 (January 1991): 57–69. A scholarly comparison of ethnography as a *record* and ethnography as *narrative.*

Ignatieff, Michael. "On Bruce Chatwin." *The New York Review of Books* 36, no. 3 (2 March 1989): 4. A deeply moving memoir of Chatwin's last year.

King, Francis. "Ties of Blood." *The Spectator* 249, no. 8047 (2 October 1982): 24. A favorable review of *On the Black Hill* that finds affinities with Mary Webb's *Precious Bane.*

Kramer, Hilton. "Patagonia Revisited." *The New York Times Book Review* (30 July 1978): 3, 16. Praises *In Patagonia* as a "wonderful read" and its author as "a marvelous storyteller."

Krizanc, John. "The Pathology of the Compulsive Collector." *The Globe and the Mail* (Toronto) (24 December 1988): 1. Favorable review of *Utz;* calls it the "first epic novella."

Lanchester, John. "A Pom by the Name of Bruce." *The London Review of Books* 10, no. 17 (29 September 1988): 10–11. One of the most comprehensive and intelligent analyses of all of Chatwin's books, with special emphasis on *Utz*'s brilliant allusions.

Mars-Jones, Adam. "Taking the Cure." *The Times Literary Supplement,* no. 4460 (23–29 September 1988): 1041. Finds, in spite of *Utz*'s compactness, a novel full of great literary riches.

Meanor, Patrick. "Bruce Chatwin." *Magill's Survey of World Literature*. Vol. 1. New York: Marshall Cavendish, 1992, 372–80. An in-depth comparative analysis of *In Patagonia* and *The Songlines* in the context of *On the Black Hill, The Viceroy of Ouidah,* and *Utz*.

Miller, Karl. "Twins." *In Doubles: Studies in Literary History*. London: Oxford University Press, 1985, 402–9. Chapter 20 of Miller's book compares several literary and mythic twins to Benjamin and Lewis in *On the Black Hill*.

Pritchett, V. S. "Make It Strange." *The New York Review of Books* 519, nos. 21 and 22 (20 January 1993): 6, 8. Favorably compares and contrasts *On the Black Hill* to Hardy's *Tess of the D'Urbervilles* and *The Woodlanders*. Finds Chatwin's greatest influences in Russian writers.

————. "Bruce Chatwin and Welsh Peasants." In *Lasting Impressions* (Essays 1961–1987). New York: Random House, 1990, 42–47. The single most enlightening essay on the Welsh in *On the Black Hill*.

Pullen, Charles. "Bruce Chatwin." In *Cyclopedia of World Authors* II. Vol. I. Pasadena, Calif.: Salem Press, 1989: 330–31. A short but trenchant discussion of Chatwin's first five books.

Rushdie, Salman. "Before the Voice We Lost Fell Silent." *The Observer* (14 May 1989): 48. Rushdie views *What Am I Doing Here* as Chatwin's "autobiography of the mind."

————. "Travelling with Chatwin." In *Imaginary Homelands: Essays and Criticism 1981–1991*. London: Granta Books, 1991, 232–36. Personal reminiscences of the journey he and Chatwin took through central Australia in 1984. Keen insights into Chatwin's complex character.

————. "Chatwin's Travels." In *Imaginary Homelands,* 237–40. A highly laudatory review of Chatwin's *What Am I Doing Here* with additional personal anecdotes.

Sage, Lorna. "Bachelor Sanctuary." *The Observer* (3 October 1982): 33. Finds the twins Benjamin and Lewis in *On the Black Hill* almost successful in rejecting the corrupting influences of the outside world.

Stone, Robert. "The Connoisseur as Survivor." *The New York Times Book Review* (15 January 1989): 3. Though Stone admires Chatwin's formidable style in *Utz,* he questions the depth of its substance.

Thubron, Colin. "Bruce Chatwin: In Love with Fantastical Tales." *The Sunday Times* (22 January 1989): G9. Declares *The Songlines* Chatwin's "masterpiece"—the culmination of more than 20 years of preparation.

Updike, John. "The Jones Boys." *The New Yorker* 59, no. 5 (21 March 1983):
    126–30. One of the keenest psychological analyses of *On the Black Hill*.
    Suggests that the twins' relationship is, in effect, a homosexual marriage.

Interviews

Bragg, Melvyn. "Bruce Chatwin." *South Bank Show*. London Weekend Televi-
    sion, 7 November 1982. Chatwin discusses the genesis of the novel *On
    the Black Hill*.
Ignatieff, Michael. "An Interview with Bruce Chatwin." *Granta* 21 (Spring
    1987): 23–37. The single most informative interview Chatwin ever gave.
    Because of Ignatieff's intelligent and relevant questions, Chatwin reveals
    crucial information about his philosophical beliefs and his enormous
    reading background, as well as biographical information, especially
    regarding his debilitating illness.

Index

The Author

Patrick Meanor, Ph.D., is professor of English at the State University of New York, College at Oneonta, and chair of the English Department. He is the editor of *American Short-Story Writers Since World War II* (1993), volume 130 of *The Dictionary of Literary Biography*, and is the author of *John Cheever Revisited* (1995), part of Twayne's American Authors Series. Dr. Meanor has also written numerous articles on such literary and cultural figures as Robert Kelly, Charles Olson, Robert Duncan, Aimé Césaire, Jean Genet, James Wright, Ethan Canin, Guy Davenport, and Charles Bukowski, among others. Dr. Meanor, who earned his B.A. and M.A. degrees under the Jesuits at John Carroll University in Cleveland, Ohio, and his Ph.D. at Kent State University, received the State University of New York Chancellor's Award for Excellence in Teaching in 1996. He lives in upstate New York with his beloved dog, Lucy, a sweet-natured and intelligent vizsla.

The Editor

Kinley E. Roby is professor of English at Northeastern University. He is the Twentieth-Century Field Editor of the Twayne English Authors Series, series editor of Twayne's Critical History of British Dramas, and general editor of Twayne's Women and Literature Series. He has written books on Arnold Bennett, Edward VII, and Joyce Cary and edited a collection of essays on T. S. Eliot. He makes his home in Sudbury, Massachusetts.